ISBN: 9781290985758

Published by:
HardPress Publishing
8345 NW 66TH ST #2561
MIAMI FL 33166-2626

Email: info@hardpress.net
Web: http://www.hardpress.net

AUGENER'S EDITION No. 9198

HARMONY SIMPLIFIED

OR

THE THEORY OF THE

TONAL FUNCTIONS OF CHORDS.

BY

DR. HUGO RIEMANN,

Professor of Musical Science at Leipzig University

TRANSLATED FROM THE GERMAN.

THIRD IMPRESSION

AUGENER LTD.
LONDON

Printed in England
by
AUGENER LTD.,
287 Acton Lane, London, W. 4.

CONTENTS.

——◦◦——

HARMONY SIMPLIFIED.

INTRODUCTION.

THE *THEORY OF HARMONY is that of the logically rational and technically correct connection of chords* (the simultaneous sounding of several notes of different pitch). The natural laws for such connection can be indicated with certainty only if the notes of single chords be regarded not as isolated phenomena, but rather as resulting from the motions of the parts ; *chord successions arise from simultaneous melodic motion of several parts.* The history of music teaches us that simultaneous melodic progression in several parts was practised and more and more perfected for centuries before the idea of harmony in the modern sense (chord) was even conceived. Thus *harmony,* in so far as it may be defined as composition in several parts (polyphony), takes root *in melody.*

Melody *is the logically rational and æsthetically satisfactory motion of a part through notes of different pitch.* With regard to the æsthetic laws for melody formation, we refer the student to the philosophy of music (*cf.* the author's " Catechism of Musical Æsthetics " [" Wie hören wir Musik "]). As the foundation of rational motion in melody common to all ages and all races, the history of music suggests the *diatonic scale,* the *simple step succession of the natural notes* of our present note system :

with its regular insertion of a semitone step (*b c′,* *e f*), alternately after two and three whole-tone steps. The age of this *fundamental scale,* counting by thousands of years, and the respect in which it has been held, are a sufficient guarantee that it is a demand of nature, that it is logical and necessary; indeed, even irregular constructions of melody may be traced back to this foundation. The notes of this fundamental scale stand in such relation to one another as the ear can apprehend with certainty, and as are expressed in acoustics and mathematics by certain simple numerical ratios. These ratios are the same as those which exist between the numbers of vibrations of elastic bodies that produce the notes, and of the air that conveys them to our ear. Such simple ratios of vibrating strings or columns of air enclosed in tubes, or—if we put aside reasoning on physical grounds and only take into consideration perception by hearing—such relations of notes to one another (recognised by the ear) as allow of their appearing musically intelligible and rational when sounded in succession, are called *harmonic* (from the Greek ἁρμόζειν = to join), and, indeed, these are after all the same relations which have to be regarded as standard in viewing the combinations of several parts, harmonies in the sense recognised nowadays. Just as harmony, then, (as chord succession) has referred us to the melody of single voices, so melody (as a succession of notes standing in harmonic relation to one another) refers us again to the original laws of harmony, so that we must say : *Every note of a melody owes its æsthetic effect* in great measure (viz., abstracting from the effect produced by its absolute pitch, or by the fact that it represents a rising or falling of the melody-line) to its harmonic meaning. And by the harmonic meaning of a note we understand *its relation, as accurately perceived by the ear, to other notes* of the same melody or—in composition in several parts—to notes of other accompanying melodies.

One NOTE compared with other notes (we shall speak now only of notes whose relation is recognised by the ear as harmonic and intelligible) is *either itself the fixed point, the PRIMA RATIO, starting from which the others are considered, or, conversely, it is in its turn considered in its relation to some other note ;* in the former case it is, therefore, the starting point of reference for other notes—the *prime ;* in the latter, a note to be referred to the prime, and whose distance from it is expressed by the ordinal number corresponding to the degree in the fundamental scale which the note occupies, counting from the prime. So, *e.g.,* if we compare *c* with *g,* either *c* is the prime and then *g* the fifth step measured from *c* upwards ; or *g* is the prime, and then *c* is the fifth step measured downwards from *g* (under-fifth). The general name for the distance of notes from each other, measured by the degrees of the fundamental scale, is *Interval.*

The verdict of the ear declares *those intervals simplest—i.e.,* understands them with the greatest certainty, and requires pure intonation for them most inexorably—which mathematics and physics reduce to the simplest numerical ratios, either by measuring the duration of vibrations in time or the extent of sound-waves in space, or by dividing a tightly stretched string in various ways. Starting with the latter as more convenient and more easily intelligible, we shall find that the simplest division of the string is into two halves ; each half of the string then gives the octave of the note sounded by the whole string, and both halves yield one and the same note. But it is evident that the ratio of the *unison*, 1 : 1, will be more easily understood than that of the whole to the half, 1 : $^1/_2$. Next to these two comes the ratio of the whole to the third part (1 : $^1/_3$), to which the musical interval of the *twelfth* (fifth of the octave) corresponds ; then follow 1 : $^1/_4$ = double octave, 1 : $^1/_5$ (major) third of the double octave, 1 : $^1/_6$ fifth of the double octave, or octave of the twelfth ; in notes, if we take *c* for the whole string :

1    $^1/_2$ $^1/_3$ $^1/_4$ $^1/_5$ $^1/_6$

If, conversely, we start with a higher note, *e.g.*, thrice-accented *e* (*e³*), and try to find those easily understood notes which lie below *e³*, then doubling the length of the string will have to take the place of halving, *i.e.*, if we take the length of *e³* as = 1, the note which corresponds to twice the length of the string (2) will be the under-octave of *e³*, therefore *e²* ; *a¹* will correspond to three times the length, *e¹* to four times, *c¹* to five times, and *a* to six times the length of the string : in notes,—

Intervals which are greater than the octave the musician does not conceive in their total extent, but divides them with the help of the octave, *e.g.*, twelfth = octave + fifth, fifteenth = octave + octave, seventeenth = octave + octave + (major) third, etc. The octave is the most easily understood of all intervals (for the unison is not really an interval, as the distance between the two notes is equal to zero) ; *notes which stand at the distance of an octave from each other are similarly named* in our modern note system, as has been the custom for thousands of years, and are regarded as *repetitions of the same note in another region* of the domain of sound. The melodic fundamental scale (see above) passes through a set of six strange notes and at the 8th degree reaches the octave, the most easily intelligible note ; but the fragments of the two harmonic natural scales, *i.e.*, the two series of notes having the closest harmonic relation, the so-called *overtone series* and *undertone series*, which we have already considered, prove that even if the intermediate degrees of the melodic fundamental scale are not all directly related to one particular note, still they are connected with one another by the relations found in the harmonic natural scales. If, instead of referring the notes from $\frac{1}{2}$ to $\frac{1}{6}$, or from 2 to 6, to 1, we compare the notes of each series with one another, we immediately find a number of the intervals of the fundamental scale.

And if we follow up the division of the string beyond ⅙, or the multiplication beyond six times, we find the missing smaller intervals, the major and minor second, and besides these, indeed, an abundance of intervals which our note-system ignores:

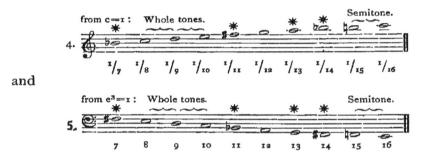

and

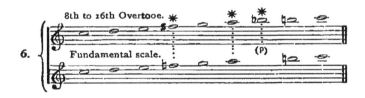

In the overtone series the notes marked * are, according to the verdict of our ears, too flat compared with the corresponding ones in our note-system; in the undertone series they are too sharp. It is, therefore, evident that the attempt to fill up the octave with the intermediate degrees thus gained, must have a result contradictory to that of our musical experience; the fourth octave of the harmonic natural scale deviates in three notes and in five intervals from the melodic fundamental scale:

and

The ear entirely rejects the replacing of the fundamental scale by either of the above, *because in both the seconds from the 8th to the 16th partial tone continually become smaller* (/), while the fundamental scale, as already remarked, is a mixture of major and minor seconds. The ear altogether fails to understand the 7th, 11th, 13th, and 14th tones of the harmonic natural scales, and refuses to recognise the intervals, formed by them with their neighbouring notes and their fundamental note (1), as fit for musical use. The rise and foundation of the natural melodic scale cannot be fathomed in this manner (the attempt was made first by F. A. Vallotti).

If we examine the two harmonic natural scales passing away into infinity with their intervals continually becoming smaller, it is clear that if our musical system is to be derived from them at all, *we must make a stop somewhere ;* for *our system knows no quarter-tones,* which the next octave must introduce. Let us, then, first sharpen our gaze, and eliminate those notes from each series which are related to other notes in the series, just as the latter are to the fundamental note, *i.e.,* let us distinguish between notes related in the first and second degree, and regard the notes $3 \cdot 2 = 6$, $3 \cdot 3 = 9$, $3 \cdot 4 = 12$, $3 \cdot 5 = 15$, etc., and $^1/_3 \cdot {}^1/_2 = {}^1/_6$, $^1/_3 \cdot {}^1/_3 = {}^1/_9$, $^1/_3 \cdot {}^1/_4 = {}^1/_{12}$, $^1/_3 \cdot {}^1/_5 = {}^1/_{15}$, respectively, as nearest related to the notes 3 and $^1/_3$, as belonging to them and derived from them, and similarly with notes found by division by $^1/_4$ or $^1/_5$ and multiplication by 4, 5, etc. :

and :

Only the following then, remain as the directly related notes
of each series :

and :

Of all the primary related notes, our ears recognise only the
first ones (up to ⅕ and 5 respectively), as the asterisks show, and
refuse to recognise all the following ones, which appear out of
tune. Those thus remaining are : the octave, fifth of the octave,
and third of the double octave in each direction ; if we shift
these into the nearest position to one another, which we may do
on account of the similar sound of octave-notes, there remain in
each case only two notes towards the filling up of the octave
interval, viz., the (major !) third, and the fifth :

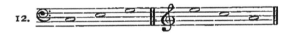

i.e., of the overtone series only a *major chord (overclang)* is left,
of the undertone series only a *minor chord (underclang)*, both
consisting of *prime, major third, and perfect fifth*, the former
measured upwards, the latter downwards.

  " *There are only three directly intelligible intervals : octave,*
[major] third, and [perfect] fifth " (Moritz Hauptmann). *All*
other intervals are to be explained musically and mathematically as the
results of multiplication and involution of these three, *e.g.*, the minor
third as $\frac{\text{fifth}}{\text{third}}$ $(^3/_2 : {}^5/_4 = {}^{12}/_{10} = {}^6/_5)$, the whole tone as $\frac{\text{fifth-fifth}}{\text{octave}}$
$\left(\frac{^3/_2 \cdot {}^3/_2}{2} = {}^9/_8 \right)$, the semitone as $\frac{\text{third-fifth}}{\text{octave}}$ $\left(\frac{^5/_4 \cdot {}^3/_2}{2} = {}^{15}/_{16} \right)$.
These secondary relationships now disclose the significance of
those degrees in the melodic fundamental scale which hitherto
seemed enigmatical : for the scale consists not only of direct
relatives of one note, but of relatives in the second degree as
well as in the first, and is, therefore, explicable not only in one
single way, but in various ways. The ancient Greek theorists
(Pythagoras) looked upon the scale as a chain of fifths ·
f, c, g, d, a, e, b, and as such it contains relatives even to the
sixth degree, according to the note that is taken as starting point

(prime), (*b* as sixth fifth of $f = \frac{(3/_2)^6}{2^3} = \frac{729}{512}$). Since the signi-ficance of the third-relationship of notes has been recognised (*cf.* the author's "Katechismus der Musikwissenschaft," p. 9 and following), it is simpler to refer the melodic fundamental scale to one principal note (prime) with its third and fifth, and its upper and under fifths with their thirds and fifths :

	I	$^4/_5$	$^2/_3$					$^3/_2$	$^5/_4$	I	
	c	*e*	*g*					*a*	*c*	*e*	
	:	:	:		or			:	:	:	
f	*a*	*c*		*g*	*b*	*d*		*d*	*f*	*a*		*e*	*g*	*b*
I	$^4/_5$	$^2/_3$		I	$^4/_5$	$^2/_3$		$^3/_2$	$^5/_4$	I		$^3/_2$	$^5/_4$	I

The ear comprehends a tone with its direct relatives (third and fifth or their octaves) *on the same side*—therefore prime, over-third, and over-fifth, or prime, under-third, and under-fifth,—*as belonging to-gether in closer unity,* and distinguishes them from *all more distant relatives* as *forming one compound sound, which we will call a* CLANG *; each of the three tones can represent the clang,* and even if the prime be not sounded itself, it is possible to understand the third or fifth as representing the clang. *Tones which belong to one and the same clang and represent it, are consonant (they blend together, appearing only as the component parts of that one clang).* *Tones which represent different clangs are dissonant.* In such cases one clang must be regarded as principal (prime-clang), while the tones representing other clangs are to be considered as merely disturbing its consonance. Thus dissonant chords arise from the circumstance that, besides tones which represent one clang (prime, third, or fifth), other tones (one or more) are sounded which do not belong to the same clang, and can be under-stood only mediately, as representatives of another clang (naturally of one standing in comprehensible relationship to the principal clang).

Just as one tone may be either principal tone (prime) or derived tone (and then either directly related, *i.e.,* plain third or plain fifth of the clang represented, or a secondary relative, *i.e.,* prime, third, or fifth of another clang, and then dissonant), *so also a clang may be either principal clang—in which case it is :alled* TONIC*—or derived clang ; and in the latter case it is either nearest related clang on the overtone side or nearest related clang on the undertone side,* or again only a secondary relative, and then must be indicated as nearest relative of a nearest related clang (ac-cessory clang of the latter). Nearest related clangs are in the first place only those known under the name of *dominants.* Starting with an overclang (major chord), the overclang (major chord) of its upper fifth is the so-called *upper-dominant* (or simply *dominant,* indicated briefly by *D*), and the overclang of

* Indicated briefly by *T.*

the under-fifth is the so-called *under-dominant* or *subdominant* (indicated briefly by *S*); but also the contra-clang of the tonic, *i.e.*, the underclang of the same principal tone, may appear as subdominant. We always indicate underclangs by a nought; thus °*S* is the under-dominant when a minor chord; in c major,—

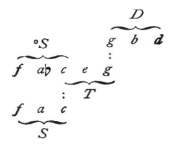

Similarly, starting with an underclang (minor chord), the underclang of its under-fifth is under-dominant (°*S*) and the underclang of its upper-fifth is upper-dominant (°*D*), but also the contra-clang of the tonic (the overclang of its prime) may appear as upper-dominant (*D*+); the overclang we generally indicate by the simple chord-signs, *T*, *D*, *S*, without any index, but in doubtful cases take the precaution to indicate it by a + in opposition to the ° : thus in A minor,—

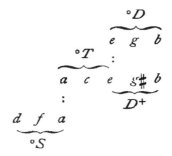

While our musical system, as we have seen, admits partial tones as representatives of a clang only as far as the interval of the third (*cf.* p. 6), it does not recognise a representation of a key by a clang beyond the fifth-clangs, *i.e.*, although the natural relationship of the upper- and under-third clangs is beyond doubt (*e.g.*, the E major chord is easily intelligible beside the c major chord as overclang of its third), yet it is not possible for the E major chord to represent the key of c major, and it generally makes its appearance, as we shall see, as a secondary relative (dominant of the parallel key, which we shall be able to explain more fully later on). We may therefore state the following principles, which explain and develop the title of the book :

I. *There are only two kinds of clangs: overclangs and under-clangs ; all dissonant chords are to be conceived, explained, and indicated as modifications of overclangs and underclangs.*

II. *There are only three kinds of tonal functions (significance within the key), namely, tonic, dominant, and subdominant. In the change of these functions lies the essence of modulation.*

By keeping both these principles well in mind, we succeed in giving the theory of harmony a form thoroughly simple and easily comprehensible, and in formulating the prescriptions and prohibitions for the progression of parts in a much more definite and binding fashion than was hitherto possible.

CHAPTER I.

WRITING CONFINED TO PURE PRINCIPAL HARMONIES (TONIC AND DOMINANTS).

§ 1. OVERCLANGS AND UNDERCLANGS.

From the combination of a tone (prime) with its (major) upper-third and upper-fifth arises the overclang (major chord); from its combination with its (major) under-third and under-fifth, the under-clang (minor chord).

To learn with certainty to know and to treat all overclangs and underclangs, with which alone we are at present occupied, and to which all that remains is easily attached as bywork, we must impress firmly on our minds the *fifth-succession of the natural notes :*

$$f \quad c \quad g \quad d \quad a \quad e \quad b$$

(*to be learnt by heart fluently backwards and forwards*), *and also the three (major) thirds without chromatic signs :*

$$f \ a, \quad c \ e, \quad \text{and} \quad g \ b.$$

The series of fifths is extended by repeating them with sharps, flats, double sharps, and double flats ($f♯$, $c♯$, $g♯$, etc., $b♭$, $e♭$, $a♭$, etc. $f×$, $c×$, $g×$, etc., $b♭♭$, $e♭♭$, $a♭♭$, etc.), in addition to which we need remark only that the connecting fifths of these series (viz., those arrived at by correction of the fifth $b\,f$, which is too small by a semitone, namely, $b : f♯$ and $b♭ : f$, and also $b♯ : f×$ and $b♭♭ : f♭$, which are derived from the same degrees) are the only fifths with unequal signature. In the case of thirds we have to consider whether the particular third is one of those indicated above as to be learnt by heart, or one derived from them : for naturally all those on the same degrees ($c♯ : e♯$, $c♭ : e♭$, $g♯ : b♯$, $g♭ : b♭$, $f♯ : a♯$, $f♭ : a♭$, etc.) must have similar signature, while those derived from the four remaining ($d : f$, $a : c$, $e : g$, $b : d$), which are too small by a semitone, must have unequal signature, just like the fifth $b : f$ (a ♯ before the upper note or a ♭ before the lower, or again a ♯ before the lower note and a × before the upper, or a ♭ before the upper note and a ♭♭ before the lower).

1ST EXERCISE.—*All the thirds arrived at in this manner (in all* 31) *are to be completed as overclangs* by adding the upper-fifth of the lower note, *and as underclangs* by adding the under fifth of the upper note ; *e.g.,* the third *c* : *e* =

$\overset{\frown}{c}\ e\ g$ = *c* overclang (*c*+, also indicated simply by *c*),

a $\overset{\frown}{c}\ e$ = *e* underclang (°*e*).

This FIRST EXERCISE is under no circumstances to be dispensed with. Another very useful preparatory exercise (SECOND EXERCISE) consists in the construction of all possible overclangs and underclangs, starting with each element of the clang, *e.g.,* if *e* be given as the third of an underclang, the other notes (prime *g*♯ and under-fifth *c*♯) are to be supplemented ; if by 1, 3, 5 we understand the prime, third, and fifth of the overclang, and by I, III, V, the prime, third, and fifth of the underclang, this exercise will be thoroughly carried out by looking upon every note in turn as 1, 3, 5, I, III, and V, and adding the other notes of the clangs (as far as the boundaries of notation will allow, *i.e.,* stopping where threefold chromatic signs would become necessary), *e.g.,* if we take the note *c*♯ as the starting-point :

13.
1   3   5   I   III   V

The more thoroughly these preparatory exercises are worked out the less we shall need to fear vague notions about keys and their principal harmonies.

§ 2. FOUR-PART WRITING.

In the introduction we pointed out, as the *task of the theory of harmony*, instruction in "the logically rational and technically correct connection of chords"; we must first of all make the supplementary remark that *four-part* writing, in the course of centuries, has proved itself the most appropriate form for exercises in this connection, because of its being at the same time so ample as not to make too many restrictions necessary, and simple enough not to be overladen and unwieldy. The four parts from whose simultaneous melodic progression chords result, are appropriately represented as the *four principal species of the human voice*, and are called after them *soprano, alto, tenor,* and *bass.* The first exercises are to be noted down in the simplest

B

fashion with the two most familiar clefs, treble and bass, the former for the two upper parts (soprano and alto), the latter for the two lower parts (tenor and bass); two parts are to be written on one stave, *on the upper the soprano with the note-stems turned upwards and the alto with the stems downwards, on the lower the tenor with stems upwards and the bass with stems downwards,* e.g.:

14.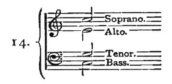

More particular directions for the actual compass of each single voice are not at present necessary, as it is not as yet a matter of real composition for voices. If we confine the *soprano and bass as far as possible within the lines,* so that only very

exceptionally the soprano proceeds as high as ♯══, and

the bass as low as ══, then with the help of the rules

to be given directly for the distance of the parts from one another, the motion of the parts in a range of pitch which corresponds to their actual compass will naturally follow.

As we are to write in *four* parts, and as the concords (over-clang and underclang), which for the present alone require consideration, contain only *three* notes of different name, either one part must always be silent (a possibility which we do not take into account at all, as it would put a stop to the four-part writing), or one note must be introduced in two parts—must, as it is termed, be "doubled." This "doubling" may occur either in the same tone region or in another octave; the latter is generally preferable, as it secures greater fulness of sound. *The note best adapted for doubling in the overclang is the prime—in the underclang, the under-fifth.* The latter assertion requires a reason. A singular acoustical phenomenon—the *attendant sounding of over-tones*—accompanies every note of our musical instruments (also voices) with the whole series of upper harmonics shown in the introduction (pp. 3–4), and the first few of these in particular sound with considerable force; thus especially the third partial tone, the twelfth (fifth of the octave), is distinctly audible, and in such a measure that the omission of the corresponding chord-note in writing is scarcely perceptible; therefore in the minor chord as well as in the major, if all three notes of the chord cannot conveniently be introduced (for reasons to be discussed later on), *the upper note of the interval of the fifth may be omitted without changing the effect materially.* In consequence of this strong simultaneous production of the twelfth, the lower note of the interval of the fifth is *the best bass-note even in the underclang,** and may appropriately be doubled.   The underclang, which, on account of the peculiar dependence of its notes on a higher principal note, appears to tend downwards, first receives a firm basis through the choice of the under-fifth for its bass-note, whence by way of the nearest overtones it projects upwards again, without, however, its nature being disturbed by this assimilation to the formation of the overclang. A certain contradiction, indeed, cannot be denied between the third of the clang and the 5th partial tone of the bass-note thus chosen, which, though comparatively weak, is still audible (*e.g.*, in the *e* underclang [A minor chord], the 5th partial tone of the bass-note *a* is *c♯*, which opposes the third of the chord (*c*), and somewhat detracts from the physical euphony of the minor chord); but the peculiar sadness in the character of the minor chord by no means arises from the harshness of this sound, but rather from the indicated

---

* In order more fully to explain the somewhat strange-looking fact that in the underclang the fifth forms the fundamental note, we submit the following short considerations :—

Unless all signs are fallacious, there has been a time which did not understand the third as part, or rather—because that remote age did not know music in parts— as representative of a harmony, but rather stopped short, in its recognition of relations of tones, at the fifth, the simplest relation after the octave. The old Chinese and Gaelic scales do not possess the semitone, which results from the introduction of the third as representative of a harmony. Also the *older enharmonic genus* of the Greeks is probably to be explained as a restriction to the fifth as representative of a harmony (*cf.* Riemann, " Dictionary of Music," under " Pentatonic Scales "). *For a music which does not understand the third as a representative of a harmony, the double modality of harmony is, of course, an unrevealed secret*—for instance, the following group of tones :

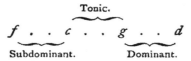

is neither C major nor C minor, or, perhaps, the one as well as the other.   Only when the third became recognised as representative of a harmony, the distinction of relations of tones as either upwards (overtones) or downwards (undertones) received practical importance and theoretical consideration.   It is impossible for us here to develop this thought so fully as its importance would deserve : we only remark that the fact of the fifth being a much older and naturally more prominent representative of a harmony, exerts its influence in this, that the third, as it was recognised much later as possible representative of a harmony, so even now is regarded only as a sort of complementary and distinctive factor of harmony—as a factor necessary, indeed, to make harmony complete and unambiguous, but one which, all the same, appears only as accessory, if compared with the two fundamental pillars of harmony (prime and fifth, whether over-fifth or under-fifth), that were much earlier recognised and stand in a much simpler relation to each other.

There is yet another consideration to be taken into account.   Tones that stand at the distance of an octave from each other are considered by the musician as identical. (No arithmetician has as yet solved the problem why it is that no involution of the interval of the octave produces a dissonance, while we understand even the second fifth as a dissonance) ; and hence theory and practice of all times and nations agree in limiting melodies or parts of a melody by the octave (which may have been suggested by the naturally limited compass of the human

downward derivation of the notes.   But this contradiction does,
indeed, explain the aversion of earlier composers to finishing a
musical piece with the complete minor chord ; their expedient,
however, in cases where they did not introduce the major chord—
omission of the third—is now no longer customary ; on the contrary, we nowadays desire to hear that note which alone decides
whether we have an overclang or an underclang before us.
Therefore *the third must not be omitted either in the overclang or
underclang ; but it must also not be doubled,* for then the clang
obtains a striking sharpness.   This doubling of the third is
particularly bad when it is produced by two parts proceeding
in the same direction.   Let us put these directions together so
as to be easily surveyed, and the result in the following form
will be easily remembered as equally applicable to overclang and

underclang (with ⊕ an overclang, with ⟨ an underclang).

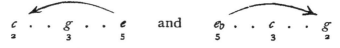

15.   ⋯ may be omitted, but may also be doubled.
             ⋯ must not be omitted, and generally not be doubled.
             ⋯ good bass-note (*fundamental note*), best for doubling.

As the aim of plain four-part writing is the harmonious combination of four parts progressing melodiously, a disagreeable effect
will be the result if the parts stand at too great a distance from

voice).   The conception of the interval of the fifth as the prototype of harmony
produced by only two tones, presupposes the identity of octave tones ; for simpler
than the ratio 2 : 3 (fifth) is the ratio 1 : 3 (twelfth).   The third appears, in the
series of related notes, only after the second octave :

$$C \,..\, c \,..\, g \,..\, c' \,..\, e'$$
$$1 \qquad 2 \qquad 3 \qquad 4 \qquad 5$$

and

$$E\flat \,..\, G \,..\, c \,..\, g \,..\, g'$$
$$5 \qquad 4 \qquad 3 \qquad 2 \qquad 1$$

Its absolutely simplest relation to the principal tone, accordingly, represents an
interval which transcends the range of an ordinary voice.   There can be little
doubt, therefore, that the natural limitation of the human voice—that musical
instrument which is the oldest and the type and standard of all others—even in
primeval times, has suggested the vicarious use of octave tones in the representation of tone relations ; and hence it is neither chance nor arbitrariness that we
are accustomed to conceive harmony in that form which places the constituent
notes in closest proximity, so that between the two more important tones—which,
without an inversion of the relation of above and below, cannot be placed closer
than at the interval of a *fifth*—the *third* enters as a middle link, as well in the
case of the overclang as in that of the underclang :

$$c \,.\,.\, g \,.\,.\, e \qquad \text{and} \qquad e\flat \,.\,.\, c \,.\,.\, g$$
$$2 \qquad 3 \qquad 5 \qquad\qquad 5 \qquad 3 \qquad 2$$

Only this genesis—which must be considered not as excogitated arbitrarily or
as having grown by chance, but as resulting necessarily from nature—fully explains
the fact that also in the chord of C minor the c, although not prime, but fifth,
forms the fundamental note.   If the third were quite on the same level with
the fifth, it would seem proper to construct the minor chord on it as foundation ;
but this is refused by the ear as being altogether impossible.

one another.   Observation of the practice of the great masters and close examination of the sound of different combinations, have led to the strict rule, that *the greatest distance allowed between the two highest parts* (soprano and alto) *is an octave, which, however, is no longer admissible between the two inner parts,* while *the bass,* which is added more for the sake of completeness and good foundation, *may at pleasure be removed further from the tenor.   Our exercises always keep to the natural relative position of the higher and lower parts, i.e.,* a lower part must not cross over a higher one (*crossing of parts*).

As has already been hinted several times, *the bass part as actual basis readily takes the fundamental notes of clangs,* i.e., *the prime* (1) *in the overclang and the under-fifth* (V) *in the underclang ; for the beginning of a period this is certainly to be recommended, for the close it is strictly the rule,* and also in the course of work it is at any time good, unless the bass, which should also be a melodious part, be by this means condemned to incoherent groping about with large intervals (*cf.* the directions for the melodious connection of chords which follow below).   There are no rules directing the use of certain notes of the chord for the other parts, though there can be no doubt that, at least in the major key, to begin and especially to close the melody with the fundamental note (1, V) gives greater decision and repose, and is therefore particularly appropriate for the special melody-part, the soprano, at least for the close of fairly long movements.

We are now in a position to arrange single chords in four parts in such a manner that they will sound well, *e.g.,* the c-major chord in the following forms :

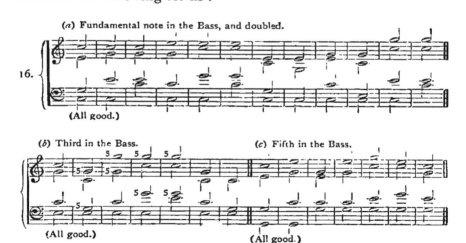

Here at (*b*) in four cases the fifth has been doubled, to which there is no objection.   The doubling of the fifths at (*c*) is in fact mostly necessary; temporary rule—*if the fifth is in the bass, it must be doubled.* The following positions of the chord are not good, but faulty:

17.

(Bad.)

A few cases with omission of the fifth may also be given:

18.

(Good.) (Bad.)

Of 18 (*b*) we may remark that, in four-part writing, according to our strict rules, *doubling of the third*, which for the present is to be avoided altogether, *sounds very bad if the fifth be omitted.* We shall come across further restrictions as regards third-doubling and also fifth-doubling directly.

3RD EXERCISE.—Write out a number of major and minor chords after the pattern of 16—18, adding the qualification "good" or "bad."

§ 3. PLAIN-FIFTH STEP (CONNECTING THE TONIC WITH THE PLAIN-FIFTH CLANG: T—D AND $°T$—$°S$).

We now take a considerable step forward in attempting to connect the two harmonies nearest related to each other, namely, the harmony of a tonic and its plain-fifth clang. By plain-fifth clang we understand that clang of the same mode as the first clang, which has as its prime the fifth of the latter. In the connection of these two clangs, the *progression of the parts* is quite *analogous* in both major and minor modes, but the *æsthetic significance* is very *different,* inasmuch as in major this connection entails rising, in minor, falling, thus in the first case *strengthening the major character,* in the latter, *strengthening the minor character.* It would be a complete misunderstanding of the peculiar and important æsthetic significance of the clang-mode, were we to expect the downward movement in minor to have the same effect as the upward movement in major. The plain-fifth clang is, in major, the nearest related clang on the overtone side (the *upper-dominant*), in minor, the nearest related clang on the undertone side (the *under-dominant*) ; the one, therefore, soars upwards, the other dives downwards, the former case entailing, for the return to the tonic, a sinking downwards, the latter, a rising aloft.

These two simplest combinations of harmonies lead directly to the most important rules for the connection of chords. If we chose to represent the harmonic relationship of these couples of chords in such a manner that for the plain-fifth step in major each part rose a fifth, and in minor fell a fifth :

19.

we should be doing about all that custom, good taste, and judgment forbid ; this would mean simply placing the two chords side by side without any actual connection, and letting the parts proceed so evenly together that not one of them would be really independent ; but that, on the contrary, each would appear to be dragged in the same direction by the others. But the principal law of part-writing is that *each part should go its own natural road*, and it should do this *as melody, i.e.*, not by the degrees of the natural harmonic scale (Introduction, p. 3), but by those of the melodic (diatonic) scale. Since, as we know (*cf.* p. 12), every note has its overtone series sounding with it, such *parallel, consecutive progressions of two parts in octaves* as above at 19 (*a*) between soprano and bass, and 19 (*b*) between alto and bass, do not really amount to two-part writing, but only to strengthened unison. Therefore, *it is strictly forbidden for two [real] parts laying claim to independence* (as is always the case with our four parts) *to proceed parallel to each other in octaves ;* indeed, in consequence of the similar sound of octave-notes, which easily deceive the ear as regards tone-region, it is not even allowable for two real parts to proceed by contrary motion from notes of the same name to notes of the same name (*b*) :

20.

(Wrong.)

But we must immediately remark that *these consecutive octaves proceeding by leap are not nearly so disagreeable as those proceeding by step* (which we shall meet with directly) ; because parts proceeding by step have in much greater measure the effect of real parts, *i.e.*, of melodies, and therefore disappoint us all the more, if their course suddenly becomes identical, and they blend into one. The same is true of *consecutive fifths* [*cf.* 19 (*a*) and 19 (*b*) between tenor and bass] ; in the case of fifths proceeding by leap, it is less the similarity of motion than the disconnectedness of the chords and the want of melodious progression that strikes us disagreeably, whereas, in the case of fifths rising or falling by step, it is the parallel motion itself which is the principal fault and causes so disagreeable an effect.   Fifths by leap in contrary motion :

21.

indeed, often occur in the works of the best masters.   No recommendation, however, can be given to their use, nor to that of octaves by leap in contrary motion, much less to that of octaves and fifths by leap in parallel motion.   The student who wishes to get acquainted with the regular methods of part-writing, to learn to know the *normal paths*, and to acquire and make a habit of *naturalness, smoothness, and fluency in the progression of parts*, so that he may judge for himself what he is doing when he turns away from the straight road, must *abstain from them entirely*.

In the connection of harmonies with which we are at present occupied, namely, the plain-fifth step and its inversion, the " retrograde plain-fifth step," or " plain-fifth close," there is no reason for making use of octaves and fifths, either in similar or contrary motion, if the simplest *fundamental law for the melodious connection of chords* be observed.   This is : *Every part should try to reach a note of the new harmony by the nearest way.*

From this main principle it follows that (1), when two harmonies have notes in common, the latter most appropriately remain in the same parts ("*notes in common are kept in the same part*") ; (2), *progressions by step are always preferable to those by leap, and steps of a minor second (semitone progressions,* LEADING-TONE *STEPS*) are specially to be recommended.

In progression by seconds rests the actual healthy life of melody (therefore, the scale is really at all times the normal *basis* of melody) ; and this is applicable even to the freest, boldest melody formation.   *Leaps are not, indeed, excluded in melody ;* on the contrary, they form the most effective factors (vigorous arousing, sudden collapse of energy, etc.) ; but they entail subsequent complete, or, at least, partial, *filling up of the gaps by means of single-step progressions.*

Only the *bass part*, whose exceptional position we have

touched upon several times, is generally emancipated in greater measure from the law of progression by seconds ; the *bass readily takes the fundamental notes of the harmonies* (1, V), particularly at the beginning and end (*cf.* p. 15), *but may at all times correctly proceed in seconds through other notes of the harmonies ; it may also take the thirds of harmonies by leap*, but then readily returns (to fill up the gaps), for the specifically melodic reasons already indicated.   But *it is altogether wrong for the bass to proceed by leap from the fifth of the major chord or prime of the minor chord ; proceeding by leap to this note* (5, I), which is contradictory to the fundamental note (therefore, not appropriate for the bass), *should also be avoided*, particularly on the *accented beat of the bar*, excepting in cases when this doubtful bass-note becomes funda-mental note of the next chord (*i.e.*, in the case of a " chord of six-four," to which we shall refer further on ; *cf.* remarks about Example 26).

If, after this rather detailed discussion, which, however, exhausts pretty well all the rules for part-writing, we again attempt to connect the tonic with its plain-fifth clang, the result will be quite different from that reached at 19 (*a*)—(*b*) :

The seven progressions in this example are transitions from the first form of the c-major chord given in Ex. 16, to the chord of G-major ; they are all good, though the third (*c*) and the last (*g*) only under the presupposition that the bass will not proceed by leap from the fifth.   The first (*a*) is absolutely normal, as the bass proceeds from fundamental note to fundamental note, and in both harmonies the latter is doubled, the note in common (*g*) remains in the tenor (**○**), the leading-tone step (*c—b*) is made in the soprano, and also the fourth part (alto) proceeds by second. At (*b*)—(*c*) the bass moves melodically to the third and fifth respectively, and the progression from fundamental to fundamental is not made at all, as the other *c* also proceeds by second [at (*b*) soprano *c"—d"*, at (*c*) soprano *c"—b'*].   Thus the doubling of the fifth is brought about, which we know to be allowed.   At (*d*) the progression 1—1 (*c"—g'*), normal for the bass, is transposed into the soprano, which is also at all times permissible.   The cases (*e*)—(*g*) are the freest ; at (*e*) and (*f*), the means of connection by sustaining one note is missing ; at (*e*) and (*g*) the leading-tone step is also missing.   But these progressions are also allowable under the presupposition that the positions of the c-major chord were reached by stricter progression of the parts, and also that the G-major chord proceed with better connection. Several such progressions following one another without real melodic support would be unwarrantable for the same reasons as those in Example 19.

On the other hand, the following progressions are faulty:

23.

(*a*) : consecutive octaves between soprano and bass ; (*b*) : the same fault, but aggravated by the doubling of the third of the dominant. [*RULE : Doubling the third of the major upper-dominant and minor under-dominant, equivalent to the DOUBLING OF THE LEADING-NOTE, is at all times—even in contrary motion—a bad mistake*] ; (*c*) : too great a distance between alto and tenor ; (*d*) and (*e*) : the same between soprano and alto ; (*f*) : consecutive octaves [by leap] between soprano and bass ; (*g*) : the same, but in contrary motion [less striking, but not to be approved of].

4TH EXERCISE.—*Imitation of the seven different progressions in Example 22*, starting with the 11 other forms of the C-major chord given in Example 16(*a*) (carrying out strictly the directions for the distance of the parts from one another and for their total compass).

The conditions for *writing in minor* are almost the same as in major ; the plain-fifth clang (the under-dominant, °*S*) has one note in common with the tonic (°*T*) (the A-minor chord [°*e*] with the D-minor chord [°*a*], the note *a*), and there is the possibility of making a leading-tone step (*e*—*f*) ; on the other hand, it must be noticed that the *treatment of the* V *as fundamental note* and as the one best for doubling, stipulates a difference in the progression, as *not the* V, *but the* I *has the possibility of proceeding by second in either direction* (*e*—*d* and *e*—*f*). Therefore, in minor, doubling of the I will occur more frequently than doubling of the 5 in major, which only confirms the correctness of the view that the minor and major chords are constructed on opposite principles. The following are normal progressions in minor in imitation of the first form of Example 16 (*cf.* Ex. 22) :

24.

Here at (d)—(f) the leading-tone step is missing; a certain disturbance of the facility of motion by the doubling of the V, which arises from the imitation of the major, cannot be denied; for this reason, the doubling of the prime often occurs in minor, excepting at the beginning and close; also, in the course of development, the bass often takes the third, by which means greater mobility is gained :

25.

5TH EXERCISE.—Imitation of the progressions in Examples 24, 25, starting with a considerable number of other minor chords.

We now proceed for the first time to the working out of a continuous example in 8 bars, which will give us occasion for a few more observations. Take the exercise :

$$\complement : T\ D \mid T\ \substack{3} \mid D\ .. \mid T\ .. \mid D\ T \mid D\ T \mid .. D \mid \overset{1}{T} \parallel$$

In the first place, we must give a short explanation of this figuring. The signs T, D we have explained (T = major tonic, D = major upper-dominant); the numbers 1, 3, 5, written below or above, imply that the particular note (prime, third, fifth) is to be in the lowest or highest part; the two dots (. .) indicate repetition of the same harmony (but the alteration of the position is always allowable and generally advisable); the perpendicular strokes are the bar-lines, $\complement$ the time-signature. No particular key is prescribed; on the contrary, *all the examples given in this species of notation are intended for working out in all keys* (or at least in a large number of keys). If we go to work, and choose for the beginning the first position of 16 (a), in the key of A-major, the attempt will probably turn out thus :

26.

(First model example.)

It should be well noted that the *middle parts* are here entrusted with the duty of *keeping the other parts together, i.e.*, they sustain notes as far as possible, and generally move within a small circle. Only when the same harmony (. .) occurs twice in succession [at (*a*) in the 2nd, 3rd, and 4th bars], progression by seconds is naturally discontinued (as *there can be no step of a second between notes of the same clang*), and all the parts (as in bar 2), or at least several, move by leap. *Such change of position of a harmony should deliberately be made use of in order to gain a good progression to the following; the student should in such cases always find out which position is rendered desirable by the bass-note required for the next chord.*—At (*b*) the bass leaps to the fifth, which, on p. 19, we indicated as unadvisable in connecting different harmonies. But when, as in this case, only the position of harmony changes, it may be done without hesitation (also, proceeding by leap from the fifth to the third or the fundamental note of *the same* chord is admissible); but at the same time a case occurs here, which we noted on page 19 as an exception, when even with change of harmonies the bass may proceed by leap to the fifth : the fifth is sustained and becomes fundamental note (of the dominant). We will not delay the explanation of this rule unnecessarily : *the tonic with the fifth in the bass* (T_5'), *which generally appears as last chord but two* (antepenultimate), *and which is followed by the dominant leading to the closing tonic, is, in reality, not tonic harmony, but rather a dissonant form of the dominant,* the so-called

Chord of six-four,

i.e., the dominant enters with two strange notes, namely, the fourth and sixth, which tend downwards to the third and fifth of the chord, that is to say, with two *suspensions*. It is true we shall not treat of suspensions till much later on ; but this chord formation is so indispensable, even for the simplest little passages, that it seems imperatively necessary to introduce it at the very beginning of the exercises, and to explain it properly. The chord of six-four is the first of the examples of dissonant chords under the cloak of consonance (*feigning consonances*), which we shall often come across ; the *doubling of the bass-note, absolutely necessary in the chord of six-four,* does not really mean doubling of the fifth, but, on the contrary, doubling of the funda- mental note (1 of the dominant). The student is to be warned, in resolving the chord of six-four into the plain dominant harmony ($^6_4$ $^5_3$), against doubling the fifth, particularly in similar motion, when it sounds simply horrible :

And thus the new numbers 4 and 6 appear in our chord signs, the former indicating the (perfect) fourth lying a semitone higher than the third, the latter the plain (major) sixth lying a whole tone above the fifth. Finally, at (*c*), in the closing chord, we have the first case of necessary *omission of the fifth* before us, because the prime is prescribed for the highest part.

EXERCISES 6—11, in major (to be worked out in all major keys up to c♯ major and c♭ major).

(6) ₵ : $\overset{3}{T}\mid D\underset{3}{..}\mid \overset{3}{T}\underset{5}{D}\mid \underset{3}{T}D\mid T\underset{3}{..}\mid D\underset{3}{..}\mid T\underset{3}{..}\mid D^{\overset{6}{\underset{4}{}}\overset{5}{3}}\mid T(\circ)$.

(7) ³/₄ : $\overset{3}{T}\underset{5}{D}\underset{3}{T}\mid D\underset{3}{..}\overset{3}{T}\mid D\underset{3}{..}\overset{5.}{}\mid T D \underset{3}{T}\mid D^{\overset{6}{4}}..\overset{5}{3}\mid T(\circ.)$.

(8) ₵ : $\overset{5}{T}\underset{3}{.\,?.}\mid D T\mid D^{\overset{6}{4}\overset{5}{3}}\mid T\,.\!?.\mid D\underset{3}{..}\mid T\underset{3}{..}\mid D^{\overset{6}{4}}D\mid T(\circ)$.

(9) ₵ $D\mid T\underset{5}{D}\mid \overset{?}{T}\underset{3}{.\,.}\mid D\underset{5\,1}{..}\mid T\underset{3}{..}\mid D T\mid D^{\overset{6}{4}\overset{5}{3}}\mid T(\circ\mid\circ)$.

(10) ³/₄ : $\overset{3}{T}\mid D\overset{3}{T}D\mid T\underset{3}{..}\mid D^{\overset{6}{4}}\mid\overset{5}{3}.\underset{3}{T}\underset{5}{D}\mid T\underset{3}{..}D\mid T\underset{5}{D}\overset{3}{T}\mid D^{\overset{6}{4}\overset{5}{3}}\mid T(\circ.\mid\circ)$.

(11) ³/₄ : $\overset{3}{T}\mid..\overset{3.}{}\mid D\underset{3}{T}\mid D\underset{5\,3}{..}\mid T\underset{5}{D}\mid T\underset{5}{D}T\mid^{3}\underset{5\,3}{....}\mid D^{\overset{6}{4}\overset{5}{3}}\mid T(\circ)$.

N.B.—The note-signs after the last figure of each exercise intimate the duration of the closing chord : those written under the beginning of Exercise 11 indicate the rhythm to be carried through.

EXERCISES 12—17, in minor (to be worked out in all minor keys).

(12) ₵ : $°T\mid°S°T\mid\underset{\text{III}}{1.}°S\mid\underset{\text{I}}{T}°S\mid°T\underset{\text{III}}{S}\mid\underset{\text{I\,III}}{T\;...}\mid°S\;..\mid°T(\circ\mid\circ)$.

(13) ₵ : $\overset{}{T}\,^{\text{III}}\mid°S\underset{\text{III}}{..}\mid°T\underset{\text{III}}{..}\mid°S\,..\mid°T\,^{\text{III}}\mid°S\,^{\text{III}}\mid\overset{}{T}(\circ)$.

(14) ³/₄ : $°T\mid°S\underset{\text{III}}{...}°T\mid\underset{\text{III\,V}}{S}\underset{}{T}°S\mid\underset{\text{III}}{T}...°S\mid°T(\circ)$.

(15) ³/₄ : $\overset{\text{I}}{T}\,^{\text{III}}\,^{\text{V}}\,.?.\mid\overset{\text{III}}{S}\overset{\text{V}}{}\;\underset{\text{I}}{T}\mid\underset{\text{III}}{S}\,^{\text{III}}\,^{\text{I}}\,.?.\mid°T(\circ.)$.

(16) ³/₄ : $\overset{\text{I}}{T}\underset{\text{III}}{°S°T}\mid°S\underset{\text{III}}{...}\overset{\text{III}}{T}\mid\underset{\text{I}}{}\overset{\text{V}}{}\underset{\text{III}}{}°S\,..\mid°T(\circ.)$.

(17) ₵ : $°T°S\mid\underset{\text{III}}{T}\,^{\text{III}}\mid°S\,^{\text{V}}.\mid\overset{\text{III}}{T}\underset{\text{III}}{...}\mid\overset{\text{III}}{S}\underset{\text{III}}{...}\mid S\underset{\text{VI\,III\,V}}{\text{IV\,III}}\mid°T(\circ)$.

We must here, before all, supplement the explanation of the figuring. As already indicated, the ° always demands an under-clang ; Roman numbers, for indicating intervals measured down-wards, likewise show that we have to do with an underclang, so that the ° is then superfluous. In the last example the *counterpart in minor of the dominant chord of six-four in the major key*, which is well intelligible, is introduced ; naturally we must avoid placing the I in the bass, for then the chord would appear merely as tonic ; similarly, the I must be doubled, for, as we shall see, *dissonant* notes must never be doubled. This minor chord of six-four is wanting in the principal means of effect of the chord of six-four in major—the tension caused by the fourth and sixth as suspensions from *above* of the third and fifth, and relaxed by their *downward* resolution. It is just this higher or lower position, this upward or downward relation, which produces the different effect of major and minor, as the relations are not congruent, but only symmetrical.

A *second series of exercises* will now follow (here and through the course of the book) which are distinguished from the first, in that *one part is given completely* (consequently also the key). *One given part often makes the best and most natural connection of har-monies impossible ;* if, *e.g.*, for the harmony step tonic-dominant, the melody step from third to third is given, then the leading-tone step is made impossible (as the leading-note must not be doubled). In these examples the harmonies are not indicated as tonic, dominant, and subdominant, but by small italic letters (*c*, °*e*) indi-cating their principal notes (1, I). *In working out, the pupil is to indicate the functions of the harmo ies* (viz., their significance as tonic or dominant, etc., but without the numbers which refer only to the progression of parts) ; in these first exercises this is a very simple matter, but later on it will become more and more difficult, and must, therefore, be made a duty from the very beginning, if the attempt later on is not to prove a failure. Take the following example :

N.B.—Where only numbers, or ⁺, or °, without clang-letter or without .. , are placed by a note, it is itself (major or minor) prime ; where there is no figuring at all (see the fifth note), it is major prime ; the number, then, indicates the particular note for the bass ; only where the latter is given, the number indicates the note for the highest part.

The given part is so to be noted on the stave that the second

part to be written on the same stave can be distinguished from
it (thus in the case in question all note-stems of the given soprano
are to be turned upwards); when the soprano is given, the chord
signs are to be placed above the upper stave, when alto or tenor
are given, between the two staves, when bass, under the lower
stave; also, at the beginning, above, or below the upper or lower
stave, it is to be indicated by *cf.* (*cantus firmus, i.e.,* given part),
which part is given (these measures are necessary to spare the
teacher error in correcting [altering the cantus firmus]). The
example, worked out with the additional indication of functions,
would then look something like this:

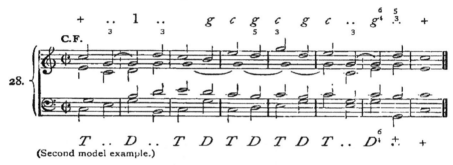

(Second model example.)

N.B.—Instead of $\frac{5}{3}$ after $\frac{6}{4}$, the abbreviated sign for the simple
overclang (major chord)$^{+}$ may be placed, as above, in the bar
before the last. This example is not wanting in progressions
which are deficient in smoothness (bars 1—2, 3, 5, 7); the student
should try to improve upon them!

I.   Major.

Exercises 18—20 (Soprano given).

EXERCISES 21—23 (Alto given).

EXERCISES 24—27 (Tenor given).

EXERCISES 28—31 (Bass given).

II.   MINOR.

EXERCISES 32—34 (Soprano given).

EXERCISES 35—37 (Alto given).

C

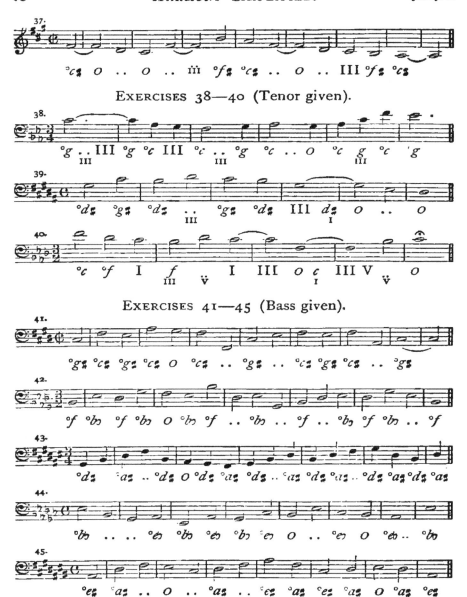

EXERCISES 38—40 (Tenor given).

EXERCISES 41—45 (Bass given).

§ 4. CONTRA-FIFTH STEP (CONNECTING THE TONIC WITH THE CONTRA-FIFTH CLANG: $T—S$ AND $°T—°D$).

If, on the one hand, the transition from the tonic to the plain-fifth clang appeared only like a natural continuation, a progression to partial notes of the second order, making the fifth of the clang independent as the bearer of its own clang, on the other hand, the transition to the contra-fifth clang (to the clang of the same mode on the fifth of the opposite side) has an entirely different significance.   It must be defined as a *forcible pressing back beyond the starting-point of harmonic relations* (the prime):

$$v \longleftarrow \overset{T\ D}{\overbrace{c\ e\ g\ b\ d}} \quad \text{and} \quad \overset{}{d\ f\ a\ c\ e} \longrightarrow {}_5$$
$$\underset{\underset{1 \longrightarrow}{}}{} \qquad \underset{{}^\circ S\ \ {}^\circ T}{}$$

The return from the plain-fifth clang to the tonic (D—T, ${}^\circ S$—${}^\circ T$) entirely coincides, indeed, in exterior, *i.e.*, as regards the means of melodious connection, with the contra-fifth step, but has an entirely different meaning; it is only a retrograde formation of that which had grown out of the tonic prime, a simple return, whereas the contra-fifth step—presupposing the consciousness of a tonic as a fixed point in the change of harmonies—causes an *artificial suspense*, which renders a marked forward motion necessary.   The contra-fifth clang is the stretched bow which slings the arrow beyond the mark (the tonic).   This applies to major as well as minor.   In major the contra-fifth clang (the underdominant, subdominant, abbreviated S) forms a receding downwards beyond the tonic, which itself strives upwards from its fundamental note : therefore, a pressing down below the level, whence it again powerfully forces the harmony upwards; in minor (as minor upper-dominant, abbreviated ${}^\circ D$) it is as a pulling upwards, an artificial lifting beyond the starting-point (the minor prime) from which the tonic develops downwards and generates the plain-fifth clang : therefore the contra-fifth clang in minor presses heavily downwards into the region of the dependencies of the tonic.   For this reason the contra-fifth clang is generally not followed by the tonic itself; this simple solution of the conflict caused by its introduction is not—at least at decisive points of the harmonic development—satisfactory or sufficient; rather, the contra-fifth clang is generally followed by the plain-fifth clang, which, then, leads back to the tonic in a thoroughly satisfactory manner, and closes restfully.   The clang successions T—S—D—T and ${}^\circ T$—${}^\circ D$—${}^\circ S$—${}^\circ T$ are, therefore, really typical for harmonic motion in general; they are so-called *complete (bilateral) cadences*.   With the addition of this new element (the contra-fifth clang), our exercises for the first time lose a certain stiffness and one-sidedness—the latter in the full sense of the word, as, so far, only *one side* of the tonic has been represented, whereas now both will be represented.   The following group of exercises still abstains from connecting the two dominants directly (on account of the risk of the worst consecutive fifths being incurred), and either the tonic or the feigning consonant formation of the chord of six-four, already known to us, is inserted between the contra-fifth clang and the plain-fifth clang.

The introduction of the contra-fifth clang after the tonic, its return to the latter, and its transition to the chord of six-four, give rise to no difficulties which would render new observations necessary.

Now, again, *exercises without given part* follow, only indicating the harmonies as tonic, dominant, etc., in the fashion of the first series in the last paragraph, which are to be worked out *in all keys ;* these exercises, as already remarked, are the easier ones, for, so long as the progression of parts is not restricted by the fixing of certain notes for the bass or for the highest part, they allow of the most normal ways of connection.

EXERCISES 46—51 (Major).

(46) ₵ : $T\ D\ |\ T\ S\ |\ T\ D\ |\ T\ D\ |\ T\ S\ |\ D^{6\ +}\ |\ \widehat{T.}$

(47) ₵ : $T\ |\ S\ ..\ |\ T\ S\ |\ T\ D\ |\ T\ \ \ |\ S\ S\ |\ D^{6\ +}\ ..\ |\ T\ (\ o\ |\ \,d\,).$

(48) ³/₂ : $T\ S\ T\ |\ D\ \ T\ ..\ |\ S\ D^{6\ +}\ ..\ |\ T\ S\ ..\ |\ D^{6}\ S\ ..\ |\ T.$

(49) ³/₄ : $S\ |\ T\ ..\ S\ |\ T\ ..\ S\ |\ T\ D\ T\ |\ D\ .\ T\ |\ S\ T\ S\ |$

$T\ S\ T\ |\ D\ :.\ :.\ |\ T\ (\,d\,).$

(50) ₵ : $T\ S\ |\ T\ ..\ |\ D\ T\ |\ D\ ..\ |\ T\ D\ |\ T\ S\ |\ D^{6\ +}\ |\ T.$

(51) ³/₂ : $T \underset{3}{D} \mid T \underset{3}{S} \underset{5}{T} \mid S \overset{3}{\cdot} \underset{3}{T} \mid \underset{3}{S} \underset{5}{T} \cdot\cdot \underset{3}{\cdot} \mid D \; T \; S \mid \underset{3}{\cdot\cdot} D^{6}_{4} \overset{+}{\cdot\cdot} \mid$

$T \underset{5}{D} \underset{3}{T} \mid S \; D^{6}_{4} \overset{+}{\cdot\cdot} \mid T (\mathrel{\mathop{\rule{0pt}{1.2ex}}}).$

EXERCISES 52—57 (Minor).

(52) ₵ : $^{\circ}T \mid \underset{\text{III}}{S} \cdot\cdot \mid \underset{\text{III}}{T} \underset{\text{I}}{D} \mid {^{\circ}T} \; {^{\circ}S} \mid \underset{\text{I}}{T} \underset{\text{V}}{D} \underset{\substack{\text{IV III}\\\text{VI V}}}{S} \mid \underset{\text{I}}{T} \underset{\text{III}}{S} \mid \underset{\text{V}}{\cdot\cdot} \underset{\text{III}}{\cdot\cdot} \mid {^{\circ}T}.$

(53) ³/₂ : $\overset{\text{III}}{T} \overset{\text{I}}{D} \overset{\text{V}}{T} \mid \underset{\text{III}}{S} \underset{\text{V}}{\cdot\cdot} \underset{\text{III}}{T} \mid {^{\circ}D} \underset{\text{III}}{\cdot\cdot} {^{\circ}T} \mid {^{\circ}S} \; {^{\circ}T} \; {^{\circ}S} \mid \underset{\substack{\text{IV III}\\\text{VI V}}}{\cdot\cdot} \overset{\text{III}}{\cdot\cdot} \mid {^{\circ}T}$

(54) ₵ : $^{\circ}T \; {^{\circ}D} \mid \underset{\text{III}}{T} \; {^{\circ}S} \mid {^{\circ}T} \underset{\text{III}}{S} \mid {^{\circ}T} \underset{\text{III}}{\cdot\cdot} \mid {^{\circ}S} \overset{\text{III}}{\cdot\cdot} \mid \underset{\text{III I}}{T} \cdot\cdot \mid \underset{\text{III V}}{S} \cdot\cdot \mid {^{\circ}T}.$

(55) ³/₄ : $^{\circ}T \underset{\text{III}}{S} \mid \underset{\text{I}}{T} \underset{\text{III}}{\cdot\cdot} {^{\circ}S} \mid {^{\circ}T} \cdot\cdot \underset{\text{III}}{\cdot\cdot} \mid {^{\circ}D} \underset{\text{III}}{T} {^{\circ}S} \mid {^{\circ}T}.$

(56) ₵ : $\overset{\text{V}}{T} \overset{\text{I}}{D} \mid \overset{\text{III}}{T} \underset{\text{III}}{S} \mid \underset{\text{I}}{T} {^{\circ}S} \mid \underset{\text{III}}{T} {^{\circ}S} \mid \underset{\text{V}}{T} {^{\circ}D} \mid \overset{\text{III}}{\underset{\text{III}}{T}} {^{\circ}S} \mid {^{\circ}T} {^{\circ}S} \mid {^{\circ}T}.$

(57) ₵ : $\overset{\text{III}}{D} \mid \underset{\text{III}}{T} \overset{\text{III}}{S} \mid {^{\circ}T} {^{\circ}S} \mid {^{\circ}T} \overset{\text{III}}{\cdot\cdot} \mid {^{\circ}D} \underset{\text{III}}{\cdot\cdot} \mid {^{\circ}T} {^{\circ}D} \mid \underset{\substack{\text{IV III}\\\text{VI V}}}{S} \mid {^{\circ}T}.$

A second series of exercises with one given part and direct indication of the clangs is intended for acquiring dexterity in smoothing interruptions in the normal connection, caused by abnormal steps in one part. The pupil is to indicate the functions of the single clangs (as tonic, dominant, and subdominant) in each exercise worked out, as was the case in Exercises 29—45:

I. MAJOR.

EXERCISES 58—60 (Soprano given).

31.

58.

$c \; f \; 3 \; g \; \cdot\cdot \; c \; f \; c \; g \; \cdot\cdot \; c \; f \; \cdot\cdot \; \cdot\cdot \; g^{\natural}_{}{}^{6} \overset{+}{\cdot\cdot}$
$_{3} _{3} _{5} _{3}$

59.

$d \; g \; d \; g \; a^{6}_{4} \overset{+}{\cdot\cdot} \; d \; a \; 3 \; 3 \; d \; g \; {}^{6}_{4} \overset{+}{\cdot\cdot} \; d$
$ _{3} \phantom{g \; a^{6}} \phantom{\overset{+}{\cdot\cdot} \; d \; a \; 3 \; 3 \; d} _{5}$

60.

$b\flat \; f \; 3 \; b\flat \; 3 \; b\flat \; f \; 3 \; e\flat \; f^{6}_{}\!{}^{4} \overset{+}{\cdot\cdot}$
$ _{5}$

EXERCISES 61—63 (Alto given).

II. MINOR.

EXERCISES 70—72 (Soprano given).

EXERCISES 73—75 (Alto given).

EXERCISES 76—78 (Tenor given).

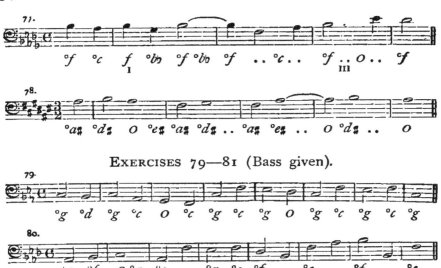

EXERCISES 79—81 (Bass given).

N.B.—For the first time in Exercise 65, a slur from the l in
the sign of the third chord from the end to the l of the last
chord is used to indicate that the bass-note (*c♯*) is to be sustained.
There the *c♯* is also an element of the middle chord (5 in *f♯* +);
later on we shall find this method of indication very useful in
expressing and explaining in a simple manner the most complicated formations of the so-called *Pedal-point.*

§ 5. THE WHOLE-TONE STEP (*S—D* AND °*D*—°*S*).

The direct connection of the plain-fifth clang with the contra-
fifth clang, as has been pointed out, brings with it the risk of
the *worst of all consecutive fifths*, viz., fifths rising or falling a
whole tone while their notes have the significance $\frac{5-5}{1-1}$ and $\frac{I-I}{V-V}$
respectively (*actual harmonic consecutive fifths*):

Our principal rules for the progression of parts form, indeed, a pretty sure guarantee against such error; why should we take whole-tone steps in all the parts, and, as in Example 17, introduce two harmonies in similar position after one another? For in so doing, are we not neglecting the best possible step, viz., the *leading-tone step? Let us make the leading-tone step, and the other parts are immediately led into their proper paths, and the danger of consecutive octaves and fifths disappears without trace:*

33.

As at (*a*) *c* proceeds to *b*, the alto cannot also take *b*, because the latter may not be doubled; consequently it is forced down to *g*. The tenor will have to take *d*, else this would be missing, if we retain the desirable bass progression from fundamental note to fundamental note. At (*c*) the relations are entirely similar: *f* must not be doubled; if *e* proceed to *f*, *g* must go to *a*, and *b* will be directed to *d*. At (*b*) and (*d*) an excellent connection of the two chords is made by doubling the 5 in *S*, and the 1 in °*D*.

The state of matters is worse, however, if one *given part* renders the above normal mode of connecting the harmonies impossible, *e.g.*, for f^+—g^+:

34.

or, for °*b*—°*a*:

35.

For, at 34 (*a*) and (*e*), and also at 35 (*a*) and (*e*), the leading-tone step is made impossible; since the leading-note itself (3 of the *D* and III of the °*S* respectively) may not be doubled, the *c* in f^+—g^+ must not proceed to *b*, if *a* has proceeded to *b* [34 (*a*)], or *f* to *b* [34 (*e*)], and in °*b*—°*a*, *e* must not go to *f*, if *g* has gone to *f* [35 (*a*)], or *b* gone to *f* [35 (*e*)]; therefore, in these four cases, the leading-tone step must be sacrificed; in major:

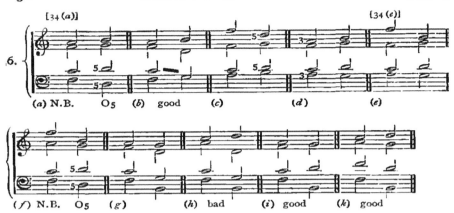

and similarly in minor :

But little need be added. At 36 (*a*) and (*f*) the bass par
leaps a third to the fifth of the dominant ; the effect is no
entirely good, for reasons already known to us (viz., becaus
taking the fifth in the bass part by leap readily gives it adde
importance, and raises the impression that we have a chord c
six-four before us, *cf.* the remarks to Example 26), but it mus
often be allowed for lack of better ways. Just in this very case
however, the actual effect of a chord of six-four is excluded, a
coming after the under-dominant the upper-dominant *in an*
position marks the key very pointedly, and a resolution of th
chord of six-four into the chord of five-three (in this case th
resolution of d_4^6 into d^+) must appear illogical, because it woul
contradict the key again. At 36 (*d*) and 37 (*d*) the third of th
subdominant is doubled in order to open up other ways ; but i
must be presupposed that the third doubling was not the resul
of parallel motion. At 36 (*g*) and (*h*) three parts proceed by leap
an expedient to be resorted to only in extreme cases.

Such cases as 34 (*b*) and 35 (*b*) are also very disagreeable
particularly when the step 5—5, or I—I respectively, is given in th
soprano or bass part ; in the former case, because then th
succession of the two fundamental notes is impossible (oi
account of consecutive fifths necessarily arising), in the secon
because the effect of two chords of six-four in succession is th

result (that placing the minor prime in the bass may produce the effect of six-four will be explained in the next chapter, which introduces the contra-clang of the tonic). The ways of evading the difficulty are:

Here at (c), (d), (e), (f), and (i) even the leading-tone step could be preserved.

There now remain the abnormal leaps given at 34 (c) and (d), and 35 (c) and (d), of which only 34 (d) gives rise to particular difficulties :

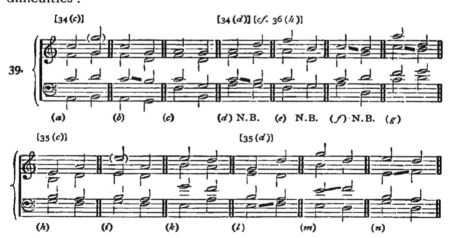

In seven of these cases, indeed, the leading-tone step had to be given up.

Another problem which this succession of harmonies for the first time brings before our notice is the possibility of *a part proceeding by an augmented interval;* the step from the prime of the contra-fifth clang to the third of the plain-fifth clang (*f—b* and *b—f* respectively) is good only as fifth (diminished, *i.e.*, too small by a semitone) ; on the other hand, it is bad as a fourth (augmented, *i.e.*, too great by a semitone, *tritone* [three whole tones: *f . . g . . a . . b*]). *Good melodious setting,* which must always be our norm, *has to avoid the tritone under all circumstances* (at least *with changing harmonies ;* when possible within the same harmony, it may be allowed without hesitation, so long as it does not incur the violation of the most important melodic principle— turning after leaps ; *i.e.*, *f—b* [rising], is good, while the same harmony is sustained, if *a* can and does follow, an exception which is of consequence in the treatment of the chord of the under seventh, as we shall see later. For the present we must accept the prohibition of augmented intervals without *any* exception).

After this detailed examination of the difficulties which meet us in writing the whole-tone step, and having settled the means of overcoming them, we may introduce the direct connection of the two dominants in our next exercises, which will thus gain in variety. We again give two series, first, such as have no given part and no key determined, in which so long as certain bass progressions or notes for the highest part are not demanded, the usual connecting of the two chords shown in Example 33 is possible, and secondly, such as cause particular difficulties on account of the given part. In working out the latter, the indica- tions *T, D, S,* or °*T,* °*D,* °*S,* respectively, are to be added, as has been done hitherto.

So as gradually to accustom the pupil to reading a *score* consisting of many staves, and, foremost, to prepare him for writing in the so-called "four clefs," the next exercises are no longer to be worked out on two, but *on four staves,* in such a manner that soprano and alto are noted, as hitherto, in the treble clef, and tenor and bass in the bass clef, but every part on a separate stave, as in the following model example :

(Third model example.)

As in this case every part has a stave to itself, it is not necessary for the soprano to have all the note-stems turned upwards, etc. ; on the contrary, *the calligraphic rules* come into force that all notes lying above the middle line should have their stems turned downwards, all lying below, turned upwards, while for notes on the middle line either way is equally good.

EXERCISES 82—93 (Major).

(82) ₵: $T \mid D\ T \mid S\ D \mid T \underset{3}{..} \mid D \underset{3}{..} \mid T \underset{3}{S} \mid D \underset{3}{..} \mid T (\text{♩})$

(83) ³/₂: $T \underset{3}{S} D \mid T \underset{3}{S} T \mid D \underset{3}{S} \underset{5}{T} \mid S\ D \underset{3}{..} \mid T\ S\ D \mid T \underset{3}{S} ..\mid$

$D^{6}_{4} S\ D \mid T (\text{♩.})$

(84) ¢: $T \mid S \underset{3}{..} D^{6\ 5}_{4\ 3} \mid T \underset{3}{S} D\ \dot{T} \mid S .. \ D .. \mid T (\text{♩.})$

(85) ³/₄: $T\ S\ D \mid T \underset{3}{S} D \mid T\ D\ T \mid D \underset{3}{..} \mid T\ S\ T \mid S\ D\ T \mid$
$\qquad (\text{♩ ♩})$
$S\ D^{6\ 5}_{4\ 3} \mid T (\text{♩.})$

(86) ³/₈: $T \mid D \underset{3}{..} \mid T\ S \mid \underset{3}{..} D \mid T \underset{5}{D} \mid T\ S \mid \underset{3}{..} D \mid T \mathrel{\vdots} \mid {}^{5}_{3} (\text{♩})$
(♩ ♩ ♩ etc.)

(87) ₵: $T\ D \mid S\ T \mid \underset{3}{S} \ D \mid T \underset{3\ 5}{D} \mid T \underset{3}{D} \mid \underset{3}{S} D \mid D^{6\ 5}_{4\ 3} \mid T (\text{♩})$

(88) ³/₄: $S\ D \mid T \underset{3\ 1}{..} \mid S\ D \mid T \underset{5}{D} \mid T\ S \mid D\ S \mid D^{6}_{4} D \mid T (\text{♩.})$
(♩ ♩ ♩ ♩etc.)

(89) ³/₄: $T \mid S\ D^{6\ 5}_{4\ 3} \mid T .. \mid S\ D \mid T .. \mid S\ D\ S \mid D\ T \mid S\ D \mid T$
$\qquad (\text{♩ ♩ ♩ ♩ ♩})\qquad\qquad (\text{♩ ♩ ♩ ♩ ♩})$

(90) ₵: $T \underset{3}{D} \mid T \underset{3}{S} D \underset{3}{..} \mid T \underset{5}{D} \underset{3}{T} D \mid \underset{3}{S} .. D^{6\ 5}_{4\ 3} \mid T (\text{♩})$

(91) ³/₄: T D | T S D T | D S T S | $D^{\circ i}$ S D .. | T
　　　　⁵　　³　　　　　　　　³

(92) ³/₈: T | S D | T .. | S D | T D | T S T | S .. | D .. | T(♩)
　　　　　³　³　　　³　　　　　　　　　³　⁵

(93) ²/₄: T .. D | T S | D .. T | D S | T S D | T S D | T D | T(♩)
　　　　　　　　³　　　　　　　　　　　　　　　　　　³

Exercises 94—100 (Minor).

(94) ¢: $^{\circ}T$ | $^{\circ}S^{\circ}T$ | $^{\circ}D$ S | T $^{\circ}S$ | T .. | $^{\circ}D$ $^{\circ}S$ | T $^{\circ}S$ | $^{\circ}T$
　　　　　　　　　　　　ɪɪɪ　ɪ　ɪɪɪ　　　　　　ɪɪɪ

(95) ³/₂: $^{\circ}T$ | S T $^{\circ}S$ | T $^{\circ}D$ | S $^{\circ}T$ $^{\circ}S$ | T $^{\mathbf{I}}_{..}$ $^{\circ}S$ | $^{\circ}D$ $^{\circ}T$ $^{\circ}D$ |
　　　　　　　　ɪɪɪ　ɪ　　　ɪɪᴄ　　　ɪɪɪ　　　　　ɪɪɪ

$^{\circ}S$ .. | $^{\circ}T$

(96) ³/₄: $^{\circ}T$ $^{\circ}D$ | $^{\circ}T$ $^{\circ}S$ | $^{\circ}T$ $^{\circ}D$ $^{\circ}S$ | $^{\circ}T$ .. $^{\circ}S$ | $^{\circ}T$ .. $^{\circ}D$ |

$^{\circ}S$ .. | $^{\circ}T$

(97) ³/₈: $^{\circ}T$ | $^{\circ}D$ $^{\circ}S$ | $^{\circ}T$ $^{\circ}S$ | T $^{\circ}D$ | S .. | $^{\circ}T$ $^{\circ}D$ | $^{\circ}S$ .. | $^{\circ}T$
　　　　　　　　　　　　　　　　ɪɪɪ　　ᴠ ɪɪɪ

(98) ¢: $^{\circ}T$ $^{\circ}S$ $^{\circ}T$ $^{\circ}D$ | $^{\circ}S$ .. $^{\circ}T$ | $^{\circ}D$ $^{\circ}S$ $^{\circ}T$ $^{\circ}S$ | T $^{\circ}S$ $^{\circ}T$
　　　　　　　　　　　　　　　　　　　　　　　　　　　　　　ɪɪɪ

(99) ¢: $^{\circ}T^{\circ}S$ | T S | T D | $^{\circ}S$ T | $^{\circ}D$ $^{\circ}S$ | .. T | D $^{\circ}S$ | $^{\circ}T$
　　　　　　　　ɪɪɪ ɪɪɪ　ɪ ᴠ　　　ɪɪɪ　　　　ɪɪɪ ɪ　ᴠ

(100) ²/₄: $^{\circ}T$ | $^{\circ}S^{\circ}T$ | $^{\circ}D$ $^{\circ}S$ | $^{\circ}T^{\circ}S$ | $^{\circ}T^{\circ}S$ | $T^{\circ}S$ | $T^{\circ}D$ $^{\circ}S$ | $^{\circ}T$
　　　　　　　　　　　　　　　　　　　　　　ɪɪɪ　ɪ

The notification of a certain rhythm (by means of ♪♩♩ or
♪♩.♩|♩. etc., under the figures) scarcely requires any further
explanation. *There would be no meaning in continuing to write*

exercises in equal notes after the manner of chorales; on the contrary, practice in four-part writing will be of the greatest advantage, if so planned as to incite and fructify the talent of a gifted pupil, instead of fettering it and sending it to sleep.

I. Major.

EXERCISES 101—103 (Soprano given).

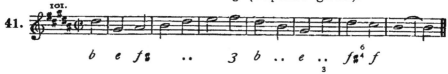

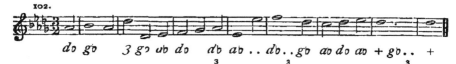

EXERCISES 104—106 (Alto given).

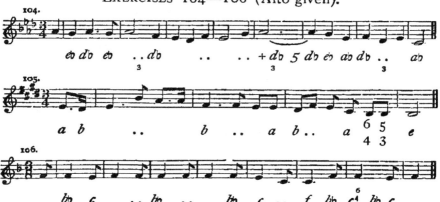

EXERCISES 107—109 (Tenor given).

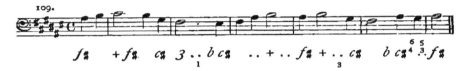

EXERCISES 110—112 (Bass given).

II. MINOR.

EXERCISES 113—115 (Soprano given).

EXERCISES 116—118 (Alto given).

§ 6. THE TURN OF HARMONY (T—$°S$ AND $°T$—^+D), CONTRA-FIFTH CHANGE ($°S$—D^+) AND FIFTH-CHANGE ($°S$—^+S AND $°D$—D^+).

If the contra-fifth clang coming after the tonic appeared like proceeding in the opposite direction beyond the uniting point of harmonic reference (pressing down below the level in major, forcible drawing upwards in minor), therefore, in a measure, as a step in the sense of the contrary clang principle (the contra-fifth is *under*-fifth of the *major tonic* and *upper*-fifth of the *minor tonic*), we cannot be surprised, if, beside the fifth of the contra-side, also the third of that side be used, and the complete *contra-clang* be placed in juxtaposition to the tonic, so that, in place of the direct relatives of the overtone series, the direct ones of the undertone series appear in company with the prime, and conversely:

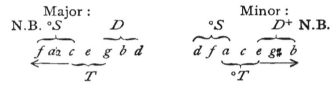

In place of the marked tension peculiar to the contra-fifth clang, the contra-clang (or "turn-of-harmony clang") of the tonic produces a transient contradiction of the mode, a *mixture of major and minor relations*, which, it must be admitted, is characterised by a certain artificiality and excitement. After the major tonic, the minor under-dominant—for the contra-clang is that—appears like a sorrowful glimpse into the gloomy region of minor relations, and, conversely, in the major upper-dominant of the minor key, we must see a yearning straining upwards into the bright domain of major relations. So much is certain—*pure minor as well as pure major, in opposition to these mixed modes arising from the introduction of the contra-clangs* (so to speak, "minor-major" and "major-minor"), *seem like healthier, more original, simpler formations;* this is sufficiently indicated by the fact that *the contra-clang contradicts the scale:* a♭ is foreign to the signature of c major, and g♯ to that of a minor. The mixed modes are an acquisition of modern times; they were unknown to antiquity and the middle ages.

The tonal function of this new harmonic formation must be explained by its origin. *The contra-clang of the Tonic is really a plain-fifth clang of the Tonic-Variant, i.e., of a tonic of the other clang-mode*);* the F-minor chord ($°c$) in c-major is really

---

* For this reason we do not indicate the contra-clang of the major tonic as $^•T$ (underclang of the tonic), but as $°S$, and the contra-clang of the minor tonic not as T^+ but as D^+, and in c major understand by $^•T$ the c minor chord, and in A minor by T^+ the A-major chord (for which more reasons will be adduced later on).

the plain-fifth clang (subdominant) of the c-minor chord, the E-major chord in A-minor is really the plain-fifth clang (dominant) of the A-major chord, so that the introduction of the contra-clang, strictly speaking, means borrowing a harmonic relation which is obvious and quite natural in the other mode. This is equivalent to saying that the contra-clang must not be looked upon as taking the place of the contra-fifth clang, but, on the contrary, as side by side with the plain-fifth clang, as another means of making a perfect cadence borrowed from the contrary mode (*hence, also, the generally recognised possibility of closing with the tonic of the opposite mode after paving the way by means of the contra-clang, at least in the minor key* [also possible in the major, but seldom used for æsthetic counterreasons]). To introduce the contra-clang simply in place of the contra-fifth clang in the two perfect cadences T—S—D—T and $°T$—$°D$—$°S$—$°T$ would not be right; in so doing we should simply be setting aside a highly important element of the cadence (the tension caused by the contra-fifth clang cannot be replaced by the contra-clang). We might sooner think of replacing the plain-fifth clang by the contra-clang :

$$T—S—°S—T \text{ and } °T—°D—D^+—°T.$$

It cannot be denied that these two cadences still contain the characteristic effects of motion towards a foreign clang (contra-fifth clang) and satisfactory closing (by means of the step contra-clang—tonic). The attempt at a contrary combination, viz., deferring the contra-clang till after the plain-fifth clang :

$$T—D—°S—T \text{ and } °T—°S—D^+—°T$$

even proves the cadential power of the contra-clang greater than that of the plain-fifth clang, *i.e.*, the contra-clang after the plain-fifth clang already seems like a decided return towards the starting-point; all that remains to be done is to turn about the prime as about a pivot. This form of cadence is generally recognised for the minor. But there is no reason for dropping either of the dominants proper to the scale in favour of those foreign to the scale, *i.e.*, ultimately the natural place for the contra-clang is at the close of the cadence, even if the contra-fifth clang and plain-fifth clang have already been introduced :

$$T—S—D—°S—T \text{ and } °T—°D—°S—D^+—°T$$

Cadences are not, of course, musical pieces, and, therefore, the importance of these remarks must not be overrated; but, on the other hand, it would be quite wrong to underrate them; for they are undoubtedly just as much types of harmonic development as scales are types of melodic motion.

With the introduction of the major upper-dominant the minor

key acquires the chord of six-four, which is so important in preparing cadences; but the chord of six-four of the $^{+}$dominant of the minor key naturally has a minor sixth, corresponding to the third of the tonic (*chord of minor sixth and fourth*). It is distinguished in figuring by a $>$ applied to the 6, which indicates that *the sixth has to be lowered a semitone* ($e\,\overset{6>}{4} = e\,a\,c$; $e\,\overset{6}{4} = e\,a\,c\sharp$!).

We must now, before proceeding to new exercises, examine the connection of the contra-clang with the tonic and the other clangs hitherto considered, in practical four-part writing. The steps $T^{+}—{}^{\circ}S$ and ${}^{\circ}T—D^{+}$ (*turns of harmony*) prove superior to the plain-fifth step, firstly, in that they offer the possibility of two leading-tone steps:

Besides, we have, as in the plain and contra-fifth-steps, a sustained note (a note in common: $c\,c\,c$ and $e\,e\,e$ respectively), with figures 1 1 1 and 1 1 1, and the unhindered succession of the two fundamental notes, the doubling of which meets with no check. But this succession of harmonies also brings a new problem with it, inasmuch as the step from the third of the one clang to the third of the other is allowable only under certain conditions:

$e—a\flat$ rising and $c—g\sharp$ falling are diminished fourths ($4>$), $e—a\flat$ falling and $c—g\sharp$ rising are augmented fifths ($5<$; [$<$, the inversion of $>$, indicates *raising a semitone*]); we have, therefore, first an augmented interval ($5<$), which is altogether forbidden as a part progression, and further a diminished one ($4>$), which is only good if it can proceed correctly. *All augmented and diminished part progressions necessitate a subsequent semitone step, the augmented ones further away in the direction of the step already made* (for which reason they almost without exception contradict the melody principle mentioned on page 18—turning after leaps— and are therefore bad), *the diminished ones, on the other hand, turning again* (by which means they attain a specifically melodic character). But *diminished* steps are good, only *on the supposition* that a turning semitone step follows; if the latter does not follow or is impossible, the diminished step also is bad. The first consequence of this is that the diminished step must be excluded in cadences:

But we must further remark that the *rhythmical position is of the greatest importance in estimating diminished as well as augmented intervals ;* as in the case of a real close, so in general in *progressions from less accented to more accented beats*, it is *not good* to introduce steps which call for subsequent proceeding by semitone (namely, augmented and diminished steps) ; whereas, in going from an accented to an unaccented beat, provided that the subsequent semitone step takes place, even augmented intervals are not very objectionable (but they must be avoided by the pupil, as he must first acquire absolutely normal ways, naturalness, smoothness, and fluency in writing). Therefore :

The connection of the contra-clang with the plain-fifth clang (D—°S and °S—D) meets with the same risks as the whole-tone step (consecutive fifths and octaves), but a few new ones in addition (augmented and diminished intervals). As, in the first place, from the one clang to the principal note of the other there is a contra-fifth step :

$$c \longleftarrow g\ b\ d \qquad \text{and} \qquad d\ f\ a \longrightarrow e$$

but the mode is also changed :

$$\longleftarrow °c \ldots g \longrightarrow \qquad \text{and} \qquad \longleftarrow °a \ldots e \longrightarrow$$

we must indicate this succession of harmonies as a *contrafifth change*. The consecutive fifths which threaten us in writing the contra-fifth change :

are not, indeed, so very bad as those in the whole-tone step, since the notes have not as in that case parallel significance (here $\frac{1}{5}$-$\frac{1}{V}$, there $\frac{1}{5}$-$\frac{1}{1}$ and $\frac{1}{V}$-$\frac{1}{V}$), but they are, nevertheless, not good.

The other hindrances in writing are (besides the *b—f* in common with the whole-tone-step, in both cases) :

another augmented fourth (bad) or diminished fifth (good), an augmented second (2 <, bad) or diminished seventh (7 >, good). But as equivalent for these hindrances, we find two leading-tone steps (3—I and 1—III):

But any way, a great number of the progressions indicated for the whole-tone-step become impossible, as a comparison, by no means superfluous, with the last § (Examples 36–39) will show, viz. :

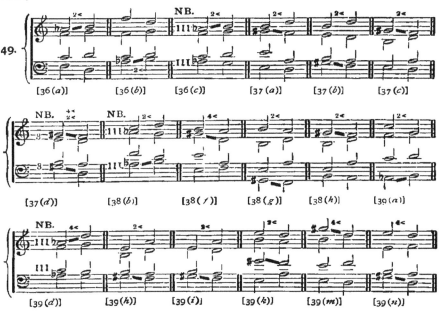

In four cases (at N. B.) even *doubling of the third* would occur, which is *altogether forbidden for the contra-clang.* A few new ways are opened to us by the step of the diminished seventh a step much better than that of the minor or major sevenths, which, for that reason, we have altogether disregarded :

The result of *connecting the contra-clang with the contra-fifth clang* is likewise a new harmony step, which we must call the (plain) *fifth-change*, since the principal note of the second clang is the plain fifth of the first, and the clang-mode changes :

The clangs constituting the contra-fifth change appeared quite foreign to each other (see above), but on the other hand, those of the plain fifth-change are very closely connected, as they have both notes of the interval of the fifth in common (though with inverted meaning) and only differ in the third :

$$f \overset{a}{\underset{ab}{\overbrace{}c}} \quad \text{and} \quad e \overset{g\sharp}{\underset{g}{\overbrace{}b}}$$

But with the introduction of this step we have a new part progression (the chromatic semitone) and also a new problem, that of *false relation*.

The *chromatic semitone step* has even more undeniable claims to consideration, than the diatonic (leading-tone step) ; if, in the fifth-change, we neglect *introducing both thirds in succession in the same part,* the result will be that ugly effect which is cried down under the name of false relation (Ger. *Querstand*). *Our ears are then not able to perceive the change of harmony,* and are rather deceived into the *belief that the same harmony is sustained ;* and so the *chromatic note only appears out of tune.* The effect is all the more disagreeable, the less marked the part is which introduces the second third, and the further the latter is distant from the first as regards octave-position (real pitch) :

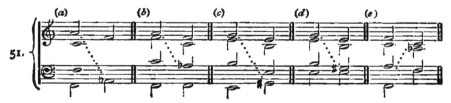

Here (*a*) and (*c*) are particularly bad, as are also (*b*) and (*d*), though the effect is somewhat mitigated at (*c*) and (*d*), because the major chord appears second; at (*e*) and (*f*) another part takes up the progression in the same octave-position, at (*g*) and (*h*) the chromatic note appears in the highest part, and is, therefore, more easily recognised. The reason given above for the bad effect of false relation also explains why the actual effect of false relation is felt only in the fifth-change, and not, for example, in third-steps of harmonies, etc., and why in certain harmony successions (tritone-step) progressions with false relation may even be normal.

The following exercises are to be worked out, similarly to those of the last paragraph, on four staves, but the *tenor* is not to be noted in the bass clef but *in the treble clef*, an octave higher than it sounds—as is usual in modern vocal scores—like the following model example :

(Fourth model example.)

EXERCISES 125—130 (Major).

(125) ₵: T | S °S | T .. | D .. | °S D | T S | °S D | T °S | T.
$\qquad\quad$ 3 1 $\quad$ 3 1

(126) $^3/_2$: T | S °S D | T .. °S | D T .. | D .. °S | $D^{\frac{6}{3}\,\frac{5}{3}}$ T |
$\qquad\qquad\qquad\qquad\qquad\quad$ 3 $\qquad\quad$ 3 1 $\qquad\qquad\qquad\qquad$ 3

$\qquad\quad$ S D °S | $D^{\frac{6}{3}\,\frac{5}{3}}$ .. | T (*o*)

(127) ³/₄: $T \mid {}^{\circ}S\ D \mid T\ S\ {}^{\circ}S \mid D^{6\ 5}_{\scriptsize{3}} \mid {}^{\circ}S\ S^{+} .. \mid T\ D\ T \mid S\ {}^{\circ}S .. \mid$
(♩ ♩ ♩) ♩ ♩
$D^{6\ 5}_{\scriptsize 3} \mid T\ (\text{♩}).$

(128) ⁹/₄: $D \mid {}^{\circ}S\ D \mid T\ S \mid {}^{\circ}S\ D \mid S\ T .. \mid {}^{\circ}S\ D \mid T\ S \mid$
(♩ ♩ ♩ ♩ ♩ ♩ ♩ ♩ ♩) ₃ ₃
$D^{6\ 5}_{\scriptsize 3} \mid T\ (\text{♩.}).$

(129) ₵: $T \mid D .. S\ {}^{\circ}S \mid D^{6\ 5}_{\scriptsize 3}\ T\ {}^{\circ}S \mid {}^{+}S\ D\ T\ {}^{\circ}S \mid T^{6\ 5}_{\scriptsize 4\ 3}.$

(130) ₵: $T .._{\scriptsize 8} \mid S\ {}^{\circ}S \mid D .._{\scriptsize 3} \mid T\ D_{\scriptsize 5} \mid T_{\scriptsize 3}\ {}^{\circ}S \mid D\ {}^{+}S \mid D^{6\ 5}_{\scriptsize 3} \mid T.$

EXERCISES 131—136 (Minor).

(131) ₵: ${}^{\circ}T\ {}^{\circ}S \mid D\ {}^{\circ}T \mid {}^{\circ}D\ {}^{\circ}S \mid D\ T_{\scriptsize III} \mid {}^{\circ}S\ T_{\scriptsize I} \mid {}^{\circ}D\ {}^{\circ}S \mid D^{6\ 5}_{\scriptsize 3} \mid {}^{\circ}T.$

(132) ³/₄: ‖: ${}^{\circ}T \mid D^{+}\ {}^{\circ}S\ D^{6\ 5}_{\scriptsize 3} \mid {}^{\circ}T\ D_{\scriptsize 5}\ T_{\scriptsize III} \mid D^{+}\ {}^{\circ}T\ {}^{\circ}D\ {}^{\circ}S \mid D^{+}$:‖
♩ ♩ ♩ ♩♩ ♩ ♩ ♩♩
II.
${}^{\circ}S\ D^{+} \mid {}^{\circ}T.$

(133) ⁴/₈: ${}^{\circ}T .._{\scriptsize III}\ D \mid S .._{\scriptsize III}\ D^{6\ 5}_{\scriptsize 3} \mid {}^{\circ}T .._{\scriptsize III}\ {}^{\circ}D\ {}^{\circ}S \mid D^{6\ 5}_{\scriptsize 3}\ {}^{\circ}T.$
♩ ♩ ♩

(134) ³/₂: ${}^{\circ}D\ {}^{\circ}S .. \mid T .._{\scriptsize III}\ D\ {}^{\circ}T \mid {}^{\circ}D\ {}^{\circ}S .._{\scriptsize III} \mid D\ {}^{\circ}S\ D^{6\ 5}_{\scriptsize 3} \mid$
♩ ♩ ♩ ♩ ♩ ♩ ♩ ♩ ♩ ♩ ♩ ♩ ♩

${}^{\circ}T\ {}^{\circ}D\ D^{+} \mid {}^{\circ}T\ S .._{\scriptsize III\ V} \mid D^{6}_{\scriptsize 4}\ S_{\scriptsize III}\ D .. \mid {}^{\circ}T.$
♩ ♩ ♩ ♩ ♩

(135) ₵: ${}^{\circ}T\ {}^{\circ}S \mid T_{\scriptsize III}\ D_{\scriptsize 5} \mid S_{\scriptsize I}\ T_{\scriptsize V} \mid {}^{\circ}D\ D^{+} \mid {}^{\circ}S\ D^{+} \mid {}^{\circ}S .. \mid D^{6\ 5}_{\scriptsize 3} \mid {}^{\circ}T$

$(136)\ ^2/_4:\ ^\circ T\ |\ ^\circ S\ ^\circ T\ |\ D^+\ ^\circ D\ |\ ^\circ S\ ..\ |\ D^+\ ..\ |\ ^\circ T\ \underset{5}{D}\ |\ \underset{\text{III}}{T}\ ^\circ S\ |$

$D^\bullet\ ^\circ S\ |\ ^\circ T.$

The examples which follow now, no longer keep to one key, but by means of a whole-tone step or contra-fifth change which breaks the bounds of the key, modulate in the simplest fashion to that of the plain or contra-fifth clang ; we thus enter a new domain, that of *MODULATION*, whose essence lies in the *change of functions of harmonies*. If, *e.g.*, from the tonic we make a whole-tone step or contra-fifth change, *a clang appears to have been passed over, which, as intervening link, is necessary to make the connection of the two clangs following each other intelligible ;* and this is revealed by the fact that we expect to hear this particular clang as the continuation of the chord succession. In other words, *the whole-tone step and contra-fifth change always appear as the succession of two dominants embracing one tonic, e.g.,* the harmony succession :

$$c^+\quad f^+\quad g^+\quad \underset{3}{c^+}\quad ..\quad \text{N.B.}\quad d^+\quad \underset{3}{..}\quad g^+,$$

at N.B. introduces after the tonic c^+ the harmony d^+ distant a whole tone from it : our ears immediately accept the succession $c^+\ d^+$ as *S—D, i.e.,* c^+, on account of the d^+ which follows, changes its significance into subdominant ; and, therefore, the succession will be correctly noted thus,—

$$T\ |\ S\ D\ |\ \underset{=\ \underset{3}{S}}{T\underset{3}{..}}\ |\ D\ ..\ |\ T$$

In the following exercises, whenever we come across the *sign of equality* $(=)$ in the indication of functions, a *change of significance from one function to another, i.e.,* modulation, takes place.

EXERCISES 137—140 (modulating).

$(137)\ \maltese:\ T\ |\ D\ T\ |\ ^\circ S\ D\ |\ T\ \underset{5}{D}\ |\ \underset{3\ =}{T}\underset{S}{..}\ |D\ T\ |\ ^\circ S\ D\ |\ T\ |\ ..\quad ^{-D}$

$S\ \underset{3}{D}\ |\ T\ \underset{3}{S}\ |\ D\ ^\circ S\ |\ T\ S\ |\ D\ ^\circ S\ |\ D^\bullet\ ^{6\ 5}_{\ \ 3}\ |\ T\ |\ ..$

(Modulation to the key of the D and back.)

(138) $^3/_4$: $°T$ | $•S\ D^{⌀\ 5}_{4\ 3}$ | $°T$ .. $\ \ ..\atop{=°S}$ | $D\ °T\ °S$ | $°T\ \ {=\atop{°D}\ \ ..}$ |

$°S\ \underset{I}{T}\ °S$ | $°T\ °S$ .. | $°T\ °S\ D^+$ | $°T$ (♩)

(Modulation to the key of the $•D$ and back.)

(139) ♭E: $T\ ..$ | $S\ D\ T\ S$ | $D\ T\atop{=D\ S}$ | $D\ T\ D^{⌀\ 6\ 5}_{\ \ \ 3}$ | $T\ ..$ $\atop{=S\ D}$ |

$T\ S\ \underset{3}{D}$ .. | $\underset{III}{T}\ S\ \underset{5}{T}\ S$ | $\underset{3}{T}\ \underset{III}{S}\ D^{6\ 5}_{4\ 3}$ | T

(Modulation to the key of the S and back.)

(140) $^3/_2$: $°T\ \underset{III}{S}\ \underset{I}{T}$ | $°S\ D\ °T\atop{=°D}$ | $°S\ °D\ °S$ | $°T\atop{=°S\ D^+}$ |

$°T\ \underset{III}{S}\ \underset{I}{T}$ | $°S$ .. | $D^{⌀\ 6\ 5}_{\ \ \ 3}$ | $°T$

(Modulation to the key of the $°S$ and back.)

In the following exercises the pupil is to determine in this manner the modulations by indicating the changes of function which take place :

EXERCISES 141—144 (Soprano given).

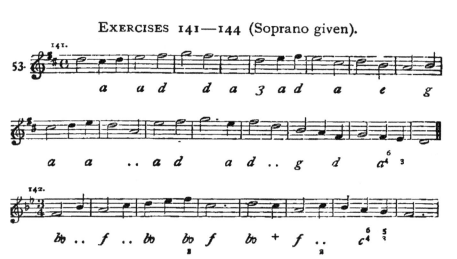

141.

53.
a   a   d   d   a   3   a   d   a   e   g

a   a   .. a   d   a   d   .. g   d a^6_4 3

142.

b♭   .. f   .. b♭   b♭   f   b♭   +   f   .. $c^{6\ 5}_{4}$

EXERCISES 145—148 (Bass given).

CHAPTER II.

CHARACTERISTIC DISSONANCES — PARALLEL-CLANGS — LEADING-
TONE-CHANGE CLANGS.

§ 7. THE CHARACTERISTIC DISSONANCES (D^7, S^{VII}, S^6, D^{VI}).

WE could not, even in our very first exercises, do without the
chord of six-four, the natural connecting member between the
two dominants, and now we are forced still further to deviate
from the current method of teaching harmony (which post-
pones the theory of discords till later), by considering the
scarcely less indispensable *characteristic dissonances* which are
usually associated with the dominants. Since the dominants
are never perfectly consonant, in so far as they are always
conceived and judged from the tonic (thus, so to speak, always
together with the latter), it cannot be wondered at that they, far
oftener than the tonic, appear with additional notes which make
their meaning still clearer, and remove all danger of misunderstanding such a succession, *e.g.*, as T^+—S^+ or $°T$—$°D$ (viz., of
conceiving it in the sense of a retrograde plain-fifth step, therefore of a close in which what was intended as contra-fifth clang
would be tonic). These characteristic dissonances are notes in
each case borrowed from the other dominant, viz.:

(A) for the major upper-dominant, the fundamental note
of the subdominant (in c-major, g b d | f; in A-minor,
e $g\sharp$ b | d).

(B) for the major subdominant, the fifth of the upper-
dominant (in c-major, f a c | d).

(C) for the minor subdominant, the prime of the minor
upper-dominant and fifth of the major upper-dominant
respectively (in A-minor, b | d f a; in c-major,
d | f a c).

(D) for the minor upper-dominant, the fundamental note
(V) of the minor subdominant (in A-minor, d | e g b).

The characteristic additional dissonant note at (A) and (C)
proves to be a *seventh* (plain, natural [minor] seventh = 7, VII),
at (B) and (D), a *sixth* (plain, major = 6, VI).

This method of connecting one dominant with a note of the
dominant lying on the other side of the tonic, circumscribes the
key in the same manner as does the succession of the two

dominants, the whole-tone step and contra-fifth change, to which, when they occurred from the tonic, we had, for this reason, to ascribe modulating power :

$$
\begin{array}{ll}
\text{(A)} \quad \underbrace{f\ [a\ \overbrace{c\ e]\ g}^{T}\ b\ d}_{S \qquad D} & \text{and} \quad \underbrace{d\ [f\ \overbrace{a\ c]\ e}^{°T}\ g\sharp\ b}_{°S \qquad D^{+}}
\end{array}
$$

$$
\text{(B)} \quad \underbrace{f\ a\ \overbrace{c\ [e\ g}^{T}\ b]\ d}_{S \qquad D}
$$

$$
\begin{array}{ll}
\text{(C)} \quad \underbrace{d\ f\ \overbrace{a\ [c\ e}^{°T}\ g]\ b}_{°S \qquad °D} & \text{and} \quad \underbrace{f\ a\flat\ \overbrace{c\ [e\ g}^{T}\ b]\ d}_{°S \qquad D}
\end{array}
$$

$$
\text{(D)} \quad \underbrace{d\ [f\ \overbrace{a\ c]\ e}^{°T}\ g\ b}_{°S \qquad °D}
$$

i.e., the combination of elements of two clangs which stand to each other in the relation of two dominants (whole-tone step or contra-fifth change) points to a clang lying between the two, and making their relation intelligible (hence their tonic), just as in the case of the succession of the two clangs.

In these four new formations we have the first examples of chords of four notes before us, thus the first *absolutely dissonant chords* (the chord of dominant six-four, which, as we have seen, contains two dissonant notes, the fourth and sixth, is yet subject to the possibility of being confounded with the tonic [$\overset{5}{T}$ and $\underset{1}{T}$ respectively], and therefore has to be defined as a *feigning consonance*, as a *discord under the cloak of consonance*); the chord of seventh, fifth, and third, or, in short, *chord of the seventh* of the major upper-dominant (major chord of the seventh) and minor under-dominant (minor chord of the seventh), and the chord of sixth, fifth, and third, or, briefly, *chord of the sixth* of a major under-dominant and minor upper-dominant, are altogether dissonant, as, besides the complete clang (prime, third, and fifth), they contain a foreign note (the seventh or sixth). The general law for the treatment of *dissonant tones* (for, as we have hitherto always spoken of prime, third, and fifth as *tones*, and not intervals, so we shall in future speak of sevenths, sixths, etc., as tones) is :

Dissonant tones are not to be doubled ; they may enter by leap, but *must resolve by step of a second*. Naturally this law was valid already for the chord of six-four, in which we had to forbid the doubling of fourth and sixth. The progression by step of a second from the fourth and sixth of this chord is not unconditionally required, because a *vicarious* (substituting) *resolution* does not strike us offensively on account of the feigning consonant nature of the chord:

Here at (*b*)—(*d*) we have vicarious resolutions in place of the really normal one at (*a*).

In the major chord of the seventh this substituting resolution is not possible for the seventh, which, on the contrary, must proceed by step of a second, if the expected harmonic progression follows at all; and, indeed, *the over-seventh regularly proceeds downwards* [55 (*a*)], on account of the striking dissonance of the seventh against the octave, whether the latter be really present next to the seventh [55 (*b*)] or be only sounded as an overtone [natural by-note, 55 (*a*), (*c*)]: *the notes forming the interval of a second always tend away from each other.* The resolution of the dissonance of a second by merging the one note into the other [55 (*d*)] has a good effect only in the case of strongly contrasting *timbres*, and is for the present strictly forbidden to the student. The upward motion of the seventh is permissible only under particular circumstances [*e.g.*, when downward motion would result in third-doubling that is not allowed: 55 (*c*)]. But naturally where the same harmony is retained, the seventh may change places with another note; then the rule for progression is simply transferred to another part [in 55 (*e*) to the bass]:

Here at (*b*) *the fifth in the chord of the seventh has been omitted:* that is quite an ordinary proceeding (as the 5 or I respectively in a chord may in any case be occasionally omitted), and is always to be recommended when we desire to make the bass progression from fundamental note to fundamental note, and to have the subsequent tonic chord complete [with fifth, 55 (*g*)]; otherwise we must forego the fifth on the tonic [55 (*f*)]. At 55 (*c*) looking upon the step *g c* as given for the tenor, and the third required as bass-note for the tonic, the downward motion of the seventh would cause a faulty third-doubling, for the *doubling of both prime and third in four-part writing is forbidden as sounding very harsh and dry.* Third-doubling sounds well only when the chord is complete; otherwise, it is *preferable to treble the fundamental note* (alto given) :

56.

(not):   (but):

As the seventh in the progression D^7—T makes the leading-tone step to the third of the tonic, or, at any rate, has to proceed by step of a second, and, on the other hand, the fundamental note of the tonic is required for the bass in the last, closing chord, *the seventh as a bass-note for the penultimate chord is impossible* [57 (*c*)]. If the chord of the seventh be not followed by the tonic, but perhaps by the subdominant, there is no necessity for this progression by second; but it will generally occur subsequently [57 (*a*) and (*b*)] :

(*a*)   (*b*)   (*c*)

57.

(good)   (good)   (wrong)

This subsequent introduction of an expected resolution, which will often occupy us hereafter (in figuration it is standard, as assuring good progression in the case of frequent leaps), also sufficiently explains why the sixth of the major under-dominant and minor upper-dominant (S^6 and D^{VI}) and the under-seventh of the minor under-dominant (S^{VII}) apparently do not require resolution by step of a second. According to our former experience the sixth, if sounded with the fifth (no matter whether in the same octave position or not), must either tend towards the seventh [58 (*a*) and (*c*)] or force the fifth to the fourth [58 (*b*) and (*d*)], as the notes of a second tend away from each other (p. 57):

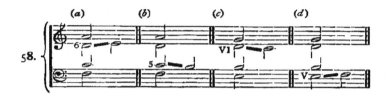

Indeed, such resolution will appear normal, if the following harmony contain the note in question :

But as the contra-fifth clang is generally followed by the plain-fifth clang, the more frequent forms of resolution will be not as at (*a*) and (*c*), but (*b*) and (*d*), *i.e., the dissonant sixth will mostly be sustained* and only subsequently proceed by step of a second. But if in the c-major cadence the 6 of the *S*⁶ chord, *d*, is in the bass and the upper-dominant follows, the *d might* be sustained [60 (*a*)], *though it need not*, but can proceed first to *g;* the *c* expected then first appears with the subsequent entry of the tonic [60 (*b*)]; even the chord of six-four may be also inserted [60 (*c*)]:

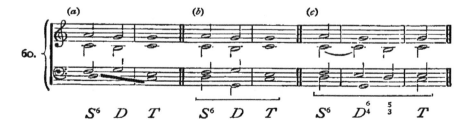

The resolution of the sixth of the minor upper-dominant, too, may be disguised by means of these intermediate notes [61 (*a*)—(*c*)]:

E

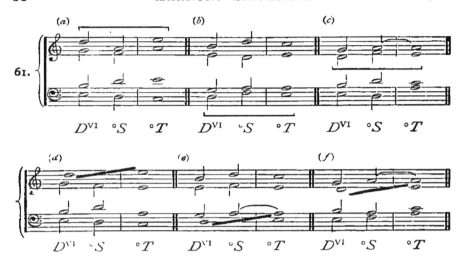

But the *d* will mostly be sustained [61 (*d*)—(*f*)]. On the other hand, the under-seventh is subject to exactly the same treatment as the over-sixth, and examples 59 (*a*)—(*b*) and 60 (*a*)—(*b*) are standard for it also, if the ♭ before the *a* be simply added :

That the chords of the over-sixth (*S*⁶) and under-seventh (*S*ᵛᴵᴵ) *readily take just the dissonant note for the bass-note* we will not conceal ; the reason for this will be quite clear to us later on (dominant of dominant) when we shall have to consider the possibilities of chromatic alteration of harmonies (*S*⁶, as soon as the 1 is raised, becomes *D*⁷ of the *D*, *S*ᵛᴵᴵ likewise as soon as the 1II and V are raised ; but then the 6 and VII respectively have become 1, *i.e.*, natural bass-note).

The introduction of characteristic dissonances into the dominant harmonies completely removes the danger of faulty consecutive fifths and octaves in the majority of cases, as it gives the chords which otherwise have no note in common, two such notes (6 of S = 5 of D, 7 of D = 1 of S or V of $°S$; VI of $°D$ = V of S, VII of S = 1 of $°D$ or 5 of D^+) :

The exercises which now follow are to be worked out, like the fifth model example, on four staves, corresponding to scores for stringed quartet, with treble clef for the two upper parts (1st and 2nd violin), alto clef for the third part (viola), and bass clef for the lowest part (violoncello); in these exercises we also keep to the normal compass of the voice as hitherto determined (regardless of the compass of the instruments) :

(Fifth model example.)

Foremost, as regards the figuring, we must remark that the 6 or 7 (or VI or VII) *beside* the clang sign (T, D, etc., or clang letter c, g, etc., or the . .) simply requires the chord of the sixth or seventh, whereas placing the numbers *above* or *below* the signs indicates particularly the note for the highest or lowest part, as hitherto.

To learn the meaning of the notes on the stave with the alto clef is easy, if we look upon the missing line for c' between the treble and bass staves as the middle line, *i.e.*, the five lines reach from the f line of the bass stave to the g line of the treble stave :

(Alto Clef.)

It must throughout be insisted upon that pupils shall not first work out the examples on an ordinary pianoforte double stave with $\oint$ and $\oint$ and then write them out in score. They are to *sketch the work directly in the desired form;* only if this be done, will it be possible to go on working quickly and with certainty from step to step!

As the introduction of characteristic dissonances does not imply greater difficulty but rather the reverse, we may venture to take another step forward in the next exercises, and practise the simplest form of *figuration* or ornamentation, *progression of one of the parts in notes of half the value.* For the present the resources alone drawn upon are:

(A) *Passing notes,* *i.e.,* notes which fill in the melodic gaps between two others entering simultaneously with the other parts, and which stand a (minor or major) second distant from both; thus, *e.g.,* if the plain unfigured movement were to introduce *e* and *g* in succession, then *f* or *f♯* would be a passing note (*e f g, e f♯ g*).

(B) *Auxiliary notes* (only a variety of passing notes), *i.e.,* the insertion of a major or minor upper or under-second, where the unfigured movement would bring the same note twice in succession, *e.g.,* *b* or *b♭* is the lower, *d* or *d♭* the upper auxiliary note for *c* (*c b c, c b♭ c, c d c, c d♭ c*). In cases where neither passing notes nor auxiliary notes can be introduced (where no third has to be filled out, nor note-repetition to be enlivened, in all steps of a fourth, fifth, sixth, or greater interval),

(C) a second *harmony note,* *i.e.,* another note of the same harmony, may be inserted as an expedient; in case of need a leap to the octave may be taken, or even the same note may be repeated; *e.g.,* in figuration of the c-major chord a *g* might be inserted between the *e* and *c'*.

The difficulty in these new exercises lies in the *increase in danger of faulty parallel progressions;* for not only may the inserted harmony note effectually produce consecutives which would not exist in unfigured writing, but the accented notes, *i.e.,* those entering simultaneously with the other parts, may form consecutives which are not removed by the intermediate notes. If, *e.g.,* the soprano in c^+—g^+ goes from *e* to *d* and the bass from *e*, inserting *g*, to *d*, these are consecutive octaves of the worst sort; but if the bass *e* goes to *c* and thence to *d*, the progression *e—d* seems to our ears to have been replaced by *c—d*, *i.e.,* the effect of octaves is not felt:

66.

Bad. Good.

We now give a model-example for these figuration exercises, in which we characterise the inserted notes by numbers; let the bass be the part to be ornamented:

67.

(Sixth model example.) N.B.—The closing chord does not need figuration.

The second chord (D^+) receives the seventh characteristic to its significance in the figuration ($e\flat$ as passing-note from f to $d\natural$); here we may remark that in figuration not only may the 7 be added to the D^+ without being prescribed, but also, when indicated in the figuring, it enters soon enough, if introduced by the inserted note. Similarly the VII of the minor subdominant and the sixth of the major subdominant and minor-upper-dominant may at any time be introduced in the figuration where not prescribed, and, where they are prescribed, may be missing at first and be added subsequently as figuration notes. If by .. it be required that a harmony with additional dissonant note be repeated, it is not necessary for the latter to be reintroduced, but the dissonant note may be dropped, as happened above (67) in the third bar at the repetition of S^{VII}.

A part of the following exercises, specially designated, is to be made more interesting by always letting one of the parts (either the bass part or soprano or one of the middle parts) proceed in note-values of double quickness. A particularly easy variety of this exercise is that of extending the figuration to all the parts, so that as far as possible only passing notes, supplemented by auxiliary notes, are resorted to, and harmony notes are inserted only in case of need, *e.g. :*

(Seventh model example.)

The pupil is to work one exercise each with figuration for soprano, alto, tenor, and bass parts, and then (each fifth exercise) with divided figuration.

EXERCISES 149—160 (for figuration).

(149) $^3/_2$: $T\ S^6\ D^7\ |\ T\ \underset{3}{.\ .\ .\ .}\ |\ °S\ D\ .\ .\ ^7\ |\ T\ \underset{=\ S^6}{.\ .^6}\ D^7\ |\ T\ .\ .\ .\ .^7\natural\ |$

$T\ S\ .\ .^6\ |\ D^{\overset{6}{1}}\ S\ D\ |\ T\ (\ _\circ\ ).$

(150) $^2/_4$: $T\ |\ S^6\ D^7\ |\ \underset{=\ S\ D}{\underset{3}{T}}\ |\ \overset{6}{\underset{\overset{5}{..}}{\overset{4}{}}}\ \overset{5}{3}\ |\ \underset{T}{=D}\ S\ |\ \underset{3}{T}\ \underset{5}{D}\ |\ T\ .\ .^6\ |$

$D^{\overset{6}{1}}\ \overset{5}{3}\ |\ T\ (\ \flat\ ).$

(151) $^3/_4$: S^6 D^7 | T_3 D^7 T | D T
$= D$ S | T D T | D T ..^{6} $= S^6$ |

D T D_5 | T $^\circ S$ $_{\overset{..}{III}}$ | D T_3' D | T (♩).

(152) $^3/_8$: T | S^6 D^7 | T ..^{6} $= S^6$ | $D^{6 +}_{4 ..}$ | $= D$ S | $D^{6 +}_{4} ..$ | T_3 S^6 |
(𝄴   ♩   𝄴 etc.) T

D^4 D^7 | T (♩).

(153) $^3/_4$: T S^6 | D $?$. T | S .. | $D^{6\ 5}_{4\ 3}$ T | ..^{6} $= T$ S |
(♩ ♩   ♩ ♩) $= S^6$ D^7 | T S

..^{6} D ..^{7} | T (♩.).

(154) ₵: T | D S^6 | $D^{6\ 5}_{4\ 3}$ | T $= D$ S | D T $= S$ | D T | S^6 D^7 | T (♩⌣♩).

(155) ₵: $^\circ T$ | S^{VII} D | $^\circ T$ $^\circ D$ | ..^{VI} S^{VII} | D ..^{7} | $^\circ T$ $_{\overset{..}{III}}$ |
S^{VII} D^+ | $^\circ T$ (♩⌣♩).

(156) $^3/_4$: $^\circ T$ D^7 $^\circ T$ | $D^{6>5}_{4\ 3}$ | $^\circ T$ ^{VI} $= D^{VI}$ S^{VII} | $^\circ T$ D | $^\circ T$ ..^{VII} $= S^{VII}$ |
(♩ ♩   ♩ ♩   ♩ ♩)

$^\circ T$ $^\circ S$ T_I | S^{VII} D^+ | $^\circ T$ (♩).

(157) $^2/_4$: $^\circ T$ | S^{VII} T_{III} | S_{VII} D | $^\circ T$ S^{VII} | D^+ .. | $^\circ T$ $_{\overset{..}{I}}$ | S^{VII} .. |
(𝄴   ♩· 𝄴 etc. Figuration in quavers).

$D^{6>5}_{4\ 3}$ | $^\circ T$ (♩.).

(158) $^3/_2$: $^\circ T$ | $^\circ D$ S^{VII} D^+ | $^\circ T$ ..^{VII} $= S^{VII}$ | D ..^{7} $^\circ T$ | D^+ .. $^\circ T$ $= ^\circ D$ |
(𝅝   ♩)

$^\circ T$ S^{VII} D | $^\circ T$ S^{VII} .. | D .. $?$. | $^\circ T$.

(159) $\natural$: $^{\circ}T \ {}^{\circ}S \ D^{+}$ | $^{\circ}T \ .. \ {}^{\mathrm{VII}}_{= \ S^{\mathrm{VII}}}$ $D^{\overset{6 > 5}{\overset{}{4}} \ \frac{5}{3}}$ | $^{\circ}T \ {}^{\overset{\scriptstyle=D^{+} \ {}^{\circ}T \ D^{+}}{\mathrm{III}<}}$

$T \ S^{\mathrm{VII}} \ D^{\overset{6 > 5}{\overset{}{4}} \ \frac{5}{3}}$ | $^{\circ}T$ ($\downarrow$).

(160) $\natural\!\!\!\!\!\!/$: $^{\circ}T \ {}^{\circ}D$ | $^{\circ}S \ .. \ {}^{\mathrm{VII}}$ | $D^{\overset{6 > 5}{\overset{}{4}} \ \frac{5}{3}}$ | $^{\circ}T_{\ =^{\circ}D \ {}^{\circ}S}$ | $^{\circ}T \ .. \ {}^{\overset{=S^{\mathrm{VII}}}{\mathrm{VII}}}$ |

$\underset{\mathrm{III}}{T} \ S^{\mathrm{VII}}$ | $D^{+} \ {}^{\circ}S$ | $^{\circ}T$ ($\circ$).

NOTE.—Besides the whole-tone step and contra-fifth change, a few more *ways of modulation* to the keys of the dominant have here been resorted to, and first of all the direct *change of meaning of a clang by the addition of the dissonance characteristic to its new significance.* Thus in 149, 152 and 153 the $^{+}$tonic changes to $^{+}$subdominant on account of the sixth characteristic for subdominant significance being added; in 156 the $^{\circ}$tonic changes to minor upper-dominant by the addition of VI, in 158 and 159 the minor tonic receives the stamp of minor subdominant by the addition of VII. The returns (retrograde modulations) are carried out in the same way; only in 159 an entirely new expedient is made use of, the *chromatic alteration of the tonic third.* Rule: *the raising of the third of the minor tonic gives the major chord which results upper-dominant significance; the lowering of the third of the major tonic gives the minor chord which results subdominant significance;* in short, the clang resulting from the chromatic alteration of the third receives the significance of the "turn-of-harmony clang" (contra-clang). Even if this rule does *not always* hold good, it yet forms a valuable hint and support.

Exercises which are in iambic rhythm ($\downarrow$ | $\downarrow$; $\downarrow$ | $\downarrow$), or alternate between the latter and notes of equal value, are to be written note against note in three parts; the fourth part to be figured then proceeds in notes of the next smaller value (for $\downarrow$ | $\downarrow$ in quavers, for $\downarrow$ | $\downarrow$ in semiquavers); the "dotted rhythm" $\downarrow$ | $\downarrow$. is to be opposed by movement in quavers. In these exercises more than one intermediate note will have to be inserted, without, however, exceeding the limits of the expedients hitherto allowed.

The following hints will, for the present, be sufficient:

Part for Figuration :

Figured Part:

i.e., the introduction of auxiliary notes on both sides cannot be avoided, and octave leaps will often have to be resorted to.

EXERCISES 161—172 (not for figuration).

(The tonal functions are to be added, as hitherto, in working out.)
161—163 (Highest part given [1st Violin]).

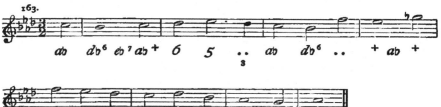

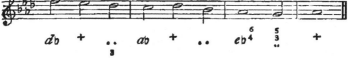

164—166 (2nd part given [2nd Violin]).

167—169 (3rd part given [Viola]).

170—172 (Lowest part given ['Cello]).

§ 8. CHORDS OF SEVEN-THREE AND PARALLEL CLANGS.

If even in the simple consonant clang of three notes we might occasionally omit one note, (for which the 5 in a major chord and I in a minor chord proved best adapted), this will naturally be the case in greater measure, when a fourth (dissonant) note is added to the clang. The omission of the fifth in the chord of the over-seventh we already met with on p. 57, as an ordinary expedient for keeping the closing tonic complete. But the omission of the prime in the chord of the under-seventh is equally permissible :

70.

The three remaining notes of the chord of the under-seventh then yield the formation known by the name of the " diminished triad," which formerly caused many scruples and much obscurity in the theory of harmony, because, in blind formalism, it was grouped beside the major and minor chords in a third class, by those who thought it necessary to regard all chords as primary that could be represented as consisting of thirds placed over one another. As we do not at all found the theory of chords on the principle of building up by thirds ($c\ e\ g$ does not appear to us like the combination of two thirds of different size, $c\ e$ and $e\ g$, but as the combination of a [major] third $c\ e$ and [perfect] fifth $c\ g$), so $b\ d f$ (S^{VII} without prime) does not appear to us comparable with $c\ e\ g$ and $a\ c\ e$, but rather with $g\ b f$ (D^I without 5), in as far as both formations arise from the omission of the note most easily dispensable in the chord of the seventh. The chord of under-seventh without prime (I) is only apparently similar to the chord of over-seventh without prime (1), *e.g.*, $b\ d f$ as D^7 in c-major with omission of the principal note. We shall express the omission of the prime by striking through the letter, and shall call the chords of the seventh with omitted prime, *chords of seven-three ;* then $b\ d f$ is either $= g\ b\ d f (= g^7)$, thus in c-major and c-minor chord of seven-three on the dominant $= D^7$, or $= b\ d f \sharp (= \sharp^{VII})$, and in A-minor and A-major chord of seven-three on the °subdominant $= S^{VII}$. Although the chord signs correspond entirely, these chords are not of equal value ; for the omission of the prime in the chord of over-seventh means omission of the fundamental note, the note best for doubling, and therefore least easily dispensed with ; therefore, correctly speaking, only comparable with the omission of the V (which is fundamental note) in the chord of under-seventh (omission of f in c^{VII} : d .. $a\flat$ c) ; both formations, indeed, only occur more frequently in three-part writing without the absence of the fundamental note making itself distinctly felt :

71.

However, the introduction of D^7 is also possible at times in four-part writing, viz., principally when the doubling of the 5 may be arrived at by steps of a second :

72.

In the chord of seven-three the fifth is the only note that may be doubled (the third [leading-note] and seventh, as we know, must not be doubled).

Another formation results from the omission of the fifth in the chords of the sixth ; first, in those hitherto considered, namely, those arising from the addition of the characteristic dissonance to the contra-fifth clangs (S^6 and D^{VI}) ; in these, by omission of the fifth a clang apparently of the opposite mode arises ; *i.e.*, $S_3^{\not5}$ (*the stroke through the 5 indicates its omission*) apparently yields a minor chord (in c-major $f\ a\ \not e\ d$ apparently $= {}^{\circ}a$), and $D_{\not y}^{VI}$ a major chord (in A-minor $d\ \not e\ g\ b$ apparently $= g^+$). Thus we become acquainted with a new category, and, indeed, a very important one, of dissonances under the cloak of consonance (*feigning consonances*). As the feigning clang (${}^{\circ}a$ as $f_3^{\not5}$ and g^+ as $b_{\not y}^{VI}$) stands to the principal clang in the relation of plain *third-change* (a is plain third in f^+, g plain third in ${}^{\circ}b$) or, which is the same thing, in the relation in which tonics of parallel keys stand to each other (F-major and D-minor, E-minor and G-major are so-called parallel keys), we will call it the *parallel clang* and, in the sign representing the functions of the harmonies, indicate the relation by a p at the side of the S or ${}^{\circ}D$. Thus Sp is the feigning minor chord arising from the omission of the fifth in the chord of the subdominant with over-sixth ($S_3^{\not5}$) ; and, similarly, ${}^{\circ}Dp$ the feigning major chord arising from the omission of the fifth in the chord of the dominant with under-sixth ($D_{\not y}^{VI}$). The parallel clangs open entirely new prospects to us, in so far as they allow of *two methods of treatment*, viz., either *in the sense of the principal harmonies represented by them* or, *with augmentation of the feigning, as really consonant harmonies ;* i.e., Sp permits [73 (a)] of the *doubling of the fundamental note of the subdominant* (which is third of the feigning harmony), even in parallel motion [73 (b)], as well as [73 (c)] of the *doubling of the fundamental note of the parallel clang* (which is actually *sixth of the subdominant*, therefore really a dissonance), also in parallel motion [73 (d)] ; indeed, also that of the I of the parallel clang, which is the third of the subdominant [73 (e) and (f)] ; and likewise in ${}^{\circ}Dp$ it is just as allowable to double the prime (I) of the ${}^{\circ}D$ [73 (g) and (h)] as to double the fundamental note or the fifth of the parallel clang [73 (*i*) and (*l*), the former (!) also in parallel motion, 73 (*k*)]. Only as regards one point the parallel clangs require great caution : proceeding by leap to the I or 5 of the parallel clang in the bass produces the undesirable *effect of six-four* already known to us, and should therefore be avoided [73 (*n*) and (*o*)] :

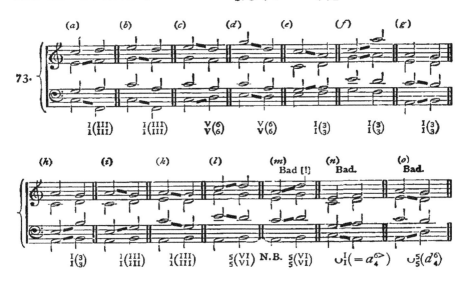

But the possibility thus manifested to us of *substituting the parallel clang for a principal clang of the key*, is not confined to the contra-fifth clang, but also possible for the others, firstly, for the tonic itself and the plain-fifth clang. These cases have to be explained, indeed, in a different way, since for the tonic there can be no characteristic dissonance (for, on the contrary, the characteristic of the tonic is *absolute consonance*), and the plain-fifth clang with its own characteristic dissonance (7, VII) cannot produce any feigning consonant formations (as the 7 [VII] is absolutely dissonant not only with the 1 [I], but also with the 3 [III]). If, in the first place, we retain the notion of "substitution," we must state its existence in the case of the parallel-clang of the tonic, particularly in the *deceptive close*, which is best explained as a *real close disturbed by a dissonant note* and as *replacing the tonic by a feigning consonance ;* three parts make their regular progression from the plain-fifth clang back to the tonic, and the fourth (in major regularly the bass), instead of the step of a fifth or fourth from fundamental note to fundamental note, makes a step of a second upwards from the fundamental note of the plain-fifth clang to the third of the contra-fifth clang (sixth of the tonic) :

The method of writing at (*a*), together with the inversions of the three upper parts—at (*d*) and (*e*)—is the properly normal four-part form of *deceptive close ;* but it is not considered necessary for the chord of dominant seventh, or even the dominant chord [*cf.* (*f*)] to be complete. *i.e.*, the fifth of the dominant may be omitted [*cf.* (*b*), (*f*), and (*g*)]. *Doubling the third of the parallel clang* (which is fundamental note of the actual harmony—therefore we have only a *feigned doubling of the third*—), is *positively characteristic in the deceptive close*, and the equally possible modes of writing as at (*b*), (doubling the fundamental note [V] of the parallel clang), or (*c*), (doubling the I of the parallel clang), remain the exceptions.

But the parallel clang of the tonic may be introduced not only at the end of a cadence (when it annuls the closing power of the tonic, and thus necessitates a new cadential formation), but also at the beginning of a cadence in *the transition from tonic to subdominant.* (In both cases, the sixth which takes the place of the tonic fifth must be understood as the third of the subdominant, and has a corresponding effect). The parallel clang appearing after the principal clang, therefore, always indicates the anticipation of an element of the harmony which follows logically ; viz. :—

in *T—Tp* the newly added note is third of *S*,
in *S—Sp* „ „ „ „ fifth of *D ;*

and the relations correspond in the minor key, viz. :—

in °*T—*°*Tp* the newly added note is third of °*D*,
in °*D—*°*Dp* „ „ „ „ fifth (V) of °*S*.

And thus, finally, also the parallel clangs of *D* in majoi and

°*S* in minor may be introduced, and must correspondingly be defined as anticipations of the third of the closing tonic; *i.e.*,

in *D—Dp* the newly added note is third of *T,*
and in °*S—°Sp* ,,   ,,   ,, ,, third of °*T.*

The introduction of the parallel clangs, therefore, signifies a very considerable enrichment of the means of cadential formation and a more detailed subdivision of them.

In the cadence of the pure major key

Tp enters between *T* and *S*
Sp   ,,   ,,   *S* ,, *D*
Dp   ,,   ,,   *D* ,, *T,*

and in the cadence of the pure minor key

°*Tp* between °*T* and °*D*
°*Dp*   ,,   °*D* ,, °*S*
°*Sp*   ,,   °*S* ,, °*T,*

by which means we gain the two following cadences, likewise to be designated as normal :

75.   *T Tp   S Sp   D Dp   T   °T °Tp °D °Dp °S °Sp   °T*

Connecting the parallel clangs with the principal clangs whose accessory harmonies they are, gives rise to no difficulties, as the two clangs have two notes in common; it is equally possible to retain the doubling of the prime [as happened at 75 (*a*)], or to double the fundamental note of the parallel clang [as at 75 (*b*)]; the latter is preferable in minor, because the doubling of the prime does not then signify doubling of the fundamental note [76 (*a*)] :

The continued fifth-doubling in the principal clangs of the major cadence [76 (*b*)] would not be happy, though not impossible.

The connecting of parallel clangs with one another ($Tp—Sp$, $Dp—Tp$, $Sp—Dp$ or $°Tp—°Dp$, $°Sp—°Tp$, $°Dp—°Sp$) corresponds entirely with the connecting of the principal clangs of the parallel key, with this difference, that in the former we have good doubling of feigning thirds in place of bad doubling of real thirds in the latter:

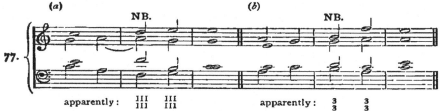

The doubling of the leading-note, otherwise so strictly forbidden, appears permissible here (at N.B.); nevertheless, in a succession of several parallel clangs, the method of writing used for the key of the opposite mode is generally to be recommended, and it has a particular charm on account of the abnormal succession of dominants, which in this case appears natural and justified:

$$77(a) \quad T \quad Tp \mid Sp \quad Dp \mid T$$
$$(-°T \mid °S \quad °D)$$
$$77(b) \quad °T \quad °Tp \mid °Dp \quad °Sp \mid °T$$
$$(=^+T \mid D^+ \quad ^+S)$$

A few new harmonic successions result from connecting each parallel clang with the other two principal clangs of the key, viz., in major—

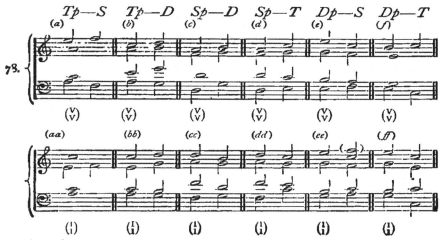

and in minor—

v

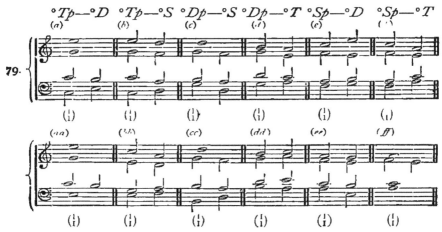

Here, at 78 (*a*)—(*f*) and 79 (*a*)—(*f*), the parallel clangs are introduced with doubling of their fundamental notes; at 78 (*aa*)—(*ff*) and 79 (*aa*)—(*ff*) on the other hand with doubling of the primes of the principal clangs, which latter at 78 (*aa*)—(*ff*) yields a more convenient result on an average than at 79 (*aa*)—(*ff*), because the doubling of the minor prime is not doubling of the fundamental note. The harmonic steps new to us which result, are :

The *leading-tone change* [78 (*a*) and (*aa*), 78 (*f*) and (*ff*), 79 (*a*) and (*aa*), 79 (*f*) and (*ff*)].
The *minor-third change* [78 (*b*) and (*bb*), 78·(*d*) and (*dd*), 79 (*b*) and (*bb*), 79 (*d*) and (*dd*)].
The *whole tone change* [78 (*c*) and (*cc*), 79 (*c*) and (*cc*)].
The *tritone change* [78 (*e*) and (*ee*), 79 (*e*) and (*ee*)].

As in all these cases it is a matter of connecting a parallel clang with a principal clang, all the steps are naturally made with *changing mode* (therefore " change "), and indeed throughout with *plain* changes.

The conditions for writing these steps singly are the following:

(A) *Leading-tone change* (*T—Dp, S—Tp;* ° *T—°Sp,* ° *D—°Tp*), *i.e.*, the step from one clang to the change-clang of its plain leading-note (= of the plain third of its plain fifth) connects clangs, which have two notes in common, show a leading-tone step from principal note to principal note, and admit the doubling of both fundamental notes without danger [80 (*a*)—(*b*)]:

Exceptional progressions [*cf.* 80 (*c*)—(*f*)] are possible in various ways, and do not imply any forbidden steps. The leading-tone change has a peculiar significance as closing step in place of the retrograde plain-fifth step, $Dp—T$ or $°Sp—°T$ instead of $D—T$ and $°S—°T$. As the notes in common are too many, the retrograde leading-tone change as close-formation in the major key is generally written so that all the parts proceed by leap (a favourite progression of Schubert's [*cf.* 81 (*a*)—(*b*)] :

81.

That this is also possible in an entirely similar manner in the minor key (only with doubling of the feigning fundamental note) we may see at 81 (*c*).

(B) *The minor-third change* ($T—Sp$, $D—Tp$; $°T—°Dp$, $°S—°Tp$), the step to the change-clang of the plain minor third, *i.e.*, to the change clang of the plain third of the contra-fifth (!, thus really the progression from the fifth-clang to the third-change clang of a third clang) connects clangs which have no note in common, and therefore give rise to danger of consecutive fifths and octaves, which may, however, easily be removed, but only if we either forego the possible leading-tone step, or double the third in the parallel clang :

82.

This step is likewise used with two entirely different meanings, in the first place at the beginning of the cadence, as transition from the tonic to the subdominant which is replaced by its parallel clang, and, secondly (retrograde), at the end of the cadence, substituting the parallel clang for the tonic, as a form of *deceptive close;* we have discussed the latter at greater length above (pp. 72, 73). The *equivalent of the ordinary major deceptive close* in the region of minor harmonies is therefore as follows (with or without seventh to the $°S$) :

Another form of deceptive close peculiar to the mixed minor (with major upper-dominant) we shall meet with later on.

(C) *The whole-tone change* (Sp—D and $°Dp$—$°S$) connects the parallel clang of the contra-fifth clang with the plain-fifth clang, and has therefore entirely the same significance as the whole-tone step without its risks. This change is highly important for modulation, and we shall have to return to it in considering the chromatic alteration of the third of the plain-fifth clang (Dorian sixth and Mixolydian Seventh.

(D) *The tritone change*, in which the distance of the principal notes from each other is an augmented fourth, *i.e.*, the most complicated of all relations in the diatonic scale (f . . [c . . g] . . b or b . . [e . . a] . . f; that is, relation of the third of the second fifth) gives rise to some difficulties in writing [risk of consecutive octaves and fifths, tritone 84 (*a*)], which can, however, be satisfactorily removed [84 (*b*) —(*d*)].

By the introduction of the parallel clangs our further exercises will gain greatly in variety, particularly as we must not lose sight of figuration. The means for *modulation* likewise appear essentially enriched: to the transitions to the upper and under dominant keys of the same mode, hitherto the only ones made, we may now add that to the parallel key, easily made by means of the parallel clangs. If we compare the cadence in the major key extended by the parallel clangs, with that of the minor key confined to the principal clangs, *e.g.*, c-major and A-minor :

$$(T— Tp—S—Sp—D—Dp—T')$$
$$c^+—°e—f^+—°a—g^+ — °b — c^+$$

$$°e — °b — °a — °e$$
$$(°T—°D — °S — °T)$$

and, conversely, the cadence of the minor key enriched by the parallel clangs with that of the major key confined to the principal clangs (the same keys) :

$$(^\circ T - {}^\circ Tp - {}^\circ D - {}^\circ Dp - {}^\circ S - {}^\circ Sp - {}^\circ T)$$
$$^\circ e - c^+ - {}^\circ b - g^+ - {}^\circ a - f^+ - {}^\circ e$$

$$c^+ - f^+ - g^+ - c^+$$
$$(T - S - D - T)$$

we are first stiuck by the reversed order of the two dominant parallels as compared with the dominants which have the same sound ; this may be turned to account in effecting a transition from one cadence to the other, *e.g.* :

$$c^+ - {}^\circ e - {}^\circ b - {}^\circ a - {}^\circ e$$
$$T - Tp$$
$$= {}^\circ T - {}^\circ D - {}^\circ S - {}^\circ T$$

or, $^\circ e - c^+ - f^+ - g^+ - c^+$
$$^\circ T - {}^\circ Tp$$
$$= T - S - D - T$$

But there is still *another possible way of deriving minor from major chords*, which we have not considered so far, viz., the (figurative) *replacing of a prime by the minor contra-second* :

In c-major : $+T^{11<} = b\,[c]\,e\,g$, apparently identical with Dp
$+S^{11<} = e\,[f]\,a\,c$, apparently identical with Tp
In A-minor : $^\circ T^{12>} = a\,c\,[e]\,f$, apparently identical with $^\circ Sp$
$^\circ D^{12>} = e\,g\,[b]\,c$, apparently identical with $^\circ Tp$

These formations arise in the simplest fashion through the plainest figuration of the harmonies by means of passing or auxiliary notes, in the first place in the more complicated form of four-note chords (major-seventh chords), *e.g.* :

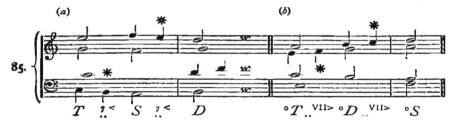

85.

$$T \quad ?^< \quad S \quad ?^< \quad D \qquad\qquad ^\circ T \quad {}^{VII>} {}^\circ D \quad {}^{VII>} \quad {}^\circ S$$

In slow movement, in order to remove the extreme dissonance of the major seventh or minor second in the major key, another part will readily move too—viz., that part which had the doubled prime (in minor the doubling of the prime given here [85 (b)] will naturally occur much more rarely than the doubling of the V). In both cases again feigning consonant chords arise, which we may not, however, identify with the parallel clangs.

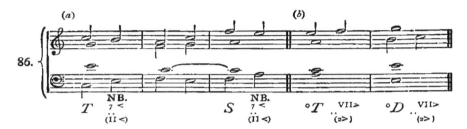

The feigning consonant accessory form of the tonic ($T^{7<}$, $T^{VII>}$ or $+T^{II<}$, $°T^{2>}$) arising from the minor contra-second (major seventh) thus forms a *natural connecting link between tonic and contra-fifth clang*, a new enriching of the cadence; also the accessory form of the contra-fifth clang arising similarly (S^7, $D^{VII>}$ or, which means the same thing, $+S^{II<}$, $°D^{2>}$) does not appear in exactly the same place as the parallel clang of the tonic (between tonic and contra-fifth clang), but rather after the pure form of the contra-fifth clang:

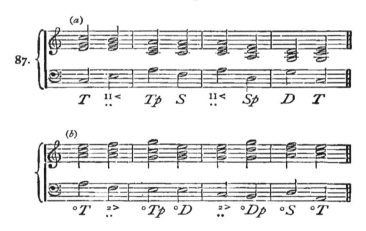

We will call these feigning consonances *leading-tone substitutes*, and adopt the following abbreviated signs for them: $\mathcal{F} = +T^{II<}$, $\mathcal{F} = °T^{2>}$, $\mathcal{S} = +S^{II<}$, and $\mathcal{D} = °D^{2>}$. The leading-tone substitutes following directly after the tonic and the contra-fifth clang (even before their parallel clangs) suggest new means for modulation:

Enriched major cadence : $(T \quad \overset{\text{\tiny II}}{\underset{\text{\tiny }}{<}} \quad Tp \quad S \quad \overset{\text{\tiny II}}{\underset{\text{\tiny }}{<}} \quad Sp \quad D \quad Dp \quad T)$
$\qquad\qquad\qquad\qquad c^{+} \quad {}^{\circ}b \quad {}^{\circ}e \quad f^{+} \quad {}^{\circ}e \quad {}^{\circ}a \quad g^{+} \quad {}^{\circ}b \quad c^{+}$

Plain minor cadence : $\qquad\qquad {}^{\circ}e \quad {}^{\circ}b \quad {}^{\circ}a \quad {}^{\circ}e$
$\qquad\qquad\qquad\qquad\qquad ({}^{\circ}T \; {}^{\circ}D \; {}^{\circ}S \; {}^{\circ}T)$

Enriched minor cadence : $({}^{\circ}T \; \overset{2}{\underset{}{>}} \; {}^{\circ}Tp \; {}^{\circ}D \; \overset{2}{\underset{}{>}} \; {}^{\circ}Dp \; {}^{\circ}S \; {}^{\circ}Sp \; {}^{\circ}T)$
$\qquad\qquad\qquad\quad {}^{\circ}e \; f^{+} \; c^{+} \; {}^{\circ}b \; c^{+} \; g^{+} \; {}^{\circ}a \; f^{+} \; {}^{\circ}e$

Plain major cadence : $\qquad\quad c^{+} \; f^{+} \qquad g^{+} \; c^{+}$
$\qquad\qquad\qquad\qquad (T \; S \qquad D \; T)$

i.e., here again we have two successions which, when inverted, are normal in the cadence of the parallel key, and will by exchange immediately suggest modulation :

88.

The next exercises, which are intended for figuration, may now make the student acquainted with the tenor clef, and for that purpose they are still to be written as if for string quartet, but with notation of the 'cello part in the tenor clef; only where more than one leger line below would become necessary, the bass clef may be resorted to. The tenor clef is, like the alto clef, a c'-clef; the line to which it is prefixed (the second from the top) has the tone-significance of once-accented c :

89.  (Tenor clef.)

The student should impress the tone-significance of these three notes on his mind, and he will easily become intimate with this clef also. For the rest we will refer him to the eighth model example. The figuration is still to be confined to passing and auxiliary notes and inserted harmony notes, and in each fifth exercise the figuration is to be divided among the four parts.

(Eighth model example.)

EXERCISES 173—184 (for figuration).

(173) $^3/_4$: $T \mid \overset{\text{II}<}{\underset{\cdot\cdot}{}} Tp \mid Sp\ D \mid Tp \qquad \qquad \mid = S\ D \mid T\ Tp \mid$
$(\flat \quad \flat \text{ etc.}) \qquad \qquad \mid = {}^\circ T\ {}^\circ S \mid D\ {}^\circ T \mid \overset{2>}{\underset{\cdot\cdot}{}} \mid$
$Sp\ Dp \mid T\ (\mathrel{\mathpalette\@d\relax})$

(174) $\mathrel{\mathrlap{E}}$: ${}^\circ T \overset{2>}{\underset{\cdot\cdot}{}} \mid {}^\circ D\ {}^\circ S \qquad \qquad \mid \qquad = {}^\circ S\ D\ \overset{7}{\underset{\cdot\cdot}{}} \mid$
$= {}^+Sp\ D\ \overset{7}{\underset{\cdot\cdot}{}} \mid \quad T\ Sp$
${}^\circ T \overset{2>}{\underset{\cdot\cdot}{}} \quad S^{\text{VII}} \quad D^7 \mid {}^\circ T\ (\mathrel{\mathpalette\@d\relax})$

(175) $^2/_4$: $D \mid T\ D \mid Tp \qquad \mid {}^\circ T\ {}^\circ D \mid = S\ D \mid T\ \overset{\text{II}<}{\underset{\cdot\cdot}{}} \mid$
$(\mathord{\mathrlap{C}} \quad \flat \text{ etc.}) \mid = {}^\circ T\ D \mid \qquad \qquad {}^\circ Sp$
$S\ \underset{3}{\overset{}{\cdot\cdot}} \mid D^{6\ 5}_{4\ 3} \mid T\ (\mathrel{\mathpalette\@d\relax} \cdot)$

(176) $^3/_2$: $Sp \mid \underset{5}{D}\ T\ S^6 \mid D\ \overset{7}{\underset{\cdot\cdot}{}}\ Tp \mid S^{\text{VII}}\ D^{6>\ 5}_{4\ 3} \mid = S\ T\ D^7 \mid$
$\qquad \qquad \qquad = {}^\circ T \qquad \qquad \mathrel{\mathrlap{F}}\ 3$
$\mathrel{\mathrlap{F}}\ Tp \mid S\ Sp\ Dp \mid Tp\ S^6\ D \mid T\ (\mathrel{\circ})$

(177) $\mathrel{\mathrlap{\$}}$: ${}^\circ T \overset{2>}{\underset{\cdot\cdot}{}} \mid {}^\circ S \qquad \mid \qquad = Sp\ D \mid T\ Sp \mid S^{\text{VII}}\ D$
$\mid = Sp\ D \mid T\ \overset{\text{II}<}{\underset{\cdot\cdot}{}} \mid Tp \qquad \qquad = {}^\circ T$
${}^\circ T\ {}^\circ Sp \mid {}^\circ T\ (\mathrel{\circ})$

(178) $^3/_4$: S^6 D^7 | $T \atop 3$ | $= {}^{\circ}Sp$ S^{VII} | D ..^{7} ${}^{\circ}T$ |

| $= S$ $D^6_4 \overset{+}{\underset{7}{\cdot\cdot}}$ | T $S \atop 3$ | $= \mathcal{F}$ |

Sp $D^{6\ 5}_{4\ 3}$ | Tp Sp D | Dp Tp S | ${}^{\circ}S$ $D^{6\ 5}_{4\ 3}$ | T (♩)

(179) ⽫: ${}^{\circ}T$ | S^{VII} ${}^{\circ}T$ S^{VII} D | $\mathcal{F}$ S^{VII} D ${}^{\circ}Tp$ |

${}^{\circ}Sp$ | $= \mathcal{D}$ $S^{VI\ V}$ ${}^{\circ}T$

$= S$ Sp $D^6_4 \overset{+}{\underset{7}{\cdot\cdot}}$ | $T \atop 3$

(180) $^3/_8$: T D^7 | T | | $= Sp$ T D^7 |

(etc.) $= {}^{\circ}Tp$ S^{VII} D | ${}^{\circ}T$ ${}^{\circ}S$ $T \atop III$ | ${}^{\circ}S$

(Figuration in Semiquavers.)

T | $= {}^{\circ}Tp$ D^7 ${}^{\circ}T$ | | ♩ ♪ | ♩.
$= D$ S D | T | $= Sp$ | D^6_4 S D^7 | T S | T

(181) $^2/_4$: T D | T S T | | $= Tp$ D T | D Tp
(etc.) $= {}^{3\ 5}_{Tp}$ | S^{VII} D ..^{7} | ${}^{\circ}T$ | $= Sp$ D |

$= D$ Tp Sp | Dp Tp D^7 | T S $\overset{6}{\cdot\cdot}$ | T
T

(182) ⽫: T D^7 | Tp $\mathcal{F}$ | $S \atop = {}^{\circ}Sp$ S^{VII} | $D^+ \atop \underline{o}$ | $= \mathcal{F}$ $Sp \atop {}^{\circ}D$ | D $S \atop III$ |

D^6_4 D | T

(183) $^3/_4$: ${}^{\circ}T$ ${}^{\circ}D$ ${}^{\circ}Sp$ | S^{VII} D $T \atop III$ | ${}^{\circ}S \atop = Sp$ $D^{8\ 7}_{6\ 5}$ | $= {}^{\circ}Tp \atop T$ S^{VII} D |

${}^{\circ}T \atop = Dp$ S^6 D^7 | T $= {}^{\circ}T \atop II>$ S^{VII} | $T \atop III$ S^{VII} D | ${}^{\circ}T$ (♩.)

(184) $^2/_4$: D ..^{7} | ${}^{\circ}T$ ${}^{\circ}D$ | S^{VII} $T \atop I$ | S^{VII} D^7 | ${}^{\circ}T \atop = \mathcal{F}$ D^7 |

$= {}^{\circ}Sp \atop T$ S^{VII} | $D^{6\ >}_{4} \overset{+}{\cdot\cdot}$ | ${}^{\circ}T$ (♩)

The connecting of parallel clangs and leading-tone substitutes with the contra-clang of the tonic we have hitherto avoided. Since this introduces clangs of the same mode in succession (of which the one, indeed, is always only a feigning consonance), the result is a number of new harmonic steps, viz. :

91.

The new steps are :

(A) *The (plain) third-step* [91 (a) and (d)], which, in the progression of parts, differs from the leading-tone change only by a chromatic step ($a-a\flat$, $g-g\sharp$),

(B) *The (plain) minor-third step* [91 (b) and (e)], differing from the third-change only by a chromatic step ($a-a\flat$, $g-g\sharp$).

(C) *The (plain) leading-tone step* [91 (c) and (f)], differing from the tritone change only by the exchange of a minor for a major second.

The next exercises introduce also these steps, of which one, viz., the leading-tone step in minor [91 (f)], requires particular notice, because retrograde, in the sense of the progression to the tonic leading-tone substitute from the major upper-dominant, it yields the most important (most frequent) form of *deceptive close in the minor key* (with or without seventh of the D) :

92.

Of 92 (b) we must remark that the *distance of alto from tenor amounts to an octave*, which, however, may be approved in this and all such cases, where *both couples of parts form thirds.* 92 (a)—(b) are the proper typical forms of the *deceptive close in minor* (also with the possible inversions of the three top parts) ; 92 (c) is rare and not so good, because the characteristic progression for the bass to the feigning fundamental note is replaced by that to the fundamental note of the principal clang.

The *exercises* which follow now are to be written in the *four old vocal clefs* (soprano, alto, tenor, and bass clefs). In working out, the tonal functions of the harmonies are, as hitherto, to be added by the student. The *soprano clef* (c-clef on the lowest line) will now be easily learned, after alto and tenor clefs have somewhat accustomed us to the varying position of the c-clef. Its relation to the treble and bass clef is :

The following ninth model example may help to set the student right :—

(Ninth model example.)

EXERCISES 185—196 (not to be figured).

(The clef prefixed indicates at the same time which part is given.)

§ 9. DORIAN SIXTH, MIXOLYDIAN SEVENTH, NEAPOLITAN SIXTH, PHRYGIAN SECOND, LYDIAN FOURTH.

The minor subdominant in major and the major upper-dominant in minor disturb the melodic flow of part progression; the thirds of each introduce the step of the augmented second into the scale :

Aversion to this unmelodic step has led composers to bridge over the gap in a like manner in both cases—viz., by chromatic alteration of the third of the plain-fifth clang, so that the latter then stands at the distance only of a whole tone from the third of the contra-clang of the tonic. The simplest and plainest cases of the introduction of the melodic neighbouring notes to the third of the contra-clang are probably those which naturally make their appearance in the figuration, whether they be used as auxiliary notes [97 (*a*), (*c*)] or as passing notes [97 (*b*), (*d*), (*e*), (*f*)] :

As proved by the ♮ against the numbers, the interval in question is in all these cases natural, and plain, in reference to the figured harmony. But these notes, conceived first on purely melodic grounds, may also be harmonised independently in such a manner that they no longer appear in the chord signs as passing or auxiliary notes added to the harmonies of the contra-clang or the tonic, but rather as chromatically altered thirds of the plain-fifth clang [98 (*a*)—(*b*)].

98 (*c*)—(*d*), indeed, may be conceived as mere figuration of the harmony of the contra-clangs, more conveniently in three-part than four-part writing:

The explanation added to 98 (*c*) and (*d*) does not necessarily imply that the contra-clang of the tonic ought to follow, for the chords *Sp*$^{2>}$ and °*Dp*$^{11<}$ may also advance in such a way that their minor contra-second proceeds to the prime [100 (*a*)—(*b*)]:

Thus we should again have two new leading-tone substitutes before us, but doubly derived ones (leading-tone substitute of the parallel clang of the contra-fifth clang), which, however, seem to point to a nearer path, viz., that struck out at 100 (c)—(d), the insertion of the contra-fifth clang of the contra-fifth clang (second under-dominant in major, second °dominant in minor). This again opens entirely new prospects to us (figuration of a dominant by means of its own dominants), which we shall have to enter further into.

At first we will confine ourselves to that introduction of the lowered ("Mixolydian") seventh of the major scale which takes place in order to bridge over to the lowered sixth (the III of the °S), and similarly to the introduction of the raised ("Dorian") sixth of the minor scale effected in order to gain a melodic transition to the major seventh of the minor scale (3 of the ^{+}D). In as far as these notes enter as chromatically altered thirds of the plain-fifth clangs, they apparently give the major key a minor upper-dominant and the minor key a major under-dominant :

But this conception is not possible in the full sense ; the principal notes of the major tonic and minor upper-dominant on the one hand, and of the minor tonic and major under-dominant on the other, would stand at the distance of a double-fifth step from each other (c^{+}—(g)—°d ; °e—(a)—d^{+}), *i.e.*, would appear related only in the second degree. The last paragraph showed us what significance the whole-tone changes (such as the harmonic successions c^{+}—°d and °e—d^{+}) would have in tonal harmony, viz., in major, the minor chord is parallel clang of the under-dominant, and the major chord is upper-dominant, and in minor correspondingly, the major chord is parallel clang of the minor upper-dominant, and the minor chord is °subdominant ; therefore, the successions °d—c^{+} and °e—d^{+} will easily and readily be understood as Sp—D [101 (a)—(b)], *i.e.*, as closing in F-major and G-major respectively, and conversely c^{+}—°d and d^{+}—°e as closing in D-minor and E-minor respectively, in the sense of °Dp—°S [101 (c)—(d)] ; indeed, even for the inverted successions the same conceptions are not excluded [101 (e)—(h)] :

$$D \quad Sp \quad T \quad D \quad Sp \quad T \quad °S \; °Dp \; °T \quad °S \; °Dp \; °T$$

But in spite of this double possibility of change of meaning and modulation, the introduction of the upper-dominant in major with lowered third and of the under-dominant in minor with raised third without altering the functions is quite possible, only presupposing that the chromatic third of the plain-fifth clang really proceeds in the same part to the third of the contra-clang of the tonic, to which the artificial note is to bridge over. Part progressions in which this is not the case, are, therefore, in the strictest sense not quite logical ; at least they are comparable to poetic licences and tropes, and purposely lead comprehension astray by means of vicarious progressions of the parts, or, as musical ellipses, require leaps in the conception. *Every entry of the Dorian sixth without the third of the major upper-dominant following in the same part*, therefore, produces that effect which is specifically called " Dorian," because it does not so much take root in our modern clarified harmonic conception, as it *reminds us of the time of the harmonic treatment of the old Church modes.*

The four principal Church modes (the four authentic ones) were the scales :

Dorian :　　$d\ e\ f\ g\ \underline{a\ b}\ c'\ d'$ (with *d* as fundamental note of the closing harmony).

Phrygian :　$e\ f\ g\ a\ \underline{b\ c'\ d'}\ e'$ („　*e* „　　　„　　„　　„).

Lydian :　　$f\ g\ a\ \underline{b}\ c'\ d'\ e'\ f'$ („　*f* „　　　„　　„　　„).

Mixolydian :$g\ a\ b\ c'\ \underline{d'\ e'}\ f'\ g'$ („　*g* „　　　„　　„　　„).

i.e., the Dorian tonic, so long as $b\flat$ or $c\sharp$ were not introduced (which proved inevitable for the final close), was deprived of plain-fifth clang as well as contra-clang, *i.e.*, of the two most important harmonies :

$$\overset{S^{III} <}{\overbrace{g\ \ b\ \ d}}\ \underset{T}{\underbrace{f\ \overset{°D}{\overbrace{a\ \ c\ \ e}}}}$$

The specially characteristic degrees of the four church modes are those printed thick above :

The sixth degree of the Dorian (Dorian sixth).

  „ second   „   „   „ Phrygian (Phrygian second).

  „ fourth   „   „   „ Lydian (Lydian fourth).

  „ seventh „   „   „ Mixolydian (Mixolydian seventh).

i.e., the major sixth in the minor scale (raised third of the °subdominant), if used unnecessarily, without modulation and without melodic rising to the third of the major upper-dominant, will always produce turns like those peculiar to the Dorian mode of the fifteenth to the seventeenth century ; likewise the minor seventh in the major scale, introduced without modulation and without the third of the °subdominant following in the same part, will reproduce the peculiarities of the Mixolydian :

The charm of such turns rests in the momentary upsetting of the tonality, in a certain *wavering of conception between the acceptance of an intended modulation and the retaining of the key*, upon which the continuation first decides.   This vagueness of key (in the sense of our modern clarified harmonic conception), was in former centuries the involuntary result of seeking for fixed rules for harmonic motion ; nowadays, it is the consequence of the study of old compositions, the wish to be able again to express their veiled sadness and unsatisfied longing ; therefore, in the first place, the result of imitation.   But it may, if theoretically understood and generalised, give rise to consciously freer motion within the clearly recognised bounds of modern tonality, by the *deliberate treatment of the abnormal for intensifying the expression*. For the Dorian sixth retains its soaring tendency and the Mixolydian seventh its lowering weight, even though the natural conclusion be drawn from neither.

The Lydian fourth and Phrygian second also bring about peculiar variations of the plain harmony proper to the scale ; they both arise from the plain-fifth clang being introduced with its *minor contra-second* as suspension (or represented by its leading-tone substitute). Thus the following are added to the forms 𝔉, ,𝔖 𝔉, 𝔇, discussed above :

𝔅, in c-major :   f♯ [g] b d   and
𝔖, in A-minor :   d f [a] b♭

The latter chord is known by the name of the *chord of the Neapolitan sixth* (b♭ is the minor upper-sixth of the fundamental note of the minor under-dominant), because it is said to have been brought into use by the opera composers of the Neapolitan school (Alessandro Scarlatti, etc.). We leave the chord its name, of course, but are clear on this point, that the introduction of the note characteristic of it (the minor second of the minor scale) makes the scale resemble the *Phrygian.* In the first place, the minor second of the minor scale must needs be conceived as an auxiliary note to the °subdominant prime [103 (*a*)—(*b*)], and even when it enters as passing note between tonic third and fifth, it must be regarded as an approach to the fifth and defined as leading-note to the latter [103 (*c*)—(*d*)] :

it, therefore, appears less natural when rising, because then there is less reason for it [103 (*d*)]. The Phrygian second (in minor), like the Mixolydian seventh (in major), seems to have a depressing influence; something like the night of the grave, and the odour of decay wafts towards us from both, or at least resignation, renunciation of the enjoyment of existence (on account of their reaching beyond the under-dominant). On the other hand, the Dorian sixth (in minor) and the Lydian fourth (in major) have somewhat of nervous strain, painful longing, yearning. The *Lydian fourth* is, in the first place, an auxiliary note of the upper-dominant fundamental note and an approach to the tonic fifth :

But the Lydian fourth and Phrygian second (Neapolitan sixth) have the most striking effect, when followed directly by the third of the contra-clang of the tonic, with which they form the interval of a diminished third (succession of both leading-notes to the tonic fifth):

About this we must remark that in cases like 105 (*a*) and (*b*) (*b♭* in soprano, *b♮* in tenor) absolutely *no effect of false relation is brought about.* This must be explained by the interval of the *diminished third,* as composed of two leading-note steps, *claiming precedence over the chromatic progression;* this, moreover, is important — *b♭* (=$^{2>}$) is the artificial note, while *b* (=5) is the natural one, whose reappearing at any time will, therefore, be easily intelligible. A similar case of "false relation" being quite natural and easily intelligible (for really no effect of false relation is brought about) takes place in the so-called "Phrygian close," at least, in that most frequent and characteristic harmonisation of the descending lower half of the Phrygian scale (*a g f e*), which gives the closing tone its major chord :

These last turns are nothing else than *half-closes, i.e.,* cases of resting on the dominant harmony, instead of on the tonic, at the end of larger rhythmical divisions. Nowadays we recognise closes of this kind only for parts of a piece of music, but not for the end of the whole piece ; formerly this was different, and the desire for a complete winding up, with the feeling that all was over and at an end, was not experienced. The strangely vague closes in the Church modes, which, as already mentioned, meant nothing more than ending on a dominant (!), have been handed down to us only as half-closes, deceptive closes, etc., of principal subdivisions, but as such they are certainly of the same efficacy now as ever.

Conforming in the main to the terminology generally accepted nowadays, but differing from it in a few points by reason of the results of our own observations, we shall now define the terms *close, half-close, deceptive close* in the following manner :

(A) *A CLOSE is the satisfactory entry of the tonic, allowing of cessation without a desire for continuation, at the end of a cadence that takes place at a point possessing rhythmical cadential power in a higher degree* (end of period or of section).

(B) *A HALF-CLOSE is the entry on a beat with rhythmical cadential power in a higher degree of a dominant (without dissonant notes or at least in feigning consonant form), necessitating continuation.*

(C) *A DECEPTIVE CLOSE is the entry of the tonic at the end of a cadence on a beat with rhythmical cadential power in a higher degree, but with progression of one or more parts to foreign notes, which give the tonic a feigning consonant form, and therefore lead on to a new cadence.*

This formulation allows of our including a larger number of harmonic formations in the separate categories; for, as regards the very first, according to the experience hitherto gained, we have a whole series of cadential formulas at our command, viz., those from both the dominants with or without characteristic dissonances :

107.
(Closes.)

[107 (*a*), (*d*), and (*f*), the closes from the upper dominant, are called *authentic;* 107 (*b*), (*c*), and (*e*)—from the under-dominant—*plagal* closes, designations which we shall drop, because they bring entirely hetero-geneous effects under one heading.]

Closes are also possible from the parallel clangs of the dominants [this category leads us naturally to the introduction of the contra-third-clang of the tonic, which is parallel clang of the contra-clang, 108 (*e*)—(*f*)]:

To these must still be added the leading-tone substitutes of the dominants [which likewise lead us to two new formations, 109 (*a*)—(*f*)] :

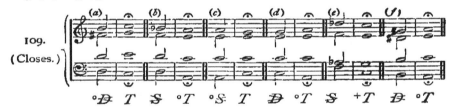

But, finally, it is possible also to close *elliptically* (skipping over the expected contra-clang of the tonic) from the chords of the Dorian sixth and Mixolydian seventh to the tonic; if in major this does not immediately sound right to our ears, yet the minor will show us that it is for want of being accustomed to it, and not for want of tenacity of tonal conception :

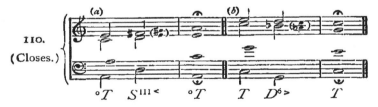

Other possible close formations will become intelligible to us as ellipses, only when we shall have become acquainted with the intermediate cadences (in the next chapter).

The term *half-close* has usually been confined to the resting on the major upper-dominant [111 (*a*)—(*h*)]; but, in the absence of sufficient reasons, this restriction is not binding on us.

III.
(Half-closes.)

T   D   Tp   D   S   D   Sp   D   °T   D+

°Tp   D+   °S   D+   °Sp   D

This small selection will suffice to show what is usually under-stood by a half-close ; of course, one can actually proceed from any chord of the key to the ⁺ dominant and pause there. But it is clear that any dominant, indeed even any parallel clang, and any leading-tone substitute of a dominant may become the bearer of a half-close, only presupposing that it falls on a beat with rhythmical cadential power in a higher degree, and is made use of as a point of rest (long note with or without a pause ; indeed, if only no rhythmical change of meaning or feminine ending destroy the effect of half-close, it is not even necessary to stop at all). We will now proceed with a few suggestions—again only a selection—as to how a half-close (principal subdivision, close of a part) may be made to one of the other dominants, and we draw special attention to the fact that just this hitherto *limited under-standing of the terms, close and half-close, bears a great share of the blame, if our modern harmony, compared with that of the flourishing period of the vocal style* in the fifteenth and sixteenth centuries under the dominion of the Church modes, *appears one-sided, stereotyped, and poor.* The suggestion of the *possibility of occasional points of rest on the under-dominant and on the parallel clangs and leading-tone substitutes of either dominant,* will lead young composers to the understanding of a number of good effects :

112.
(Half-closes.)

T   S   Tp   S   T   Sp   Dp   Sp   S   Dp

We have already discussed the *deceptive close* in its simplest forms (pp. 72, 77, 84) ; if we now define it quite generally as a close disturbed by foreign notes, but in feigning consonant form, all closes introduced in 107—110 must be looked upon as deceptive closes as soon as the tonic does not enter in pure form, but as feigning consonance, thus in the first place as parallel clang or leading-tone substitute :

113.
(Deceptive Closes.)
cf. 107.

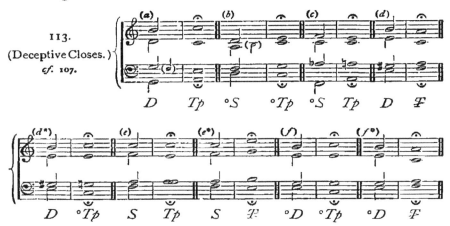

Above (111—112) we avoided the parallel clang of the contra-clang among the half-closes, for the reason that, in close-formations, it is not looked upon as parallel clang of the contra-clang, but rather as a chromatic transformation of the tonic, viz., as *leading-tone substitute of the tonic-variant, i.e., of the tonic of the opposite mode :* e.g., $a\flat^+$ in c-major, not as $^\circ Sp$, but as $T^{6}_{\substack{8\\3}>}$, more simply $\mathcal{F}$; and $^\circ g\sharp$ in A-minor, not as ^+Dp, but as $T^{\tilde{x}}_{\text{III}<}$, more simply $\mathcal{F}$. In other words, the succession $g^+—a\flat^+$ in c-major [114 (a)] denotes a *quick change from c-major to c-minor, making use of the most customary form of deceptive close of the latter* [$D—\mathcal{F}$ *cf.* 113 (d)], and similarly in A-minor $^\circ a—^\circ g\sharp$ [114 (b)] is a quick change from A-minor to A-major, making use of one of the forms of deceptive close of the latter [$^\circ S—\mathcal{F}$, *cf.* 113 (e*)] ; however, not only the leading-tone substitute, but also the *parallel clang of the tonic-variant may be borrowed for deceptive closes,* by which means we gain two more new deceptive close-formations, viz., for A-minor first $e^+ - {}^\circ c\sharp$ $[= D - {}^+ Tp$, really $\mathcal{T}^{\text{VII}\natural}_{\text{III}<}$, cf. 114 $(c)]$, and for C-major ${}^\circ c - e\flat^+$ $[= {}^\circ S - {}^\circ Tp$, really $\mathcal{T}^{7\natural}_{3<}$, cf. 114 $(d)]$. But the close to the parallel clang of the tonic-variant is possible not only from the contra-clang, and that to its leading-tone substitute not only from the plain-fifth clang; we therefore gain a whole series of new possible forms of deceptive close $[114 (e)—(m)]$:

114.
(Deceptive Closes.)

Certainly all the deceptive closes from 114 $(a)—(m)$ give rise to difficulties in the further retaining of the tonality, and come rather near to a real transition into the fifth-change key (key of the tonic-variant); at least they necessitate the use of the chords of the Dorian sixth or Mixolydian seventh for the return over the contra-clang and the quickest possible regaining of the plain-fifth clang or its parallel clang, *e.g.* :

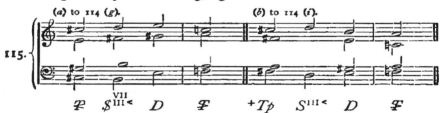

115.

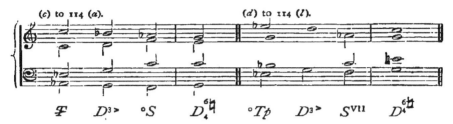

These last observations have introduced an abundance of new harmonic steps. The introduction of the Mixolydian seventh and Dorian sixth each yield two new feigning consonances (in c-major: $D^{3>} = {}^{\circ}d$ and $\mathcal{D}^{7\natural}_{3>} = b\flat^{+}$; in A-minor: $S^{\mathrm{III}<} = d^{+}$, $\mathcal{S}^{\mathrm{VII}}_{\mathrm{III}<} = {}^{\circ}f\sharp$), whose combination with the principal clangs indeed only reproduce harmonic successions already discussed (c^{+}—${}^{\circ}d$ and ${}^{\circ}e$—d^{+} = whole-tone change, g^{+}—${}^{\circ}d$ and ${}^{\circ}a$—d^{+} = fifth-change, f^{+}—${}^{\circ}d$ and ${}^{\circ}b$—d^{+} = minor-third change; ${}^{\circ}d$—${}^{\circ}c$ and d^{+}—e^{+} = whole-tone step); their connection with the parallel clangs also yields no new steps (${}^{\circ}d$—${}^{\circ}e$ and d^{+}—c^{+} = whole-tone step, ${}^{\circ}d$—${}^{\circ}a$ and d^{+}—g^{+} = contra-fifth step, ${}^{\circ}d$—${}^{\circ}b$ and d^{+}—f^{+} = minor-third step, $a\flat^{+}$—${}^{\circ}d$ and d —${}^{\circ}g\sharp$ = tritone change). But, on the other hand, the two new harmonies arising from the introduction of the Phrygian second and Lydian fourth, in c-major: ${}^{\circ}f\sharp$ ($= \mathcal{D}$) and d^{+} ($= {}^{+}D^{2>}_{\mathrm{II}<}$); in A-minor: $b\flat^{+}$ ($= \mathcal{S}$) and ${}^{\circ}d$ ($= {}^{\circ}S^{2>}_{\mathrm{II}}$), supply a few new combinations:

(A) ${}^{\circ}c$ d^{+} (${}^{\circ}S$—${}^{+}D^{2>}_{\mathrm{II}<}$) and e^{+}—${}^{\circ}d$ (D^{+}—${}^{\circ}S^{2>}_{\mathrm{II}<}$) are *contra-whole-tone changes*.

(B) ${}^{\circ}c$—${}^{\circ}f\sharp$ (${}^{\circ}S$—$\mathcal{D}$), $a\flat^{+}$—d^{+} (${}^{\circ}Sp$—${}^{+}D^{2>}_{\mathrm{II}<}$), e^{+}—$b\flat^{+}$ (${}^{+}D$—$\mathcal{S}$), ${}^{\circ}g\sharp$—${}^{\circ}d$ (${}^{+}Dp$—${}^{\circ}S^{2>}_{\mathrm{II}}$) are *tritone steps*.

(c) f^{+}—${}^{\circ}f\sharp$ (S—$\mathcal{D}$) and ${}^{\circ}b$—$b\flat^{+}$ (${}^{\circ}D$—$\mathcal{S}$) are *chromatic-semitone changes*.

(D) $a\flat^{+}$—${}^{\circ}f\sharp$ (${}^{\circ}Sp$—$\mathcal{D}$) and ${}^{\circ}g\sharp$—$b\flat^{+}$ (${}^{+}Dp$—$\mathcal{S}$) are *augmented-sixth changes*.

To these we must add the connecting of the parallel clang of the tonic-variant with the leading-tone substitute of the plain-fifth clang:

(E) $e\flat^{+}$—${}^{\circ}f\sharp$ ($T^{7\natural}_{3>}$—$\mathcal{D}$) and ${}^{\circ}c\sharp$—$b\flat^{+}$ ($T^{\mathrm{VII}\natural}_{\mathrm{III}}$—$\mathcal{S}$), an *augmented-second change*, a step which is also the result of the connection of the parallel clang of the contra-clang with the parallel clang of the plain-fifth clang ($a\flat$—${}^{\circ}b = {}^{\circ}Sp$—${}^{+}Dp$, and ${}^{\circ}g\sharp$—$f^{+} = {}^{+}Dp$—${}^{\circ}Sp$).

Finally, the combination of the parallel clang of the contra-clang with the parallel clang of the tonic furnishes the step:

(F) $a\flat^{+}$—${}^{\circ}e$ (${}^{\circ}Sp$—${}^{+}Tp$) and ${}^{\circ}g\sharp$—c^{+} (${}^{+}Dp$—${}^{\circ}Tp$) = augmented-fifth change (*double-third change*),

while the combination of the same with the parallel clang of the subdominant ($ab^+—°a = °Sp—^{+}.Sp$, $°g\#—g^+ = {^+}Dp—°Dp$) repre-sents the chromatic-semitone change already introduced at (c).

If we still add the *leading-tone substitute of the contra-clang* ($\mathcal{S}$ in major, $\mathcal{D}$ in minor), this will produce, besides the already mentioned rare steps (in c-major and a-minor: $dp^+—°e$ and $°d\#—c^+ =$ augmented-second change, $db^+—°b$ and $°d\#—f^+ =$ augmented-sixth change), two more new steps:

    (G) *The augmented-third change,* $\mathcal{S}—\mathcal{D}$ ($db^+—°f\#$) and $\mathcal{D}—\mathcal{S}$ ($°d\#—bb^+$), and

    (H) *The chromatic-semitone step:* $\mathcal{S}—{^+}D^{\overset{2}{\text{II}}<}$ ($db^+—\dot{a}^+$) and $\mathcal{D}—°S^{\overset{2}{\text{II}}>}$ ($°d\#—°d$).

The parallel clang of the leading-tone substitute of the plain-fifth clang (by the way, the most complicated of our formulas, ${^+}D^{\overset{2}{\text{II}}<}$ and $°S^{\overset{2}{\text{II}}>}$) may be comprehended more simply as plain-fifth clang of the plain-fifth clang, *i.e.,* as *dominant of the dominant* ($\mathcal{D}$), or *°subdominant of the °subdominant* ($°\overset{\circ}{S}$); we shall further on become acquainted with many a possibility of intro-ducing the dominants of clangs proper to the scale, but we preserve the special significance of these two, which are the first we meet, by affixing a special sign, viz., the doubled D or $°S$. The second dominant and the contra-clang stand in intimate relation to each other, as the one harmony may be transformed into the other by chromatic alterations; if the characteristic dissonance be added, this will prove even more striking ($S^{\overset{\text{VII}}{\underset{\text{V}}{\text{III}}<}}=\mathcal{D}^7$; $D^{\overset{7}{\underset{3>}{5>}}} = \mathcal{S}^{\text{VII}}$).

The *contra-whole-tone change,* the simplest of the new steps (connecting the contra-clang with the second dominant of the other side: $°S—\mathcal{D}$ or $D^+—°\overset{\circ}{S}$), therefore, requires two chro-matic progressions:

116.

    $°S$ $\mathcal{D}$ D T $\mathcal{D}^7$ S^{VII} ${^+}D$ $°\overset{\circ}{S}$ $°S$ $°T$ D^7 $\mathcal{S}^{\text{VII}}$

Part progressions which should be avoided are the augmented sixth ($ab—f\#$, $g\#—bb$; inverted—as a diminished third—good at any time), and the augmented fourth ($ab—d$ and $g\#—d$; in-verted—as a diminished fifth—good).

The *tritone step* ($°S—\mathcal{D}$, $°Sp—\mathcal{D}$, ${^+}D—\mathcal{S}$, ${^+}Dp—°\overset{\circ}{S}$) has, besides the three tritone steps (1—1, 3—3, 5—5, or I—I,

III—III, V—V), also an augmented-second step (5—3, or III—V) to be avoided, but is very simple if the possible diminished-third step (I—3, III—I) be made :

The *chromatic-semitone change* (S—D, °D—°$\bar{S}$, °Sp—^{+}Sp, ^{+}Dp—°Dp) contains only one possible augmented step, which is, however, obviated if the leading-tone step be made :

The *augmented-sixth change* (°Sp—D, Dp—S, S—^{+}Dp, D—°Sp) is simple if the possible step of a diminished third be practicable ; it has the possibility of two augmented seconds (I—V, I—5), two augmented fourths (I—III, 3—I), an augmented fifth (5—III), and an augmented sixth (I—I) which are allowable only in inversion :

The *augmented-second change* ($T_{3>}^{7\natural}$—D, $T_{III<}^{VII\natural}$—S) shows two leading-tone steps and a chromatic step, which are confronted by an augmented-second step (I—I) and an augmented-fifth step (I—V) :

The *double-third change* (augmented-fifth change : °*Sp*—+*Tp*, +*Dp*—°*Tp*) gives occasion for a sustained note (3 III), and has also two chromatic steps, but likewise risk of consecutive fifths (⁵₁ ₁ᵥ) and of steps of an augmented fifth and of an augmented fourth ·

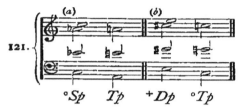

121.

°*Sp*   *Tp*   +*Dp*   °*Tp*

The *augmented-third change*, connecting the two most artificial chords (*S*—*D*), gives occasion for making both those diminished third steps simultaneously (2ᵇ —3, III—IIᶜ), but, for the rest, an augmented second 5—V, an augmented fifth 3—V, and two augmented sixths (1—V, 5—I), obstruct the way [122 (*a*)—(*b*)].

122.

S +*D*ᴵᴵ˂¹   *T*   *D*· °*S*ᵃ˃¹   *D*   *S*   *D*   *D*   *T*

D· °*S*   °*S*   °*T*

The *chromatic-semitone* step [122 (*c*)—(*d*)] is not difficult, if use be made of the proper doubling (V of °*S*, and 5 of *D*⁺ respectively).

If we now proceed to make the numerous new expedients shown here our own by practical exercises, we choose the simplest forms for this purpose—*i.e.*, write note against note (*without figuration;* but in order to make a smoother progression to the following chords possible, a *change of position* by way of figuration may occasionally be resorted to). We also forego modulation for the present, so as not to lose the power of surveying the whole on account of the abundance of possibilities. The exercises following next are therefore to be worked out simply in the *four vocal clefs.*

EXERCISES 197—220 (not for figuration).

(197) ₵: $T\ D\ |\ T\ D^{3>}|\ {}^{\circ}S_{\underset{\text{VII}}{\cdots}}|\ D^{6\ 5}\ |\ Tp\ Sp\ |\ \mathcal{D}\ D\ |\ \mathcal{F}\ {}^{\circ}S\ |\ T$

(198) ³/₂: ${}^{\circ}T\ S^{\text{III}<}\ D\ |\ {}^{\circ}T\ {}^{\circ}Tp\ {}^{\circ}Dp\ |\ S^{\text{VI}\ \text{V}}\ D^{\gamma}\ |\ \mathcal{F}\ D\ \mathscr{S}^{\overset{\text{VII}}{\text{III}}<}\ |$
$\quad\quad D\ {}^{\circ}T\ \mathcal{S}\ |\ D^{\overset{6>}{4}}\ \overset{..}{.}\ ..^{\gamma}\ |\ \mathcal{F}\ D\ ..^{\gamma}\ |\ {}^{\circ}T$

(199) ³/₄: $T\ |\ {}^{\circ}S\ \mathcal{B}\ 1\ |\ \mathcal{F}\ Sp\ \mathcal{D}\ |\ D\ S\ \mathcal{S}\ |\ D^{\overset{6}{4}\ \overset{5}{3}}\ {}^{\circ}Tp\ |$
$\quad\quad S\ ^+Sp\ \mathcal{B}\ |\ D\ Tp\ {}^{\circ}S^{2>}\ |\ \overset{!}{..}\ D^{6\ 5}\ |\ T$

(200) ₵: ${}^{\circ}T\ {}^{\circ}Tp\ |\ \mathscr{S}^{\overset{\text{VII}}{\text{III}}<}\ ^+D\ \mathcal{F}\ \mathcal{S}\ |\ D^{\overset{6>}{4}\ \overset{5}{3}}\ ^+Tp\ ^+Dp\ |$
$\quad\quad \mathscr{S}^{\overset{\text{VII}}{\text{III}}<}\ {}^{\circ}S\ ^+D^{\text{II}<}\ ^1\ |\ {}^{\circ}T$

(201) ₵: $T\ |\ Sp\ D\ |\ \mathcal{F}\ {}^{\circ}S\ |\ ..^{2>}\ ^+D^{\text{II}<}\ |\ ..^{\overset{1}{3}>}\ {}^{\circ}Sp\ |\ S^{\text{VII}}\ {}^{\circ}Tp\ |$
$\quad\quad S^{\text{VII}}\ D\ |\ T$

(202) ⁶/₈: ${}^{\circ}T\ |\ {}^{\circ}S\ {}^{\circ}Sp\ {}^{\circ}S^{2>}\ \overset{!}{..}\ |\ ^+Dp\ ^+Tp\ \mathscr{S}^{\overset{\text{VII}}{\text{III}}<}\ {}^{\circ}S\ |\ \mathcal{S}\ D$
$\quad\quad \mathcal{C}\ \mathcal{F}\ \mathcal{C}\ \mathcal{F}\ \text{etc.}$
$\quad\quad {}^{\circ}Tp\ S^{\text{III}<}\ |\ \mathcal{S}\ D\ {}^{\circ}T$

(203) ₵: $T\ |\ \mathcal{B}\ D\ |\ \mathcal{F}\ \mathcal{D}\ |\ \mathcal{S}\ D\ |\ Tp\ S^{\text{VI}}\ |\ {}^{\circ}Tp\ \underset{3}{..}\ |$
$\quad\quad ^+D^{\text{II}<}\ ^1\ |\ T$

(204) ³/₂: $S\ D\ Tp\ |\ Sp\ \mathcal{S}\ \mathcal{S}\ |\ D\ Sp\ \mathcal{B}\ |\ \mathcal{F}\ S^{\text{V}}\ D^{\gamma}\ |$
$\quad\quad T\ {}^{\circ}S\ \mathcal{D}\ |\ D\ \mathcal{F}\ {}^{\circ}S\ |\ T\ (\overset{\frown}{\circ\cdot|\circ}\cdot)$

(205) ₵: $S^{\text{III}<}\ \mathscr{S}^{\overset{\text{VII}}{\text{III}}<}\ ^+D^{\text{II}<}\ ^1\ |\ ^+Dp\ ^+Tp\ \mathcal{S}\ {}^{\circ}Sp\ |\ {}^{\circ}\mathcal{S}\ {}^{\circ}S\ D^{\overset{6>}{4}}\ \overset{..}{.}\ |$
$\quad\quad {}^{\circ}Tp\ {}^{\circ}S\ {}^{\circ}T\ (\downarrow)$

(206) ₵: $D^{3>}\ \mathcal{D}^{\overset{7}{3}>}\ {}^{\circ}S^{2>}\ ^1\ |\ {}^{\circ}Sp\ {}^{\circ}Tp\ \mathcal{B}\ Dp\ |\ \mathcal{D}\ D\ S^{\overset{\text{IV}}{\text{VI}}<}\ \overset{\text{III}}{\text{V}}\ |$
$\quad\quad Tp\ D\ T\ (\downarrow)$

(207) $^3/_4$: T $\overline{S}$ I | D $\overline{F}$ $°D\!p$ | $°\overset{\circ}{\overline{S}}$ $°S$ $°T$ | $S^{\text{III}}\overset{\text{VII}}{<}$ D $\overset{..}{}$ |
       $\overset{..}{7}$

 T $\underset{\text{III}}{S^{\text{III}<}}$ $\underset{\text{III}}{T}$ | $\underset{\text{III}}{S^{\text{III}<}}$ D $\overline{S}$ | $°\overset{\circ}{\overline{S}}$ $°S$ D | $°T$ $(\;\downarrow.)$

(208) E: T $\underset{3}{D^7}$ | $\overline{F}$ $+Tp$ | $\slashed{D}$ D | $\overline{F}$ $°S\!p$ | $\overline{S}$ $+S\!p$ | $+D^{\text{II}}$ ^{1} |
 $S^{\overset{\text{IV}}{\text{VI}}<\overset{\text{III}}{\text{V}}}$ | T

(209) E: $°D$ $°S$ | $+D\!p$ $+Tp$ | $°S^{2>}$ ^{1} | D $\overline{F}$ | $S^{\text{III}<}$ $\overset{\text{VI}}{S^{\text{III}<}}$ |
 $+D\!p$ $°T$ | $°S$ $°D$ | $°T$

(210) $^3/_4$: T | S D | T $D^{3>}$ | $°S\!p$ $\overline{S}$ | $D^{\overset{6}{4}}$ $\overset{..}{\overset{7}{..}}$ | $°S$ $..^{\text{VII}}$ |
 ρ $\overset{3}{\rho}$ etc.
 $°Tp$ $\overline{S}$ | $+S\!p$ D | T

(211) $^3/_4$: $°T$ $..^{2>}$ $°Tp$ | $\underset{\text{V}}{D}$ $\underset{\text{VI}}{°S}$ | $D^{6>}$ ^{7} ^{5} | $\overline{F}$ $\underset{3}{°Tp}$ $°S^{2>}$ |
 $\overset{\text{I}}{..}$ D $+D\!p$ | $+Tp$ $S^{\text{III}<}$ $\overset{\text{VII}}{S^{\text{III}<}}$ | D $°S\!p$ D | $°T$

(212) ¢: T Tp | $°S$ $D\!p$ | Tp S | $S\!p$ | $°S$ D $\overset{..}{}$ | $°S\!p$ $\overline{S}$ |
  ρ ρ
 $+S\!p$ S | T

(213) ¢: $°T$ | $°D$ S^{VII} | $°Tp$ $°S\!p$ | $°S$ $\underset{\text{III}}{T}$ | $°D$ $°S$ | $\underset{\text{III}}{T}$ T $\overline{S}$ |
 D^7 $°Tp$ | $\overline{S}$ $..^{\text{VII}}$ | $°T$

(214) $^3/_4$: $°T$ | $°S^{2>}$ ^{1} D | $\overline{F}$ $\overline{S}$ $°D$ | $°S\!p$ $S^{\overset{\text{III}<}{\text{VII}}\natural}$ VIII |
 D^+ $°D$ $°S\!p$ | $°Tp$ $°T$ $S^{\text{III}<}$ | D^+ $+Tp$ $°S^{2>}$ |
 $\overset{..}{}$ D $°S\!p$ | $°T$

(215) ¢: $\overline{F}$ $S\!p$ | $+D^{\text{II}<}$ ^{1} | $\overline{F}$ $D\!p$ | Tp $\overline{S}$ | D^6 ^{5} | $°S^{\overset{2\natural}{\text{II}}}$ $\overset{\text{I}}{\text{III}}$ |
 $D^{\overset{6}{4}}$ $\overset{..}{\overset{7}{..}}$ | T

(216) $^3/_4$: $°T$ | $S^{\overset{\text{V}}{\text{III}}<}$ $\overset{\text{VI}}{}$ $\overset{\text{VII}}{S^{\text{III}<}}$ | D $\overline{F}$ | $\overline{S}$ S^{VI} D | $+Tp$ $°S$ |
 ρ $\rho\cdot$ ς ρ ρ ρ $\rho\cdot$ ς ρ ρ ρ
 D^{VI} $\overset{\text{I}>}{..}$ | $°S^{2>}$ ^{1} D | $°T$ $°S^{\overset{2>}{\text{III}}}$ ^{II} | $°T$
 ρ ρ $\rho\cdot$ ς ρ ρ $\rho\cdot$ ς ρ

(217) $\mathfrak{C}$: $^+D^{\mathrm{II}\,<}$ I | $\underset{\mathrm{III}}{S}$ $..^{\mathrm{VII}}$ $D^{\overset{6}{3}>}$ S^{VII} | $D^{\overset{6}{4}}$ $^{\overset{5}{3}}$ $\mathcal{F}$ $^\circ Tp$ | $S^{\overset{\mathrm{VII\ VIII}}{\mathrm{V\ \ VI}}}$

  $\mathcal{D}$ D | $^\circ T$

(218) $\mathfrak{C}$: $^\circ S$ | D $\underset{3}{S}$ | S^{VII} $\mathcal{D}$ | $^+D^{\mathrm{II}\,<}$ I | Sp Dp | $^\circ Sp$ $^\circ S$ |

  Tp Sp $..^{\mathrm{VII}}$ | T

(219) $^3/_4$: $^\circ S$ | $^\circ T$ S^{VII} $^\circ T$ | $^\circ D$ $\mathcal{F}$ $\mathcal{D}$ | S^{VI} $^\circ D$ $^\circ T$ | $\mathcal{S}$ $^\circ T$ |

  $..^{\mathrm{VII}\,>}$ S^{VII} $\overset{\mathrm{VII}}{S}^{\mathrm{III}\,<}$ | $^+D^{\mathrm{II}\,<}$ I $?$ | $^\circ T$ S^{VI} ^{V} | $^\circ T$

(220) $^4/_4$: $S^{\mathrm{III}\,<}$ | $^\circ T$ $\overset{\mathrm{VII}}{S}^{\mathrm{III}\,<}$ D $\mathcal{F}$ | $^\circ Dp$ S^{V} ^{VI} $^\circ D$ $\overset{\mathrm{VII}}{S}^{\mathrm{III}\,<}$ |

  D^7 $\mathcal{F}$ D^{VI} $S^{\mathrm{III}\,<}\overset{\mathrm{VII}}{}D$ | $\mathcal{F}$ S^{VII} $^\circ T$

These exercises go as far as is at all possible in the combination of feigning consonant formations that are intelligible as related to one and the same tonic; if any other formation beyond those displayed here be found intelligible, it will have to be judged and treated according to the same principles. The great majority of the harmonic progressions considered in this paragraph generally induce modulation; but we again draw attention to the fact that the greatest power of expression in harmony lies not in the frequent (and only too easy) change of tonality, but rather in extending the boundaries of the key; progressions like $b\flat^+$—b^+ ($\mathcal{S}$— $\mathcal{D}$) in A-minor or $^\circ f$—$^\circ f\sharp$ ($= {}^\circ\overset{\circ}{\mathcal{S}}$ — $\mathcal{B}$) in c-major (without modulation) signify a powerful respiration, as if to burst the fetters of the mortal frame. Naturally the student of composition should be most imperatively warned against the misuse of these strongest means of expression.

Our view has now become extensive, and the following chapters, which lead us back into the more trodden paths will introduce easier work again.

CHAPTER III.

THE THEORY OF DISSONANCE.   SEQUENCES.   INTERMEDIATE
CADENCES.

§ 10. COMPLETION OF THE THEORY OF DISSONANCE.

WE have gradually, and as occasion offered, become acquainted
with the significance of dissonant formations of all kinds ; it is
now time to arrange them according to fixed points of view, and
group them clearly, so that other analogous formations, when
introduced, will immediately be understood.   The most important
distinction is that of *characteristic* dissonances from those only
figurative ; the former class we have already become acquainted
with, as the most important marks of clangs in their functions as
dominants, within the key as well as for modulation (6 added to
the ^+S, VII to the $^{\circ}S$, 7 to the D^+, VI to the $^{\circ}D$), and of the latter
class we have written a great number in our figuration exercises,
without, however, giving them special consideration.   Now it is a
matter of extending the category of characteristic dissonances
and of arranging the large number of figurative ones in groups.
If we begin with the latter, we shall find that figuration by means
of passing and auxiliary notes quite naturally makes us acquainted with a lot of dissonant chords, to which, in the usual
method of teaching harmony founded on the " figured bass," far
too much importance is attached by their being placed on a level
with the characteristic dissonances.

If, in the figuration of the prime or fifth of the major and minor
chords by their upper or under seconds, the figured note be
doubled, and thus remain present (generally in another octave-
position) simultaneously with the foreign note (second or
seventh), then *chords of four notes* will result of a construction
partly contradictory to the chords of four notes with which we
have hitherto become acquainted :

123.

H

The figuration of the third yields similar formations :

If the figurative note (the 7<, 2, 6, 4, or VII⁾, II, VI, IV)
proceed immediately by step of a second, *i.e.*, if the 7< coming
from the 8 lead to the 6 or back to the octave, if the 2 coming
from the 3 go to the 1 or back to the 3, etc., therefore—if the
foreign note (entering on an unaccented beat) really prove to be
the most natural insertion between two harmonically significant
notes, we have before us the most easily intelligible but weakest
kind of dissonant formation, and that on the lowest footing as
regards effect, so-called

Passing Dissonances.

As auxiliary notes, the leading-notes (minor upper and under
seconds) of the note to be ornamented are often introduced, even
where they are not proper to the scale, by which means the
formations of 123 and 124 receive a somewhat different aspect :

By this approximation to the ornamented note the more close
connection with the latter is very sharply marked : in many cases,
however, the effect becomes weak and artificial.

Many of the chords written down at 123—125 have three
notes on degrees next to one another (even though in different
octave-positions), thus *c d e* in 123 (*b*) and (*f*) and 124 (*k*);

a b c in 123 (*h*) and 124 (*m*), whereas all the dissonant chords considered hitherto (S^6, D^{VI}, S^{VII}, D^7) had only two notes on degrees next to each other ($^6_5$, $^V_{VI}$, $^{VII}_{VIII}$, $^8_7$). It is evident that such chords, unless they arise in the fashion already discussed, *as it were casually* in the figuration, would make themselves very noticeable by their striking dissonance, and they therefore remain alien to plain, unfigured writing, which avoids all that is remarkable; this style in general prefers feigning consonant clangs, parallel clangs, and leading-tone substitutes. It, therefore, seems quite explicable that successions of consonant harmonies, comparatively very difficult to understand, should have become quite at home in musical literature much earlier than even the simplest chords of the seventh and of the sixth arising from the addition of the characteristic dissonances to the dominants. In one form of introducing, certainly, not only these last mentioned formations, but also those shown in Examples 123—125 were common for centuries, even in the strictest style of writing for several parts, viz., as so-called

Prepared Dissonances.

If in the transition from one harmony to another ($T-S$, $S-D$, $D-T$, $S-T$, etc.), a note foreign to the second be at first sustained and only subsequently proceed by step of a second to a note belonging to the new harmony, a so-called *suspension* arises (the note belonging to the first clang *suspends* one of the second for a time).

We will enumerate the most important cases for the principal harmonies :

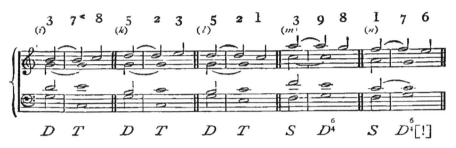

To these examples in major the following examples in minor correspond :

To these must be added the formations arising from the introduction of the contra-clang of the tonic :

By the combination of two suspensions possible in the same harmony step, other chord-forms arise, but only some of them are more complicated :

Composition in more than four parts, which we shall have to practise later on, admits a great number of new possible harmonies through suspensions ; good effect, as regards the sound of prepared suspensions, is certain so long as we avoid writing the sustained note simultaneously in the same octave-position as the chord-note which it retards :

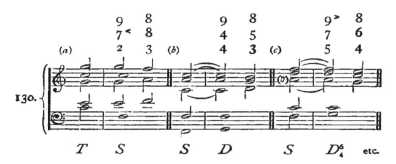

Those dissonances which arise from *chromatic alteration of a chord-note* (so-called *altered chords*), belong as a rule to the class of *passing* dissonances, *i.e.*, a chromatically altered (raised or lowered) note may be inserted as a figurative element, when, in unfigured writing, there would be a step of a major second. Such chromatic passages are generally quite easily intelligible, as inserting a leading-note to the following chord-note, *e.g.* :

But our ears often refuse to understand formations like
$1^>$, $I^<$, $3^<$, $III^>$, because the interval of the augmented third
arising from them ($1^>$—3, I—$3^<$, III—$I^<$, etc.) sounds too
much like the fourth, and may under circumstances lead to a
wrong conception of the harmony :

(Naturally the $3^<$ of the *T* and *D*, the $I^>$ of the *T* and *S*, the $5^>$
of the *S*, in major, and likewise the $III^>$ of the °*T* and °*S*, the
$I^<$ of the °*T* and °*D*, and the $V^<$ of the °*D* in minor, have no
claim to be admitted, as they coincide enharmonically with an
easily intelligible note proper to the scale ; moreover, it should be
remembered, that in chromatic passages it is only a question
of gaining a leading-tone step to the next note.)   In cases like
132 (*a*) and (*d'*), it would be preferable to write and conceive the
figurative note as an auxiliary note (*f*♯ auxiliary note to *g*),
although it does not return, but, on the contrary, is chromatically
altered in the next chord (quitted auxiliary note) :

Perhaps many would prefer to write also $b\flat$ ($4\natural$ or VII$^>$) instead of $a\sharp$ in 132 (b) and (c). One would also rather see the 5$^>$ of the ^+T and the V$^>$ of the $^\circ T$ and $^\circ S$ written as auxiliary notes to 5$\natural$ and V$\natural$ [134 (a)—(f)], whereas the 5$^>$ of the D and V$^<$ of the $^b S$ are quite intelligible [134 (g)—(h)]:

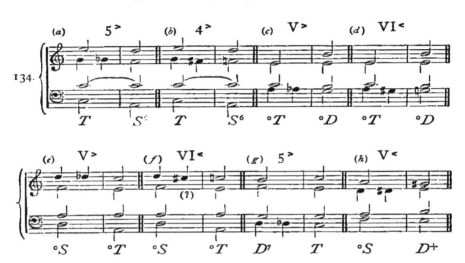

In general, it must be confessed that chromatic raising is altogether much more familiar to us than chromatic lowering, for which the practice of the present day may in part be responsible.

But now both the "passing dissonances," arising from diatonic progression by second through intermediate degrees, and "altered chords," arising chromatically, come in a line with "prepared dissonances," and indeed outdo the latter in harshness and power of dissonance, as soon as they are moved to the accented beat in the bar; in this manner we obtain the third and most important category of dissonant formations,

Unprepared Dissonances.

All the dissonant formations introduced as prepared dissonances above (126—130), may also enter freely, without preparation of the dissonance, and with more or less good effect; this third category therefore includes *all* dissonant formations. Certainly we should be very wrong in assuming that any dissonance might with impunity enter unprepared; on the contrary, it will under any circumstances be well to bear in mind, that any such *free entry is always more or less the result of substitution or ellipse.* The following examples throughout confront the unprepared dissonance with the prepared, that entering by step of a second on the accented beat, with the passing note on the unaccented beat, as with the more original and more perfect form [cf. (*a*) with (*aa*), (*b*) with (*bb*), etc.].

The following examples are throughout to be compared with the prepared dissonances at 126, of which the progressions given here are only *vicarious* forms :

The examples in minor (Example 127) by means of vicarious progressions yield the following unprepared dissonances :

The bracketed ♯ or ♭ in 136 and 137 changes the whole-tone suspensions into leading-tone suspensions, and marks the melodic relation of the note in question to that following in the same part even more unequivocally ; but, on the other hand, disposes of the theory that this combination results from mere vicarious progression (with change of position of the chord), or, at least, demands in addition the assumption of a chromatic passage after the kind at 135, *e.g.* :

The transformation of the examples from 131 onwards into

unprepared dissonances will now scarcely be necessary ; besides, they all yield leading-note suspensions as it is.　But now we may say in general that, *before any chord-note, unprepared whole-tone or semitone suspensions from above or below are possible,* but that they are by no means of equal value.　*Leading-note suspensions from below are at all times easily intelligible, those from above, on the contrary, only when they are proper to the scale, or at least introduce*

nearly related harmonies (III of °S in major, III of °S̊ in minor). *But we most emphatically warn all against the misuse of suspensions foreign to the scale.*　Too much pepper and salt spoil a dish.

The enlightenment we have now acquired as regards the theory of dissonance we shall first turn to advantage in diversifying our figuration exercises.　The following group of exercises is to be worked out in such a manner that every example, as far as possible, introduces *prepared dissonances on the accented beats,* and, as in Exercises 149 and those following, one example each with figuration of the soprano, of the alto, of the tenor, and of the bass, and every fifth with distribution of the figuration among all four parts.　The following remains to be noticed as regards the execution of these exercises :

(A) For *the preparation of the dissonance* a chord-note entering on the preceding unaccented beat will serve (prime, third or fifth of a real harmony or of a feigning consonance [!], or also the seventh of the $+D$ or °S or sixth of the $+S$ and °D).

(B) The *dissonance has to proceed by step of a second ;* only the VII of the °S and the 6 of the S may first proceed to the fundamental note of the $+D$, and let the progression by second follow subsequently.

(c) When the part to be figured gives no opportunity for the introduction of a prepared dissonance on the accented beat, the syncopation is to be carried through, by *tying a note common to both harmonies ;* in such cases the syncopated part is absolved from the necessity of proceeding by step of a second, and, if possible, it will proceed to a chord-note which yields a prepared dissonance for the next accented beat.

(D) In figuration for bars of three beats, or where the figuration is to introduce three or even more notes to each chord of the other three parts, only the note immediately preceding the accented beat is to be tied, so that the syncopation is only partial, as may be seen from the following commencements :

The following (tenth) model example may serve to render the application of these rules intelligible; we will take the alto part for figuration:

(Tenth model example.)

At NB., as the note falling on the accented beat is consonant, a chord-note follows, at bars 3 and 4 the same one, at bar 6 another, in bar 8 the seventh, and at NB.† chromatic alteration of the third takes the place of simple repetition (°S instead of S⁺).

EXERCISES 221—236 (for syncopated figuration).

(221) ₵ : T | ..$^{II<} Tp$ | $S\ Sp$ | D^{6}_{4} ?. | $T\ Tp$ | °$S\ D$ | $Dp\ Tp$ |
$S^{6}\ D$ | T

(222) $\oplus$: S^{VII} | $D+$ S^{VII} | $D+$ $^\circ T$ | $S^{VII<}_{III}$ D | $^\circ T$ $^\circ D$ | $^\circ Sp$ $\mathcal{S}^{VII}$ |

$D^{6>}_{4}$ $\therefore$ | $\mathcal{F}$ $^\circ S$ | $^\circ T$

(223) : $^3/_4$: T | S^6 D | $\mathcal{F}$ S | Sp Dp | Tp $^\circ S$ | D^6_4 $\therefore$ | etc.

$\mathcal{F}$ $^\circ S$ | D S | T

(224) $^3/_4$: $^\circ T$ S^{VII} | D $\mathcal{F}$ | $^\circ S$ $^\circ D$ | $^\circ Dp$ S_1 | D_3 $^\circ L$ | $^\circ S$ T_1 | etc.

S^{VII} $D+$ | $^\circ T$

(225) $^2/_4$: T | D Tp | $\mathcal{F}$ S | D Sp | D D | Tp $\mathcal{F}$ | etc.

Sp $\colon S$ | D^6_4 $\pm$ | T

(226) $^2/_4$: $^\circ T$ | S^{VII} D | $^\circ T$ $^\circ D$ | $^\circ Sp$ $\mathcal{S}^{VII}$ | D $^\circ D$ | $..^{?>}$ $^\circ S$ | etc.

D $\mathcal{F}$ | $^\circ S$ D | $^\circ T$

(227) $^3/_4$: S D | Sp $..$ | Dp T | Sp D | T $^\circ S$ | D Dp | Tp D | T etc.

(228) $^3/_4$: $^\circ T$ | $..$ $^\circ S$ | $^\circ Dp$ $^\circ T$ | S^{VII} D | $^\circ T$ $^\circ Dp$ | $^\circ Tp$ $^\circ T$ | etc.

$^\circ S$ $..^{VII}$ | D^6_4 $\therefore$ | $^\circ T$

(229) $\oplus$: T | S^6 T S^6 D | T $^\circ S$ D Dp | Tp Sp D^6_4 $\therefore$ |

Tp S T (Figuration : ♪♩ ♫ ♩ ♩ ♩ ♪♩ ♪)

(230) $\oplus$: $^\circ T$ $..$ $^\circ S$ | $^\circ T$ S^{VII} D $^\circ T$ | $^\circ D$ $^\circ T$ S^{VII} $..$ |

D^7 $\mathcal{F}$ S^{VII} D^7 | $^\circ T$

(231) $^3/_2$: T S $\therefore$ | D Dp T | Tp D $..^7$ | T Sp D | T Tp Sp |

D Tp S | Sp D^6_4 $\therefore$ | T (Figuration : 𝄴 ♩ ♩ ♩♩ ♩)

(232) $^3/_2$: $^\circ T$ | $^\circ S$ D^7 | $\mathcal{F}$ $^\circ Tp$ | $^\circ S$ $^\circ Dp$ | $^\circ Sp$ $+D$ | $^\circ T$ |

$\mathcal{S}$ $\mathcal{F}$ | $^\circ S$ D | $^\circ T$

(233) ₵: T | S $+S$ | D Sp | $+D^{II<1}$ | F Tp | $°S$ Dp |

F S | $D^{6♮}_4$ $∴$ | T

(234) ₵: T_{III} S^{VII} | D F | D_{III} $°Sp$ | Tp $°S$ | D $°T$ | S T_{I} |

$D^{7}_{2>\ 1}$ | $°T$

(235) ₵: $°T$ | $°Sp$ $°S^{2>}$ | $∴$ D | F $°S$ | D $°Tp$ | S^{VII} $\mathcal{D}$ |

Dp D^{7} | $°T$ (♩)

(236): ₵ : $°T$ | $S^{III<}$ D | F $°D$ | $°S$ S^{VII} | $°D$ D^{+} | $+Dp$ $+Tp$ |

$°S$ S^{VII} | $°Tp$ $°Sp$ | $°T$

§ 11. SEQUENCES.

The method of teaching harmony founded on thorough-bass
was for a long time at fault, owing to the similarity of the figuring,
counting from the bass, in putting on the same level chord-
formations which, according to their harmonic sense (their
" function "), were of widely different value, and thus in
assuming, for each degree of the scale, not only a triad, but a
chord of the seventh, and at the time of the worst formalism
(about 1800 A.D.) even a chord of the eleventh, and of the
thirteenth :

141.

(a) Major.
T Sp Dp S D Tp D^{7}
     (F) (S)

(b) Minor.
$°T$ S^{VII} $°Tp$ $°S$ $°D$ $°Sp$ $°Dp$
      (D) (F)

(c) Major.
$T^{7<}$ S^{6} D^{6} $S^{7<}$ D^{7} T^{6} D^{7}_{2}

(d) Minor.
T^{VI} S^{VII} $D^{VII>}$ S^{VI} D^{VI} $T^{VII>}$ S^{VII}_{II}

To these we must first add those formations resulting from the introduction of the raised sixth and seventh degrees of the minor key (taken from the ascending melodic minor scale) :

142.

$$S^{\mathrm{III}<}\quad T^{\mathrm{v}}\quad S^{\mathrm{III}<}\quad D+\quad T^{\mathrm{VII}\natural}\quad D^7$$
$$(D^{6>}_{8})\qquad\qquad (S^{\mathrm{v}}_{\mathrm{III}<})$$

(b)

$$T^{\mathrm{VI}<}\quad S^{\mathrm{III}<}\quad D^{6>}_{5}\quad S^{\mathrm{III}<}\quad D^7\quad T^{\mathrm{VII}\natural}\quad D^{9>}\quad [S^{\mathrm{III}<}]$$
$$(D^{7>}_{2})$$
$$(S^{\mathrm{IX}<})$$

and also those formed by the lowering of the seventh as a bridge to the third of the °*S* in major :

143.

$$D^{7>}_{3}\quad T^{6>}_{8}\quad D^3\quad °S\quad T^{7\natural}\quad S^{\mathrm{VII}}$$
$$(S^{\mathrm{VI}<}_{\mathrm{v}})$$

(b)

$$T^{6>}_{5}\quad D^{7>}_{3}\quad S^{\mathrm{VI}<}\quad D^{6>}_{3}\quad S^{\mathrm{VII}}\quad T^{7\natural}\quad D^{9>}\quad [D^{9\natural}_{3<}]$$
$$(S^{\mathrm{IX}<})$$
$$(D^{7>}_{2})$$

It is evident that such formalism can have no object, as we should never see an end of it ; we merely need to remember the Lydian fourth in major and the Phrygian second in minor, or even the chromatic leading-notes of the former paragraphs. But the representation we have hitherto given now dispenses us completely from the necessity of devoting particular attention to these "accessory triads" of all sorts and even accessory chords of the seventh and of the ninth, etc. The nucleus of all harmonic motion, in our estimation, is formed by the three principal pillars of the cadence :

tonic, subdominant, and dominant,

around which all the rest adheres as bywork, thus in the first place the characteristic dissonances (S^6, D^7, S^{VII} ; D^{VI}, S^{VII}, D^7), then the feigning consonant, vicarious, accessory forms of the principal harmonies (parallel clangs and leading-tone substitutes), furthermore the chords of the Dorian sixth and Mixolydian seventh, which are also feigning consonances rendered necessary on melodic grounds, and finally the absolutely dissonant formations (those proper to the scale and those with notes foreign to the scale) arising variously by means of passing notes, auxiliary notes, anticipations, and suspensions.

Only in so-called *sequences* these incidental—as it were, casual —formations enter with the appearance of equal rights beside the characteristic dissonances ; this led theorists astray quite long enough, until Fr. J. Fétis opened their eyes for them. *Sequences* are, as Fétis was the first to recognise and express, not really harmonic, but *melodic formations*—i.e., *their ruling principle is not the logical progression of their harmonies, but the proceeding by degrees through the scale.* Briefly, a *sequence is the imitation several times of a motive, proceeding upwards or downwards through the scale of the key.* If we formulate the definition thus, it sufficiently expresses that even passages for one part like the following are sequences :—

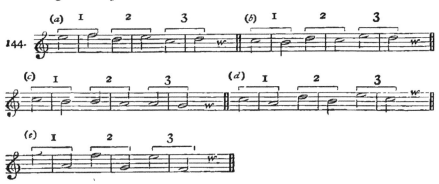

The single imitation of a motive does not form a sequence ; the name sequence rather implies that that *manner of progression of the motive is to be adhered to,* which would stipulate at least two repetitions of the motive.

Any sequence in a part to be harmonised will more or less certainly give occasion for the other parts to proceed sequentially ; but it is only when they do so proceed that we call part-writing a sequence. Now as regards the harmonies, the sequence (harmonic progression) thus formed is the *imitation, proceeding by step through the notes of the scale, of a succession of harmonies ;* the model of the harmonic progression must consist of a succession of harmonies which has logical sense in itself—that which follows in the imitation is accepted as the result of a sort of *necessity of nature ;* and only when the sequence is relinquished, do the tonal functions resume their efficacy. This, indeed, goes so far that *within the sequence even the doubling of leading-notes and of dissonances may be unhesitatingly introduced, which outside of it* (and also in the initial motive) *would be altogether faulty.*

We will sketch a few beginnings of sequences in explanation of the above :

Here we find all those "accessory chords of the seventh," etc., enter with rigid necessity into the chain, but without their tonal significance exerting the least influence on the progression, only so to speak as a mechanical impress of the harmonic succession at the beginning of the sequence.

But, naturally, motives for sequences may be longer than those we have hitherto given; any figuration of the motives of 145 (*a*)—(*f*) may be strictly imitated, *e.g. :*

I

146.

Sequences apparently *imitating at the interval of a third* and not by degrees, as—

147.

are yet founded on progression through the scale, as a glance at the three lower parts at 147 (*a*) and at the bass of 147 (*b*) will show, they are the only uniform harmonisations of the scale possible without consecutive octaves and fifths (one would almost feel inclined to call the scale itself a sequence !).

Beautiful effects are obtained when the extent of the sequence motive does not coincide with the species of bar, and so the harmonies which correspond with one another come at points of different rhythmical value, *e.g.* :

148.

As the tonal functions are suspended during the imitations of the sequence motive, there can be no object in indicating them; we therefore only give indications for the harmonies of the motive, and just intimate at the first imitation, whether the sequence rises or falls; but, for the rest, abbreviate the indications by means of brackets (as many brackets as imitations), as was the case already at 145 (*a*)—(*f*) (the figures added below may therefore be omitted as being understood).

The following exercises devoted to initiating into the writing of sequences are again easy, and give us an opportunity at the same time of making a first attempt at *five-part writing*. This will require no new rules. Naturally we need fear exceeding the maximum distance of the parts from one another favourable to euphony still less than in four-part writing, as we shall have to find room for five parts within the same total compass (which we shall retain throughout the book); but, on the other hand, we must remark that the two lower parts may quite well occasionally be distant a whole octave from the three upper parts, or the three lower from the two upper, without a sense of isolation arising. Doubling of thirds and fifths will occur more frequently in five-part than in four-part writing, but is still limited by the same restrictions (doubling of thirds by parallel motion is permissible only in parallel clangs and leading-tone substitutes; thirds which form leading-tones with notes of the tonic, may never be doubled). The following (eleventh) model example may serve to guide the student. The highest part is to be written in the treble clef :

(Eleventh model example.)

EXERCISES 237—248 (in five parts).

(237) ₵ : T | D^7 T | S^6 D^7 | $\mathcal{F}$ $S^{7<}$ | 　 | 　 | S^6 |
D S | $°S$ D | T

(238) ³/₂ : $°T$ | $°S$ $\overset{VII}{..}$ D | $\mathcal{F}$ T^{VI} $S^{III<}$ | D $S^{\overset{IX<}{III<}}$ $D^{6>}$ |
$S^{III<}$ $S^{VII\ VIII}$ | D^+ $S^{\overset{VII}{III<}}$ D^+ | $°T$ S $..$ | D $^{6>5}_{4\ 3\ 7}$ | $°T$

(239) ³/₄ : T | S^6 D $?.$ | Tp $S^{\overset{6}{6}}$ $\overset{5}{-}$ | D T | 　 | 　 |
Sp D^1 $!.$ | T $°S$ D | T

(240) ₵ : $°T$ $S^{\overset{VI}{V<}}$ | D $°T$ | S $..$ | D T | $S^{\overset{VII}{III<}}$ $\overset{}{..}$ | $D^{\overset{6}{8>}}$ |
　　　　$_V$　　　　$_V$　$_{III}$　　　$_{III}$　　　　$_V$
$S^{III<}$ | D^{1} $^{6>5}_{3}$ | $°Sp$ S^{VII} | D $..$ | $°T$
　　　　　　　　　　　　　　　　　　$_3$

(241) ³/₂ : $°Sp$ S I | $D^{\overset{6}{4}}$ $?.$ Tp | Sp Tp Sp | D T S |
　　　　　　　　　　　　　　　　　　　　　　　$_3$　$_3$
D^7 | 　 | 　 | S $D^{\overset{6}{4}}$ $\pm$ | T

(242) ₵ : T | $S^{7<}$ $D^{\overset{9}{7}}$ | $\overset{8}{\therefore}$ Tp | $°S$ $D^{\overset{6}{4}}$ | $\pm$ T | D Sp | 　 | 　 |
D^7 | T

(243) ₵ : S^{VII} D^7 | °T °D | °Sp °S | ⌐ ¬ | ⌐ ¬ | °T |

⌐S¬ D | °T

(244) ³/₄ : Tp Sp D | T S D | T D Tb | ⌐ ¬ | ⌐ ¬
                     ₃   ₃

Sp D | T

(245) ³/₂ : °T | ..$^{VII>}$ S^{VII} D | °T $S^{III}_{IV}{}_{V}^{III}$ | °Dp $D^{III}_{IV}{}_{V}^{III}$ |

⌐ ¬ ⌐ ¬ | $D^{7>1}_{2}$ | °T S^{VII} .. | D^4_1 S^{VII} D^7 | .. | °T

(246) ³/₂ : T | S Sp D | Dp Tp S^{VII} | $D^{7>}_{2}$ ₃ | T $S^{7<}$ | D^7 |

$S^{7<}$ | D^6 | T

(247) ♯ : T S^6 | D^7_2 Tp | ⌐ ¬ | Sp D | T T S^6 D |

Tp Dp | ⌐ ¬ | Tp S^6 D | T

(248) ♯ : T .. S^8 $^{7<}$ | D^7 .. | ⌐ ¬ | D ⌐ ¬

⌐ ¬ ⌐ ¬ | ⌐ ¬ | ⌐ ¬ | T

§ 12. INTERMEDIATE CADENCES.

More gifted pupils will very likely often have felt the avoidance of familiar chromatic alterations in our exercises hitherto, as a rather unnatural restraint ; at least, many of the turns to be developed in the following may by experience often have entered their minds, while we, with the single exception of a few harmonies anything but commonplace (S, D, $S^{III<}$, $D^{3>}$, D, ', °D, °S), kept strictly to harmonies proper to the scale. The result will, however, justify our procedure. *Our aim was to develop the feeling of tonality to the utmost extent,* and to teach the student to still understand, in their relation to the ruling tonic, harmonies apparently very remote from it; this paragraph only seemingly takes a step in the opposite direction, by introducing the harmonic turns which are generally called *transitions,* in contradistinction to real modulation, the actual change of tonality.   Under any circumstances a rational method of teaching harmony must always strive to *obtain an ever wider field for unity of conception.*   So, in the end, actual modulation must be compared to a harmony step from the tonic to some nearly related chord, *i.e.,* new tonics reached by modulation must always be comprehended similarly as harmonies within the key—they have *tonal functions in an extended sense. In transitions we express this very definitely by leaving unchanged the indication of the functions of the tonics reached.*   We now make, to express it briefly, *cadences to the several harmonies hitherto characterised according to their position in the key (real and feigning consonances); these harmonies, then, are to be considered as tonics, without, however, their tonal functions being altered.*

Let us return to the simplest forms of cadence, the connection of the tonic with its dominants of the same mode :

$$T—S—D—T \text{ and } °T—°D—°S—°T.$$

These acquire quite a different aspect, if *by addition of a note foreign to the scale* (7♮ or VII♮ of the tonic), or by *chromatic alteration* of a chord-note, we change each harmony to the dominant of the next :

150.

Here the indication of the alteration of tonal harmonies (by 7♭, VII♮, 1$^<$, 1$^>$) still seems the more convenient and easily intelligible (that which, in reading, renders most easy the translation of the chord signs into conceptions of harmonies).   But when more than one chord is to be referred to a following chord as tonic (for the time being), *the indication of harmonies as dominants of the following harmony* will not only be more convenient, but also more correct (corresponding to the real course of thought).   We express such relation by placing the chords in question in *rounded brackets* (as we did by way of supplement at 150 in the lower row).

Rule : *Chord signs in brackets are not to be understood as relating to the principal key, but as circumscribing the chord immediately following the bracket, as tonic, e.g. :*

151. $\quad T \quad (S \quad D^7) \quad S \quad (S \quad D^7) \quad D \quad ..^7 \quad T$

$\circ T \quad (S^{VII} \quad D) \quad \circ D \quad (S^{VII} \quad D) \quad S \quad ...^{VII} \circ T$

This new expedient leads to a number of new turns, for similar intermediate cadences may be made not only to the principal harmonies, but also to all the parallel clangs and leading-tone substitutes :

152. $\quad T \,(S^{VII} D^7)\, \mathcal{F}\,(S^{VII} D^7)\, T\!p \,(\circ S \, D)\, S\!p \,(S \, D^7)\, D \,(S^{VII} D^7)$

$D\!p \quad D^7 \quad T \qquad T \quad (\circ S \quad D^7) \quad \circ S \quad (S^6 \, D) \quad \circ S\!p \quad S \quad \text{\textit{\char`lp}}^{9>}$

$D \quad T \quad \circ T \quad (\circ S \quad D^+) \quad \circ S \quad (S^+ \, D) \quad \circ S\!p \quad S^{VII} \quad D \quad \circ T$

At times such cadential formation with the dominants may result from a harmony intelligible within the key, without returning to it; then an *arrow pointing backwards* under the bracketed harmony succession, shows that the preceding chord is its tonic :

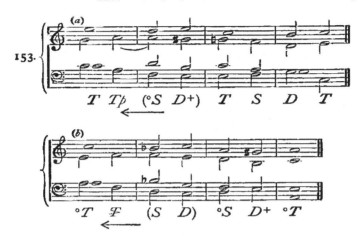

In such cases, in place of the chord circumscribed by the
intermediate cadence, and positively expected to follow, another
comes in.   But if, by chance, this chord do not even precede the
intermediate cadence, and the harmony to which the cadence
leads be skipped, then we indicate the chord expected in *angular
brackets after the rounded ones :*

Rule : *The harmony indicated within the angular brackets is
the merely imagined tonic of the preceding intermediate cadence
indicated in the rounded brackets, and is itself not introduced at
all, but skipped over.*
So as to be able to read quickly the chord signs enriched by
these new expedients, and to have present at once to the mind
the required harmonic successions, the student must, as soon as
he comes across rounded brackets, look directly to the chord

following them, and understand the bracketed indications of functions as referring to that chord as tonic.

The exercises which follow now are to be worked out for *four wind instruments,* viz., for *oboe, clarinet, horn, and bassoon.* Of these the notation for the oboe is in the treble clef, for the bassoon in the bass clef; but the clarinet and horn are so-called *transposing instruments,* and the manner of writing for them is quite different. So as to be clear, once for all, about transposing instruments, it should be noticed that *the fundamental note of the key whose name they bear is written as c,* e.g., written note *c* on an *F* horn means the note *f;* on an *A* clarinet, note *a;* on a *Bb* trumpet, note *bb,* etc.; all the other notes should be read as *interval signs, written in their relation to c,* but to be *understood in their relation to the fundamental note of the instrument,* e.g., the note *f♯* is to be read as an augmented fourth, and on an *A* horn would signify the augmented fourth from *a,* therefore *d♯,* on a *Bb* clarinet the augmented fourth from *bb,* therefore *e,* on an *E* trumpet the augmented fourth from *e,* therefore *a♯.* But, further, the student must know whether an instrument transposes upwards or downwards. The clarinets and horns, with which we are firstly concerned here, transpose *downwards.* In the following exercises we shall make use of the clarinets only in *C, Bb,* and *A,* customarily used in the symphonic orchestra; *C* clarinets do not transpose (*c'* retains the significance of *c'*), *Bb* clarinets transpose a whole tone, and *A* clarinets a minor third lower. *The C clarinet is to be used only in exercises in the key of c-major, the Bb clarinet in all exercises with key-signature in flats, the A clarinet for all keys with sharps, and also for A-minor.* Horns (natural horns) we assume as existing in every tuning of the twelve semitones: *B, Bb (A♯), A, Ab (G♯), G, F♯ (Gb), F, E, Eb (D♯), D, Db (C♯), C,* and also in low *B, Bb* and *A,* the latter transposing another octave lower. The part for horn is written in the treble clef and without any key-signature (according with the usage of composers of symphonies), and each *b* or *♯* needed is placed before its particular note; in the case of the clarinet, the number of flats or sharps in the signature of the natural key of the instrument (Bb clarinet: Bb-major = 2b, A clarinet: A-major = 3♯) is to be subtracted from those in the key-signature of the exercise, *e.g.:*

Key of the exercise Ab-major = 4b
Tuned in Bb-major = 2b
Remainder (for key-signature) = 2b

Key of the exercise G♯-minor = 5♯
Tuned in A-major = 3♯
Remainder (for key-signature) = 2♯

If the key of the exercise have fewer flats or sharps than the natural key of the instrument, then the excess is represented by the opposite signature ($\flat$ for $\sharp$, and $\sharp$ for $\flat$) :

$$\begin{array}{rl}
\text{Tuning of the instrument B$\flat$-major} & = 2\flat \\
\text{Key of the piece D-minor} & = 1\flat \\
\hline
\text{Key-signature} & = 1\sharp
\end{array}$$

$$\begin{array}{rl}
\text{Tuning of the instrument A-major} & = 3\sharp \\
\text{Key of the piece A-minor} & = 0\sharp \\
\hline
\text{Key-signature} & = 3\flat
\end{array}$$

Retaining the normal compass for voices, with the clarinet for the alto part and the horn for the tenor part, the pupil may be sure that he is not expecting impossible things of the instruments; more detailed explanations of the nature of the instruments are therefore not needed here (on this point cf. the author's "Catechism of Musical Instruments"). Our principal aim now is to prepare the pupil gradually and thoroughly in the practice of reading from score, and with the introduction of transposing instruments an important step forward has been taken.

The following (twelfth) model example is calculated to illustrate the above clearly :

(Twelfth model example.)

EXERCISES 249—263 (for Oboe, Clarinet, and Bassoon).

(249) ¢ : T ($\mathcal{D}^7$ | D ?.) | $S\flat$ $\mathcal{D}$ | D ?. | (S^{VII} D) | [$S\flat$] $\mathcal{S}$ S |
     $\mathcal{D}^7_2$ $\overset{\frown}{D}$ ^{5} | T

(250) ¢ : $^\circ T$ $^\circ D$ | $T^{VII}\natural$ $\mathcal{D}$ | D ?. | $\mathcal{F}$ $^\circ S$ | D (D^7) | [$^\circ S$] $^\circ S\flat$
     $\mathcal{D}^{9>}$ | $D^{6>}_4$ $^5_3$ | $^\circ T$

(251) ¢ : $\mathcal{F}$ | S^{VII} $\underset{3}{D}$ | $^\circ T\flat$ $\mathcal{D}^{9>}$ | $^8_{5>}$ D^7 | $\mathcal{F}$ (D^7) | $^\circ S$ ..^{VII} |
     D $^\circ T$ | $\underset{VII\natural}{..}$ D^7 | $^\circ T$

(252) ¢ : $\mathcal{D}^7$ S^{VII} | D^7 $^\circ T$ | $^\circ S$ (S^{VII} | D) .. | $\mathcal{S}^{VII}$ ^{VIII} |
     D $\mathcal{F}$ | $S^{III<}$ D | $^\circ T$

(253) ¢ : $^\circ T$ | $\underset{VII\natural}{..^{II<}}$ ^{I} | S^{VII} $\underset{III<}{D}$ | $^\circ T$ $^\circ S$ | D (D) | D (S^{VII} |
     D^7) $^\circ S$ | $D^{6>}_4$ ∴ | $^\circ T$

(254) ¢ : T | ?.$\natural$ $^\circ S$ | D ($^\circ S$ | D ?.) | [$T\flat$] S (D^7) | $\mathcal{S}$ $l\!\!l^{9>}$ |
     D^6_4 ∴ | $\underset{1}{T}$ $^{6>}_2$ | $^5_3_1$

(255) ³/₂ : $\underset{3}{\mathcal{D}^{9>}}$ $\underset{7}{D}$ | ($\mathcal{D}^{9>}$) $S\flat$ $\underset{3}{D}$ | T $S^{7<}_{5<}\,{}^6_6$ | D^6_4 $\mathcal{D}$?. | D $^7_{?>}$ |
     $T\flat$ $S\flat$ $D\flat$ | T ?.$\natural$ S | D^6_4 S^6 D | T

(256) 𝄵 : $S^{VII}_{IV}\,{}_{III}$ | $D^{7}_{2>}\,{}^3_1$ (S^{VII} D^7) | [$^\circ S$] $\mathcal{S}$ I $\underset{VI<}{IV}\,\underset{V}{III}$ |
     $\mathcal{D}^{9>}$ $^{10>}$ $D^{6>}_4$ ∴ | $^\circ T$

(257) 𝄵 : $\mathcal{D}^{9>}_5$ S^{VII} | D^7 $\underset{=D}{\mathcal{F}}$ | ..^{7} T | S D^7 | $\mathcal{S}$ $\mathcal{l\!\!l}^{9>}_3$ |
     $\underset{3\natural}{..}$ D | $^\circ T$

(258) ³/₂ : S^6 D ..^{7} | T $T\flat$ $\underset{=S^{VII}}{.._{VI}^{I>}}$ | D^5_4 ∴ ?. | (D) $T\flat$ .. $^{=D\flat}$ |
     $S\flat$ $^\circ S$ $\mathcal{S}$ | D^6_4 $^{8<}_{6>}\,{}^8_5_3$ | T

(259) E: T (D^7) | Tp (D^7) | Sp (D^7) | D ..⁷ | T ..⁷♮ | S $\mathbb{D}^{o>}$ |

D_4^6 ?. | T

(260) ³/₄: D | $°T$ $°Sp$ | $°S^{2>1}$ | D ..⁷ | $\mathcal{F}$ (D^7) | .. $\mathbb{D}_5^{o>}$ |
　　　　　•ı | ⏚ |　　　　　　　　 ₃

$D_4^{6>}$ ∴ | $°T$

(261) ₵: $°T$ ..²ᐳ | S^{VII} D | $°T$　| $=°Tp$ D | $°T$
　　　　　　　　　　　　 | $=\mathcal{F}$ D^7 | T　　　　　| $=Sp$ D |

$=°Tp$ S^{VII} | $D_4^{6>}$?. | $°T$
T

(262) ₵: $T^{6\ 5}$ | $S^{7<\ 6}$　| ..ⱽᴵᴵ (D^7) | D $=S^{VII}$ | D^+
　　　　　　　 $=S^{VI}$ |　　　　　　　　 $\ \ _{3>}^{5>}$ | $=S^{III<}$ D^7|

$=Dp$ Sp | D_4^6 ∴ | T
$°T$

(263) ₵: T ..⁷˂ | S $\mathbb{D}^{o>}$ | D_4^6 ..⁷˂ | Tp (D^7) | S T ı

S^6　　　 | $=D_1^6$˂ ⁵♮ ⁝ T
$=S^{VI}$ ..ⱽᴵᴵ | D

EXERCISES 264—280 (for 2 Trumpets and 2 Tenor Trombones).

For trumpets the notation is the same as for horns (without key-signature); but they sound an octave higher. Trumpets exist in all tunings from high B♭ to low A. Tenor trombones do not transpose, and are written in the tenor clef with the usual *key-signature*. These exercises are therefore to be arranged like the following (thirteenth) model example (with a stave for each couple of instruments with similar notation):

(Thirteenth model example.)

i.e., the trumpets are always to be taken in the tuning corresponding to the key of the exercise. The notation for the trombones does not vary, as they are not transposing instruments. For these school-exercises the trumpets in low A and B♭ are preferable to those in high A and B♭, as they necessitate fewer leger-lines.

(264) ₵: °T ..| °D S^{VII} |.. D | °T (D⁷) | °S .. | T °S^{III} |
        D⁹⁻ D | °T

(265) ₵: S D⁹⁻ | D F | S^{VII} ^{VIII} | D (D⁹⁻) | °S °T |
        ..^{VII}♮ D⁷ | S^{VI}_{III} D⁷ | °T

(266) ₵: T Tp | S Sp | D ..⁷ | Tp (D⁷) | .. (D⁷) | Sp S^{VII} |
        D⁶₄ ..⁷ | T

(267) ₵: T..⁷♮ | S ..⁷ | (S^{VII} ^{VIII} | D ..⁷)| Tp (S^{VII} | D ⁷) |
        Dp D⁹⁻ | D⁶₄ ∴ | T

(268) ₵: S⁶ | D⁶ ₅⁷ | (D) [Tp] S | S (D) | °Sp D⁹⁻ |
        D⁹⁻ T | ⁺D^{II} ¹ | T ₆ | T

(269) ₵: T °Sp | D³⁻ _{VII} = S^{III} D | =°S ..^{VII} | D ..⁷ | F S |
        °T
        D⁶₄ ∴ | T

(270) ₵: °T | S^{VII} D⁷ | D⁺ Tp | °Sp D | °S D | °T S |
        D⁶⁻₄ ∴ | °T

(271) ₵: °T Tp |(D Dp | S) °S | D (D⁷) | °Tp (D⁷) | °S ..^{VII} |
        D⁵⁻₄ ∴ | °T

(272) $^3/_2$: $\mathbb{D}^{9>}$ D ($\mathbb{D}^{9>}$) | T_p S (D^7) | .. $^\circ S_p$ $\mathbb{D}^{0>}_{5}$ | $D^{6\natural}_4$ $\pm$ | T

(273) ₵ : T | ($S^{III<}$ D) | [T_p] S (S^6 | D) S | (S^{VII} D) | S_p S^{VII} |
D^8_6 $^?_5$ | T

(274) ₵ : F D | $S^{III<}$ $+D_p$ | $S^{\overset{VII}{,II}<}$ D | $^\circ S_p$ $..^{7<}$ | (S^6 D^7) |
[$^\circ T_p$] (S^{VII} D) | [$^\circ S$] S^{VII} D | $^\circ T$

(275) ₵ : T S | D T_p | (S^{VII} D) | D $\overset{..}{_3}$ | ($T^{.VII\natural}$ D) | F S |
$\mathbb{D}^{\circ\natural}$ D | T

(276) ₵ : T | S_p (D) | $\overset{VII}{.._{=S^{VII}}}$ | D $^?_{..<}$ | $\overset{=D_p}{T_p}$ D | $\overset{T_p}{=D^{11<}}$ $^._7$ |
T $\mathbb{D}^{9>}$ | D^4_2 $^3_1$ | T

(277) ₵ : T^6_4 $^5_{3>}$ | $\mathbb{D}$ S^{VII} | ($D^7_{2>}$ $_1$) | [T_p] (S^{VII} D^7) |
[S_p] S^6_4 $^5_{3>}$ | l $^7_{5\natural}$ D^7 | T

(278) $^3/_2$: ($\mathbb{D}^{0>}_{5}$ D) [T_p] S | (D $^?_1$) [F] T | (D $^?_1$) S |
$\mathbb{D}^{9>}$ D^7 T

(279) ₵ : S $^{9>}$ | ($\mathbb{D}^{9>}$) T_p | (S^{VII} D) | D ($\mathbb{D}^{?}_{5>}$ | D) [T_p] S |
(D) S | $\mathbb{D}^{9>}_{5}$ D | T
  $_7$

(280) ₵ : $^\circ T$ | (S $\mathbb{D}^{9>}$ | D) [$^\circ D$] S^{VII} | D (S^{VII} | D) $^\circ S$ |
$^\circ T$ (S^{VII} | D) [$^\circ D_p$] $\mathbb{D}^{9>}$ | S^{VII} D^7 | $^\circ T$

EXERCISES 281—289 (for 2 Valve Trumpets in high B♭ and
2 Valve Horns in F).

Here all the instruments transpose. Valve trumpets in high
B♭ are written without key-signature, in so-called *cornet-notation*, an
octave higher than the trumpets in the preceding exercises, otherwise most of the notes would continually lie under the stave.
The following (fourteenth) model example may render this clear:

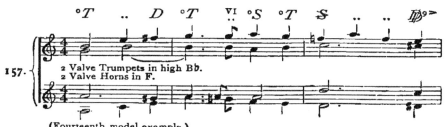

157.

(Fourteenth model example.)

(281) ₵ : D $\cancel{D}^{9>}_{3}$ | D_{7} ($S^{\overline{VI}}_{5}$ | $D_{5>}^{7}$) | $\cancel{D}$ (D^{7}) | $S\!\!\!\!S$ (D^{7}) | $°Sp$ .. |

$D^{7<}_{2>}$ $^{8}_{1}$ | T

(282) ₵ : (D^{7}) | $°S^{2>\;I}$ | D_{7} (S^{VII} | D ..^{7}) | [$°S$] $\cancel{D}^{6>}_{2>}$ $_{1}$ $^{5}_{3}$

S^{VI} (D^{7}) | $°Tp$ (S^{VII}) | $D^{3}_{6>}$ $_{5}$ $^{?}_{.}$ | $°T$

(283) ₵ : ^{c}T | $S^{\overset{III<}{VII}}$ ($\cancel{D}^{9>}$ | D) .. | $^{III}\natural$ D^{7} | $F\!\!\!\!F$ D^{+} | $°T$

(284) ₵ : $°T$ | $\cancel{D}^{9>}_{5>}$ $D^{6>}_{4}$ | S^{VI} $\cancel{D}^{7}$ | D ($\cancel{D}^{9>}$) | ^{+}Tp (D^{7})

^{c}Sp $S\!\!\!\!S$ | $\cancel{D}^{9>}_{5>}$ D | $°T$

(285) ₵ : $\cancel{D}^{9>}$ ^{c}T | S^{VII} $S\!\!\!\!S$ | ═$°Sp$ | S^{VI} D | ^{+}Tp (D) | .. $\overset{═══S^{VI}}{\underset{..VI}{^{1>}}}$ |

D^{7} $F\!\!\!\!F$ | S^{VII} D^{7} | $°T$

(286) ₵ : $°T$ ($°S$ | D) [$°Tp$] D | $°T$ ($°Sp$ | $°S$ D) | [$°S$] $°Sp$?. |

$S\!\!\!\!S$ $\cancel{D}^{9>}$ | $D^{6>}_{4}$ $^{5}_{3}$ | $°T$

(287) ₵ : T Tp | $^{+}D^{II\;1}$ | $°S$ ($S\!\!\!\!S^{IX<}$ | D) Tp | (D^{6} $^{7}_{1<}$) |

[S] Sp $°S^{2}$ | ^{1} D | T

(288) ₵: °T | S̄ ᴅ̶⁹⁼ | D (Sⱽᴵᴵ | D ..⁷) | [°S] ⁺Sp Sⱽᴵᴵ |

D⁷ (Dⱽᴵᴵ | D⁷) [°S] S̄ | .. D | °T

(289) ₵: T °Sp | ᴅ̶ D⁷ | Tp S̄ | ᴅ̶⁷ (D) | Dp (D⁷)
                                   ⁹⁼ ᴄ ₂

°Sp S̄ | (S) D⁷ | T

EXERCISES 290—300 (for 2 Oboes, 2 Clarinets, 2 Bassoons,
                    and 2 Horns),
to be written on four staves, the two clarinets in unison with
the oboes, the two horns in unison with the bassoons, as in
the fifteenth model example.

(Fifteenth model example.)

(290) ₵: T °Sp | (D) [Tp] T | S̄ ᴅ̶ | (ᴅ̶ D) | [Tp] T °Sp |
           1 ᴄ 3

(D) [Tp] D⁷ | T

(291) ₵: $°T$ $\underset{\text{vi}}{..}$ | S^{VII} D | $\mathcal{F}$ $\underset{\text{7}}{(D)}$ | $\underset{= S \; \mathcal{D}^7 \mid D \; ?< \mid}{S}$

$\underset{T\!p}{=°S}$ $..^{\text{VII}}$ | $D_4^{6>}$ $\therefore$ | $°T$

(292) ₵: $S_5^{7<}$ | ${}_6^8$ ${}_1^{6<}$ | $D\!p$ $(\mathcal{D}^{9>})$ | $\underset{\text{VII}}{T\!p}$ S | $\underset{5>}{D_4^7}$ ${}_3$ T | $S_2^{7<}$ ${}_3^6$ |

$D_{9>}^6$ ${}_8$ $\overset{5}{.}$ | T

(293) ₵: T $\overset{5<}{..}$ | S $\mathcal{D}^{9>}$ | D $..\overset{?}{1<}$ | $T\!p$ (D^7) | S (D^7) | $S\!p$ $\mathcal{D}_{5>}^{9>}$ |

$D_4^{6\natural}$ ${}_3^5$ $?.$ | T

(294) ₵: T $\overset{4<}{\underset{..}{2<}}$ | ${}_3^5$ $\underset{3}{..}$ | S $\overset{4<}{\underset{..}{2<}}$ | ${}_3^5$ $..$ | $\underset{3>}{\mathcal{D}^7}$ $\underset{5>}{8}$ | $\underset{6>}{7}$ $\underset{5>}{D}$ | $\widehat{T}$

(295) ₵: ³/₂: $\underset{1}{T}$ $\mathcal{D}^7$ $\underset{1}{T}$ | S_5^6 D (D) | $S\!p$ $\mathcal{D}^7$ D | $(D^7$ ${}_4^{6>}$ ${}_3^5)$ |

$[S\!p]$ S_4^6 ${}_{3>}^5$ D^7 | T (D^7) $\mathcal{S}$ | $\mathcal{D}$ D $D\!p$ | T

(296) ³/₄: $T^{\text{VII}\natural}$ D | $°T$ $(S^{\text{VII}}$ $D)$ | $[°S]$ $(S^{\text{III}<}$ D $?.)$ | $[°S]$ $\mathcal{S}$

D $\underset{3 \;\; \infty \; \text{III}}{?.\lfloor}$ $(S^{\text{VII}}$ D^6 ${}_7^5)$ | $[T\!p]$ $°T$ $\mathcal{D}_5^3$ ${}_4^4$ | ${}_3^5$ $S_{\text{V}}^{\text{III}}$ $\underset{\text{IV}}{}$ |

$\underset{\text{III}}{\overset{\text{V}}{}}$ D $?.$ | $°T$

(297) ₵: $T\!p$ | $(\mathcal{D}^{9>})$ $..$ | D^7 T | $S^{6<}$ T | $\mathcal{D}$ D^7 | (D) $T\!p$ |

$°S$ $°S\!p$ | T

(298) ₵: T $°S\!p$ | $\mathcal{D}^{9>}$ D | $\mathcal{F}$ D | (D) $T\!p$ | $°S$ $°S\!p$ | $\mathcal{D}$ D |

T_4^6 $\overset{4<}{\underset{2<}{}}$ | ${}_3^5$

(299) ³/₄: T $(S^{\text{III}<}$ $D)$ | $T\!p$ $(S^{\text{III}<}$ $D)$ | $°S$ $(\mathcal{S}$ $D)$ | $[°S]$ ${}^+\!S\!p$

$D\!p$ $(\mathcal{D}^{9>})$ | $T\!p$ $°S\!p$ $\mathcal{S}$ | $\mathcal{D}^{9>}$ D_4^5 ${}^+$ | $°S\!p$ $°S$ $..^{\text{VII}}$ | T

(300) ³/₂: $°D\!p$ | $°S\!p$ $°T\!p$ $°S$ | D $°T$ (D^7) | $\mathcal{S}$ $(S$ $D)$ | $..$ $°S$ $\mathcal{D}^{9>}$ |

$°T$ $°S$ $\mathcal{D}^{9>}$ $!$ $D_4^{6>}$ ${}_5^9$ ${}^{8}_{}$ ^{7} | $°T$

The sign $\overline{\smash{\omega}}$ occurring in a few of these examples between two numbers, indicates an *enharmonic tie ; e.g.*, in 290, if we assume D-major to be the key of the exercise, then *b♭* (the prime of the parallel clang of the minor under-dominant) is to be sustained as *a♯* (third of the dominant of the tonic parallel).

All these examples, as indeed all those merely indicating the functions of harmonies, should be worked out *in a number of different keys.* As no part is given, and also but little of the bass part is indicated, it is possible for *each working to turn out different. The great value of this kind of exercise arises from its leaving complete free play for melodic progression.* The aspiring student will not be satisfied with a merely correct connecting of each two chords which follow each other, but will soon learn to look for the melody lines of the exercise as a whole, at least in the soprano and bass.

CHAPTER IV.

THE CHANGE OF TONAL FUNCTIONS (MODULATION).

§ 13. CHANGE OF MEANING OF THE SIMPLEST HARMONY STEPS. CHARACTERISTIC FIGURATION.

IN our exercises hitherto we did not, indeed, entirely avoid modulation, but only resorted to a very few means of transition, and those only occasionally and without particularly discussing them, merely for the sake of giving animation and variety to the examples; our principal aim was directed towards strengthening the feeling of tonality and extending to the utmost the circle of harmonic formations intelligible in their relation to one and the same tonic. Our formulas for the tonal functions gradually became more complicated, but became simpler again with the introduction of intermediate cadences. We, indeed, succeeded in characterising every chord not only as a transformation of another major or minor chord, but also as a more or less equivalent representative of some tonic, dominant, or subdominant.

We now set ourselves the opposite task, that of finding out in which direction harmony steps which, according to the observations made in the previous chapters, are intelligible without denial of the tonality, are calculated to incite modulation. In so doing we shall soon perceive that the very simplest succession of harmonies may help to bring about modulation, if we call to our aid either characteristic dissonances or characteristic figuration-notes, or again rhythmical expedients.

Even in our first explanations we could not but acknowledge the fact that the contra-fifth step in its outer form coincides entirely with the retrograde plain-fifth step, and likewise the plain-fifth step with the retrograde contra-fifth step :

$(T—S)$ in c-major : $c^+—f^+$ = contra-fifth step ;
  in F-major : $c^+—f^+$, plain-fifth close $(D—T)$
$(T—D)$ in c-major : $c^+—g^+$ = plain-fifth step ;
  in G-major : $c^+—g^+$, contra-fifth close $(S—T)$
$(°T—°D)$ in A-minor : $°e—°b$ = contra-fifth step ;
  in E-minor : $°e—°b$, plain-fifth close $(°S—°T)$
$(°T—°S)$ in A-minor : $°e—°a$ = plain-fifth step ;
  in D-minor : $°e—°a$, contra-fifth close $(°T—°D)$.

The step to the contra-clang of the tonic also coincides with the close from the contra-clang to the tonic in another key :

$(T+-{^\circ}S)$ in c-major : $c+-{^\circ}c$ = turn of harmony ;
$\qquad$ in F-minor : $c+-{^\circ}c$, turn-of-harmony close $(D+-{^\circ}T)$
$({^\circ}T-D+)$ in A-minor : ${^\circ}e-e+$ = turn of harmony ;
$\qquad$ in E-major : ${^\circ}e-e+$, turn-of-harmony close $({^\circ}S-T+)$

It is, therefore, evident that we only require to add the 6 to the T to prompt its change of meaning to S, or the VII to make ${^\circ}S$ of the ${^\circ}T$, or 7♮ to stamp the T as D; similarly the sudden entry of 4< in the figuration of the major tonic will give the latter under-dominant significance, the merely passing 7♮ will prepare its change of meaning to dominant, and the minor tonic, with a IV>, becomes minor upper-dominant, with a VII♮, under-dominant.

The *types of figuration*, true to the scale, for the principal harmonies are :

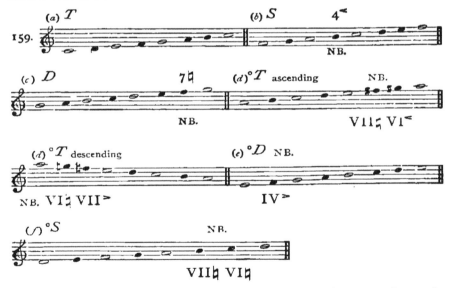

The figuration in scale form of the contra-clang of the tonic, as we know, necessitates besides the third, foreign to the scale, the introduction of the Mixolydian seventh or Dorian sixth :

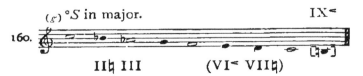

(*h*) D^+ in minor.

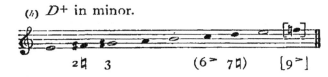

2♮   3   (6⁻ 7♮)   [9⁻]

but what is striking in the natural figuration of these harmonies, does not lie in the sixth and seventh being greater or less, but rather in the plain second and third contradicting the scale of the key (for which reason the second or ninth, where not proceeding to or coming from the third, is, as a rule, taken minor [9>, IX<, as auxiliary note to the octave, or 2>, II<, as auxiliary note to the prime]).

The parallel clangs and leading-tone substitutes, when the aim is to give expression to their meaning as strictly as possible in figuration, should be ornamented as far as possible with the notes of the scale of the key:

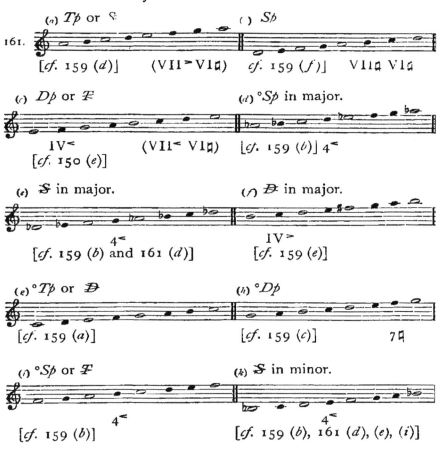

161.

(*a*) *Tp* or $\mathcal{S}$ ( ) *Sp*

[cf. 159 (*d*)]   (VII⁻ VI♮)   cf. 159 (*f*)]   VII♮ VI♮

(*c*) *Dp* or $\mathcal{F}$ (*d*) °*Sp* in major.

IV<   (VII< VI♮)   [cf. 159 (*b*)] 4<
[cf. 150 (*e*)]

(*e*) $\mathcal{S}$ in major.   (*f*) $\mathcal{D}$ in major.

4<   IV⁻
[cf. 159 (*b*) and 161 (*d*)]   [cf. 159 (*e*)]

(*g*) °*Tp* or $\mathcal{D}$ (*h*) °*Dp*

[cf. 159 (*a*)]   [cf. 159 (*c*)]   7♮

(*i*) °*Sp* or $\mathcal{F}$ (*k*) $\mathcal{S}$ in minor.

4<   4<
[cf. 159 (*b*)]   [cf. 159 (*b*), 161 (*d*), (*e*), (*i*)]

(*l*) +*Dp* in minor.   (*m*) *ᴮ* in minor.

IV⁼   IV⁼
[*cf.* 159 (*c*)]   [*cf.* 159 (*b*), 161 (*d*), (*e*), (*i*), (*k*)

but in this manner no forms at all result which would deviate from those at 159 and 160; the fact, however, that the parallel-clangs coincide also in their figuration with the principal clangs of the parallel key, is a welcome help in modulation, as it, at least, does not prevent change of meaning. The most important results of this examination into the scale figuration of the most essential chords are :

(A) The prominent rôle which falls to the *augmented fourth* (4< in the +*S*, IV⁼ in the °*D*; but also [in major] 4< in the °*Sp* and *S* and IV⁼ in the *Dp* and *ᴮ*, and [in minor] IV⁼ in the +*Dp*, *ᴮ* and 4< in the °*Sp* and *S*).

It should be noticed that the 4< is introduced only into harmonies with + under-dominant significance, the IV⁼, only into harmonies with °upper-dominant significance; for in °*Sp* and *S* in major, the heightening of the under-dominant significance is unmistakable, and similarly in +*Dp* and *ᴮ* in minor, the heightening of the upper-dominant significance.

(B) The significance of the *natural seventh* (7♮, VII♮), which always gives the major chord upper-dominant significance, and the minor chord under-dominant significance (in major 7 to the *D*, VII to the °*S* and the +*Sp*; in minor, VII to the °*S*, 7 to the +*D* and the °*Dp*).

It will be sufficient to keep these two points well in mind; in so doing we shall in many cases choose a path different from that followed by the all-levelling custom of the day, which carries out all figuration more or less in the sense of tonic significance by introducing the plain fourth in place of the augmented and adopting the leading-note to the prime (octave), *e.g.*, 159 (*b*) and 161 (*i*) with *b♭* instead of *b*, 159 (*c*) and 161 (*h*) with *f♯* instead of *f*, 159 (*e*) and 161 (*c*) with *f♯* instead of *f*, 159 (*f*) and 161 (*a*) with *c♯* instead of *c*, etc. The (three-part) new exercises in figuration asked for later on [ex. 304 (*f*)] will give the student an opportunity of turning these observations to the right use.

As regards the *assistance of rhythm in the change of meaning* of clangs, we will at present only remark that chords falling on accented beats receive increased attention, whereas to those entering on unaccented beats we readily ascribe only transitional importance; *i.e.*, for example, we should look upon a chord entering on an unaccented beat between two harmonies of the same sound which are related to it, and are placed upon accented beats, as a kind of ornamentation of them (in the sense of the intermediate cadences of the preceding chapter), as harmonic figuration. *So long, therefore, as the accented beats retain the same harmony, no actual harmonic motion takes place.* In the following example :

$$\mathbf{C} : T \; \overset{3}{D} \; | \; T \; \underset{5}{D} \; | \; T \; D \; | \; T \, .. \; | \; \overset{3}{D} \; T \; | \; \underset{3}{D} \; \underset{5}{T} \; | \; D$$

the G-major chord in the second half is just as much ornamented by the c-major chord as in the first half the c-major chord is by the G-major chord ; in other words, we should figure this more correctly thus :

$$T \; (D \; | \; T \; D \; | \; T \; D) \; | \; T \, ..$$
$$= S \; | \; T \; (S \; | \; T \; S) \; | \; T$$

a conception whose correctness is immediately proved if we add the characteristic dissonances (D^7 instead of D, S^6 instead of S) :

162.

The continuation as at II differs from that at I only in that the upper-dominant (d^7) instead of the under-dominant is taken as figuration for the new tonic. The possibility of changing the meaning of the very simplest harmony steps is thus proved (c—g transformed from T—D into S—T, *without the aid of notes foreign to the scale*) ; but it should be noticed that the incitement to modulation does not lie in the step itself, but outside of it. We may, by making use of the same expedient (transferring the dominant to the accented beat and the tonic to the unaccented), similarly give changed meaning to the following steps :

$$T \quad S \text{ changed into } D \mid T$$
$$°T \,°S \qquad ,, \qquad ,, \quad °D \mid °T$$
$$°T \,°D \qquad ,, \qquad ,, \quad °S \mid °T$$
$$+T \,°S \qquad ,, \qquad ,, \quad +D \mid °T$$
$$°T \; D+ \qquad ,, \qquad ,, \quad °S \mid +T$$

for which every pupil will easily construct examples. But after this it will be quite intelligible that a plain-fifth step or a turn of harmony must be all the more likely to lead out of the key, when made from a dominant in the direction opposite to the tonic; the successions $D(D)..$, $S(S)..$, $°S(°S)..$, $°D(°D)..$, are perfectly familiar to us from § 12 as passing treatments of a dominant as tonic (intermediate cadences). They become real modulations if the harmony settles on the new tonic, *i.e.*, if a period closes with it, or indeed a new one starts in the key reached. Rule: *Any harmonic step going beyond a dominant (i.e., resorting to the dominant, foreign to the scale, of a dominant) is sufficient impulse for a modulation to the dominant in question*, but to overcome the resistance offered by our feeling of tonality, in the first place the *assistance of rhythmical relations* is needed (the elements of which have been explained above, and further details have yet to follow).

§ 14. MODULATING POWER OF HARMONY STEPS.

If even proceeding by step beyond a dominant may incite modulation, then naturally *proceeding by leap beyond it* must be all the more calculated to render the dominant the central point, to make a tonic of it. *Every whole-tone step, because it corresponds to the transition from one dominant to that on the other side* ($'S—D$, $D—S$, $°D—°S$, $°S—°D$), *has power to modulate to the clang skipped.* The extended tonal system of harmony, as we have developed it in the preceding chapters, presents an entire series of whole-tone steps, whose *latent* modulating power may at any time become *active*, by mere resort to characteristic dissonances or expedients in figuration, or simply by proper use of rhythm (the varying accent of time-beats). As whole-tone steps, besides the connecting of the two dominants, we find the successions:

(A) in Major: (A) $Sp—Dp$, in c-major: $°a—°b$, skipping $°e$ (Tp).
(B) $T—Sp$, ,, ,, $°b—°a$, ,, $°e$ (Tp).
(c) $T—D$, ,, ,, $c^+—d^+$, ,, g^+ (D).
(D) $T—S$, ,, ,, $c^+—b\flat^+$, ,, f^+ (S).
(E) $Tp—D^{3>}$, ,, ,, $°e—°d$, ,, $°a$ (Sp).
(F) $Tp—D$, ,, ,, $°e—°f\sharp$, ,, $°b$ (Dp).
(G) $D^{3>}—°S$, ,, ,, $°d—°c$, ,, $°g$ ($°T$).
(H) $S—°Sp$, :, ,, $b\flat^+—a\flat^+$, ,, $e\flat^+$ ($°Tp$).
(I) $°Tp—S$, ,, ,, $e\flat^+—d\flat^+$, ,, $a\flat^+$ ($°Sp$).

(Here we put aside the harmonies that may be introduced in intermediate cadences, because they form very pronounced dominant steps to new tonics, and therefore require no more explanation.)

(B) in Minor : (A) $°Dp—°Sp$, in A-minor : $g{+}—f{+}$, skipping $c{+}(°Tp)$.
   (B) $\mathscr{F}—°Dp$, ,,   ,, $f{+}—g{+}$,   ,, $c{+}(°Tp)$.
   (C) $°T—°\mathscr{S}$, ,,   ,, $°e—°d$,   ,, $°a\ (°S)$.
   (D) $°T—°\mathcal{D}$, ,,   ,, $°e—°f\sharp$,   ,, $°b\ (°D)$.
   (E) $°Tp—S^{111<}$, ,,   ,, $c{+}—d{+}$,   ,, $g{+}\ (°Dp)$
   (F) $°Tp—\mathscr{S}$, ,,   ,, $c{+}—b\flat{+}$,   ,, $f{+}\ (°Sp$
   (G) $S^{111<}—D{+}$, ,,   ,, $d{+}—e{+}$,   ,, $a{+}({+}T)$.
   (H) $°\mathcal{D}—{+}Dp$,,   ,, $°f\sharp—°g\sharp$,   ,, $°c\sharp\ ({+}Tp)$.
   (I) $^{+}Tp—\mathscr{D}$,,   ,, $°c\sharp—°d\sharp$,   ,, $°g\sharp\ ({+}Dp)$.

Surprising effects (in the best sense) are obtained, when the composer introduces one and the same succession of harmonies under similar conditions (*i.e.*, at corresponding places in the thematical construction), proceeding from it at one time without change of tonality, and another time making use of the modulating power of the step (compare with each other the examples with single and double letter indications):

Like the whole-tone step, also the *contra-fifth change*, lying tonally between the plain-fifth clang and the contra-clang, circumscribes a tonic (T or $°T$). This step, which occurs but once between harmonies of the same key, may therefore be employed very effectively for modulations; and, as it is very easily intelligible, there is nothing to hinder its being made from any harmony of the key. The typical forms are $°S—D^+$ and $D^+—°S$; the following progressions are the result of imitation:

(1) in Major:

$Sp=°S—D^+$, in c-major : $°a—e^+$ { leads to the tonic } $°e\ (Tp)$ or a^+.

$Tp=°S—D^+$ „ $°e—b^+$ „ $°b\ (Dp)$ or e^+.

$Dp=°S—D^+$ „ $°b—f\sharp^+$ „ $°f\sharp\ (D)$ or b^+.

$D^{3>}=°S—D^+$ „ $°d—a^+$ „ $°a\ (Sp)$ or $d^+\ (D)$.

$T=D—°S$ „ $c^+—°f$ „ $f^+\ (S)$ or $°c\ (°S)$.

$S=D—°S$ „ $f^+—°b\flat$ „ $b\flat^+\ (S)$ or $°f\ (°S)$.

$D=D—°S$ „ $d^+—°g$ „ $g^+(D)$ or $°d\ (D^{3>})$
    etc.

(2) in Minor:

$°T=°S—D$, in A-minor : $°e—b^+$ „ $°b\ (°D)$ or $e^+\ (D^+)$.

$°D=°S—D$ „ $°b—f\sharp^+$ „ $°f\sharp\ (°D)$ or $b^+\ (^+D)$.

$°S=°S—D$ „ $°d—a^+$ „ $a\ (°S)$ or $d^+\ (S^{III<})$.

$°Tp=D—°S$ „ $c^+—°f$ „ $f^+\ (°Sp)$ or $°c$.

$°Dp=D—°S$ „ $g^+—°c$ „ $c^+\ (°Tp)$ or $g°$.

$S^{III<}=D—°S$ „ $d^+—°g$ „ $g^+\ (°Dp)$ or $°d\ (°S)$.
    etc.

The difference of mode of the two dominants produces the double possibility of turning to a new $°T$ or ^+T; but the former or latter will have to be preferred, *i.e.*, it will be expected with greater probability, according as it is or is not a clang of the tonal harmony. *Of course there is no meaning in accumulating unexpected turns one on top of the other*; the saying of a harmonist, to whom a prize was awarded, that any chord might follow any other chord, may be true for two chords considered in isolation; but the third chord is, as we shall see, anything but free, and the choice can waver only within a small circle, according to the ambiguity of the combination started from.

We now come to the *fifth-change,* which we came across tonally as the changing of the contra-fifth clang into the contra-clang of the tonic $T—S—°S—T$; $°T—°D—D^+—°T$, *i e.,* the opposition of the contra-fifth clang is more marked than that of the contra-clang, in proceeding to which a kind of retrograde step is taken, in as far as we return from the contra-fifth of the tonic to its prime, *e.g.,* $c^+—f^+—°c—c^+$; $°e—°b—e^+—°e$. *It should be noticed that here the minor chord arising from the lowering of the third of the major chord ($f^{3>}=°c$) becomes ° sub-dominant, and the major chord arising from the raising of the third of the minor* *chord*, $^+$ *dominant;* to this the most frequent and important modulating significance of this step entirely corresponds, no matter from what clangs it occurs, *i.e.*, in general terms : *the alteration of a major chord into a minor chord* (by lowering the 3) *gives the latter the significance of a* °*S; the alteration of a minor chord into a major chord* (by raising the III) *gives the latter the significance of a* $^+$*D.* Thus from the clangs of the tonal harmony we again obtain an abundance of new turns, most of which we have already considered among the intermediate cadences, and which we shall therefore only briefly indicate :

A. (Major) :

T—$^{3>}$=°S, in c-major : c^+—°g leads to g^+ (D).
D—$^{3>}$=°S,   „   „ g^+—°d „   „   °a (Sp) or d $(\not D)$.
Sp—$^{III<}$=D, „   „   °a—d^+ „   „ g^+ (D).
Tp—$^{III<}$=D, „   „   °e—a^+ „   „   °a (Sp) or d $(\not D)$.
Dp—$^{III<}$=D, „   °b—e^+ „   „   °e (Tp).

B. (Minor) :

°T—$^{III<}$=D, in A-minor : °e—a^+ „   „   °a (°S).
°S—$^{III<}$=D,   „   „   °a—d^+ „   „ g^+ (°Dp) or °d (°$\mathbb{S}$).
°Dp—$^{3>}$=°S,   „   „ g^+—°d „   „   °a (°S)
°Tp—$^{3>}$=°S,   „   „ c^+—°g „   „ g^+(°Dp) or °d (°$\mathbb{S}$).
°Sp—$^{3>}$=°S,   „   „ f^+—°c „   „ c^+ (°Tp).

But since the fifth-change is tonally intelligible also in the sense of $D-{}^{3>}$ in major and °$S-{}^{III<}$ in minor, the above rule is not without exceptions ; *on the contrary the major chord arising chromatically may also proceed as chord of the Dorian sixth* $(S^{III<})$, *and the similarly formed minor chord, as chord of the Mixolydian seventh* $(D^{3>})$; thus the following progressions arise :

A. (Major) :

T—$^{3>}$=$D^{3>}$, in c-major=c^+—°g, leads over °f to °c(°S) or f^+(^+S).

S—$^{3>}$=$D^{3>}$,   „   =f^+—°c,   „   „ °$b\flat$ „ °f(°$\mathbb{S}$) „ $b\flat^+$($\mathbb{S}$).
Sp—$^{III<}$=$S^{III<}$,   „   =°a—d^+ „   „ e^+ „ °e(Tp) „ a^+.
Tp—$^{III<}$=$S^{III<}$,   „   =°e—a^+ „   „ b^+ „ °b(Dp)„ e^+.
Dp—$^{III<}$=$S^{III<}$,   „   =°b—e^+ „   „ $f\sharp^+$ „ °$f\sharp$($\not D$)„ b^+.

B. (Minor) :

°T—$^{III<}$=$S^{III<}$, in A-minor=°e—a^+ „   „ b^+ „ °b(°D)„ e^+(D^+)
°D—$^{III<}$=$S^{III<}$,   „   =°b—e^+ „   „ $f\sharp^+$„°$f\sharp$(°$\not D$)„ b^+($^+\not D$)
°Dp—$^{3>}$=$D^{3>}$,   „   =g^+—°d „   „ °c „c^+(°Tp)„ °g.
°Tp—$^{3>}$=$D^{3>}$,   „   =c^+—°g „   „ °f „f^+(°Sp)„ °c.
°Sp—$^{3>}$=$D^{3>}$,   „   =f^+—°c „   „ °$b\flat$ „ $b\flat$($\mathbb{S}$)„ °f.

Another different interpretation of the fifth-change, more important than these, which are but seldom successfully carried out, is that based on *the change of the second upper-dominant back into the parallel clang of the under-dominant* in major ; I say the change *back*, as the second upper-dominant in reality arises chromatically from the parallel clang of the under-dominant $(Sp^{\text{III}<} = \mathbb{D}$; conversely therefore $\mathbb{D}^{3>} = Sp)$. By this means the rule that the minor chord arising chromatically becomes °sub-dominant, receives the new addition, "or parallel clang of a major sub-dominant," and a few new modulations are added to those developed above on p. 151 :

T—$^{3>}$=Sp, in c-major : c^+—°g, leads over f^+ to $b\natural^+(\mathbb{S})$;
similarly in A-minor : °Tp—$^{3>}$=Sp.
D—$^{3>}$=Sp, in c-major : g^+—°d, leads over c^+ to $f^+(S)$;
similarly in A-minor : °Dp—$^{3>}$=Sp.
S—$^{3>}$(°S)=Sp, in c-major : f^+—°c, leads over $b\natural^+$ to $e\natural^+$(°Tp) ;
similarly in A-minor : °Sp—$^{3>}$=Sp, etc.

The examination into the inversion of the relation (in minor °$Dp^{3>}$=°$\mathbb{S}$, returning °$\mathbb{S}^{\text{III}<}$=°Dp), we leave to the pupil (*e.g.*, °T—III<=°Dp—°S—°T, from A-minor to B-minor).

§ 15. MODULATIONS BY MEANS OF CHORDS OF SEVEN-THREE AND OF MINOR NINE-THREE.

Continuing with chromatic alterations, we find quite similar changes of meaning of harmonies, first by raising the major prime and lowering the minor prime, *e.g.* :

$$c^+—^{1<}=c\sharp\ e\ g\ ;\ °e—^{1>}=a\ c\ e\flat.$$

The chord arising in both these cases is dissonant, and is a chord of seven-three, which may proceed either in the sense of major $(\mathbb{D}^7)$ or of minor $(\mathbb{S}^{\text{VII}})$. This formation occurs tonally as Sp—$^{1>}$=$\mathbb{S}^{\text{VII}}$ or °Dp—$^{1<}$=$\mathbb{D}^7$, and in both cases it is only the mode that changes and not the tonal function (alteration of the contra-fifth clang into the contra-clang, thus fifth-change) ; also the change of the chord of the Neapolitan sixth back into the minor sub-dominant chord of seven-three ($\mathbb{S}$—$\mathbb{S}^{\text{VII}}$), and the change of the chord of the Lydian fourth back into the major dominant chord of seven-three ($\mathbb{D}$—$\mathbb{D}^7$) outwardly yield the same formation, *e.g.* :

in c-major $\begin{cases} f\sharp\ \ b\ \ d\ \ (=°f\sharp)—f\natural\ \ b\ \ d\ \ (=g^7)\ ; \\ f\ \ a\natural\ d\flat\ (=d\flat^+)—f\ \ a\natural\ d\natural\ (=\varepsilon^{\text{VII}})\ ; \end{cases}$

in A-minor $\begin{cases} d\ \ f\ \ b\flat\ \ (=b\flat^+)—d\ \ f\ \ b\natural\ \ (=d^{\text{VII}}) \\ d\sharp g\sharp\ b\ \ (=°d\sharp)—d\natural\ g\sharp\ \ b\ \ (=\varepsilon^7) \end{cases}$

and here, too, the function remains the same (°*f*♯ and *g*⁷ with dominant significance, *b*♭⁺ and *d*ᵛᴵᴵ with sub-dominant significance).

But now any feigning consonance in tonal harmony may, with unerring effect, be changed, by similar chromatic alteration of the prime, into a chord consisting of two minor thirds, and the latter may proceed equally well in major sense or in minor :

A. (Major) :

$$T — ^{!<}_{..} = \begin{cases} D^7 \\ S^{VII} \end{cases}$$ in c-major : *c*⁺—*a*⁷ leads to °*a* (*Sp*) or *d*⁺ (*D*).
,, : *c*⁺—*b*ᵛᴵᴵ ,, °*f*♯ (*Dp*, *D*) or *b*⁺.

$$S — ^{!<}_{..} = \begin{cases} D^7 \\ S^{VII} \end{cases}$$,, : *f*⁺—*d*⁷ ,, *g*⁺ (*D*) or °*d* (*Sp*, *D³*˃).
,, : *f*⁺—*e*ᵛᴵᴵ ,, °*b* (*Dp*) or *e*⁺.

$$D — ^{!<}_{..} = \begin{cases} D^7 \\ S^{VII} \end{cases}$$,, : *g*⁺—*e*⁷ ,, °*e* (*Tp*) or *a*⁺.
,, : *g*⁺—*f*♯ᵛᴵᴵ ,, °*c*♯ or *f*♯⁺.

$$D — ^{!<}_{..} = \begin{cases} D^7 \\ S^{VII} \end{cases}$$,, : *d*⁺—*b*⁷ ,, °*b* (*Dp*) or *e*⁺.
,, : *d*⁺—*e*♯ᵛᴵᴵ ,, °*g*♯.

$$°Sp — ^{!<}_{..} = \begin{cases} D^7 \\ S^{VII} \end{cases}$$,, : *a*♭⁺—*f*⁷ ,, *b*♭⁺ (*S*).
,, : *a*♭⁺—*g*ᵛᴵᴵ ,, *g*⁺ (*D*) or °*d* (*Sp*, *D³*˃).

$$Tp — ^{!>}_{..} = \begin{cases} D^7 \\ S^{VII} \end{cases}$$,, : °*e*—*f*⁷ ,, *b*♭⁺ (*S*).
,, : °*e*—*g*ᵛᴵᴵ ,, *g*⁺ (*D*) or °*d* (*Sp*), *D³*˃).

$$Sp — ^{!>}_{..} = \begin{cases} D^7 \\ S^{VII} \end{cases}$$,, : °*a*—*b*♭⁷ ,, *e*♭⁺ (°*Tp*).
,, : °*a*—*e*ᵛᴵᴵ ,, *c*⁺ (*T*, thus tonally) or °*g* (°*T*).

$$Dp — ^{!>}_{..} = \begin{cases} D^7 \\ S^{VII} \end{cases}$$,, : °*b*—*e*⁷ ,, *f*⁺ (*S*) or °*c* (°*S*).
,, : °*b*—*d*ᵛᴵᴵ ,, °*a* (*Sp*) or *d*⁺ (*D*).

NB. °*S*—$^{!>}_{..}$ = $\begin{cases} D^7 \\ S^{VII} \end{cases}$,, : °*c*—*d*♭⁷ ,, *g*♭⁺.
,, : °*c*—*e*♭ᵛᴵᴵ ,, *e*♭⁺ (°*Tp*).

$$D — ^{!>}_{..} = \begin{cases} D^7 \\ S^{VII} \end{cases}$$,, : °*f*♯—*g*⁷ ,, *c*⁺ (*T*, thus tonally).
,, : °*f*♯—*d*ᵛᴵᴵ ,, °*e* (*Tp*).

B. (Minor) :

$$°T — ^{!>}_{..} = \begin{cases} S^{VII} \\ D^7 \end{cases}$$ in A-minor : °*e*—*g*ᵛᴵᴵ ,, °*d* (°*S*) or *g*⁺ (°*Dp*).
,, : °*e*—*f*⁷ ,, *b*♭⁺ (*S*).

$$°D — ^{!>}_{..} = \begin{cases} S^{VII} \\ D^7 \end{cases}$$,, : °*b*—*d*ᵛᴵᴵ ,, °*a* (°*S*).
,, : °*b*—*e*⁷ ,, *f*⁺ (°*Sp*).

$$°S — ^{!>}_{..} = \begin{cases} S^{VI*} \\ D^7 \end{cases}$$,, : °*a*—*e*ᵛᴵᴵ ,, *c*⁺ (°*Tp*).
,, : °*a*—*b*♭⁷ ,, *e*♭⁺.

$$°S — ^{!>}_{..} = \begin{cases} S^{VII} \\ D^7 \end{cases}$$,, : °*d*—*f*ᵛᴵᴵ ,, *f*⁺ (°*Sp*) or °*c*.
,, : °*d*—*e*♭⁷ ,, *a*♭⁺.

$$+Dp — ^{!>}_{..} = \begin{cases} S^{VII} \\ D^7 \end{cases}$$,, : °*g*♯—*b*ᵛᴵᴵ ,, °*f*♯ (°*D*).
,, : °*g*♯—*a*⁷ ,, °*a* (°*S*) or *d*⁺ (*S*ᴵᴵᴵ˂, °*Dp*).

$$°Tp — ^{!<}_{..} = \begin{cases} S^{VII} \\ D^7 \end{cases}$$,, : *c*⁺—*b*ᵛᴵᴵ ,, °*f*♯ (°*D*).
,, : *c*⁺—*a*⁷ ,, °*a* (°*S*) or *d*⁺ (*S*ᴵᴵᴵ˂, °*Dp*).

$$°D\!\!\flat — \overset{!<}{\because} = \begin{cases} \mathcal{S}^{\text{VII}} \text{ in A-minor} : & g^+ — f\sharp^{\text{VII}} \text{ leads to } °c\sharp \; (^+T\!p). \\ L^7 & ,, \qquad : g^+ — e^7 \quad ,, \quad °e \; (°T, \text{ thus tonally}) \\ & \qquad\qquad\qquad\qquad\qquad \text{or } a^+ \; (^+T). \end{cases}$$

$$°S\!\!\flat — \overset{!<}{\because} = \begin{cases} \mathcal{S}^{\text{VII}} & ,, \qquad : f^+ — e^{\text{VII}} \quad ,, \quad °b \; (°D) \text{ or } e^+ \; (D^+). \\ D^7 & ,, \qquad : f^+ — d^7 \quad ,, \quad g^+ \; (°D\!\flat) \text{ or } °d \; (°\mathcal{S}) \end{cases}$$

$$\text{NB. } D^+ — \overset{!<}{\because} = \begin{cases} \mathcal{S}^{\text{VII}} & ,, \qquad : e^+ — d\sharp^{\text{VII}} \quad ,, \quad °a\sharp. \\ L^7 & ,, \qquad : e^+ — e\sharp^7 \quad ,, \quad °c\sharp \; (^+T\!p). \end{cases}$$

$$\mathcal{S} — \overset{!<}{\because} = \begin{cases} \mathcal{S}^{\text{VII}} & ,, \qquad : b\flat^+ — a^{\text{VII}} \quad ,, \quad °e \; (T, \text{ thus tonally}). \\ D^7 & ,, \qquad : b\flat^+ — g^7 \quad ,, \quad c^+ \; (°T\!p). \end{cases}$$

Like the chords of seven-three (D^7 and $\mathcal{S}^{\text{VII}}$), also the *chords of minor nine-three* ($D\overset{9>}{{}^7}$, or briefly $D^{9>}$ and $\mathcal{S}^{\overset{\text{IX}<}{\text{VII}}}$ or $\mathcal{S}^{\text{IX}<}$), are characteristic and particularly effective forms of the dominants; any chord of minor nine-three may, like any chord of seven-three, proceed either in the major sense or the minor, but either way will lead to the same tonic :

$$b \; d \; f \; a\flat = \left\{ \begin{matrix} g^{9>}, & \textit{i.e.} \; D^{9>} \\ e^{\text{IX}<}, & \textit{i.e.} \; \mathcal{S}^{\text{IX}<} \end{matrix} \right\} \text{ of c-minor or c-major.}$$

Chords of minor nine-three arise in the first place from raising the prime of a chord of the over-seventh or lowering the prime of a chord of the under-seventh :

A. (Major) :

$$D^7 \; \overset{!<}{\because} = \begin{cases} D^{9>} \text{ in c-major}: & g^7 — e^{9>} \\ \mathcal{S}^{\text{IX}<} & ,, \qquad : g^7 — d^{\text{IX}<} \end{cases} \left.\begin{matrix}\\\\\end{matrix}\right\} \begin{matrix} \text{both lead to } °e \, (T\!p) \\ \text{or } a^+. \end{matrix}$$

$$S^{\text{VII}} \; \overset{!>}{\because} = \begin{cases} \mathcal{S}^{\text{IX}<} & ,, \qquad : c^{\text{VII}} — e2^{\text{IX}<} \\ D^{9>} & ,, \qquad : c^{\text{VII}} — b2^{9>} \end{cases} \left.\begin{matrix}\\\\\end{matrix}\right\} \begin{matrix} \text{both lead to } e\flat^+ \\ (°T\!p) \text{ or } °b\flat. \end{matrix}$$

B. (Minor) :

$$S^{\text{VII}} \; \overset{!>}{\because} = \begin{cases} \mathcal{S}^{\text{IX}<} \text{ in A-minor} : & a^{\text{VII}} — e^{\text{IX}<} \\ D^{9>} & ,, \qquad : a^{\text{VII}} — g^{7>} \end{cases} \left.\begin{matrix}\\\\\end{matrix}\right\} \begin{matrix} \text{both lead to } c^+ (T\!p) \\ \text{or } °g. \end{matrix}$$

$$D^7 \; \overset{!<}{\because} = \begin{cases} D^{9>} & ,, \qquad : e^7 — e\sharp^{9>} \\ S^{\text{IX}<} & ,, \qquad : e^7 — f\sharp^{\text{IX}<} \end{cases} \left.\begin{matrix}\\\\\end{matrix}\right\} \begin{matrix} \text{both lead to } °c\sharp \\ (^+T\!p) \text{ or } f\sharp^+. \end{matrix}$$

Moreover, chords of minor nine-three may be formed at any time quite simply by altering the prime of the clang and simultaneously adding the natural seventh, *e.g.* :

$$c \; e \; g \; — c\sharp \; e \; g \; b\flat \text{ or } a \; c \; e \; — f\sharp \; a \; c \; e\flat$$

But by adding the natural seventh in this manner ($T — \overset{!<}{\because}\overset{\flat}{7}$ and $°T — \overset{!>}{\text{VII}\natural}$) one of the two possible ways of progression which, as we saw above, were open to us by alteration of the prime, falls away ; *i.e.*, whereas $c\sharp\ e\ g$ is intelligible either as d^7 or b^{VII}, and may therefore either proceed to D-minor (D-major) or B-minor (B-major), after the addition of the $b\flat$ only the road to D-minor (D-major) remains open, since the chord tends that way both in major and minor sense.   The pupil should now find out which of the paths opened on pp. 153-4 fall away when the seventh is added with the chromatic alteration of the prime (instead of $.!.^<$, read everywhere $..!^{<}_{\natural}$, instead of $.!.^>$, everywhere $..^{VII}{}^{I\,>}_{\natural}$).

The nine-three chords acquire fresh importance from the possibility of enharmonic change of meaning of single notes, which we have already turned to advantage here and there in our exercises.   We will, in the first place, establish the relation of the notes in major and minor sense without enharmonic change of meaning, then, *e.g.*, in $b\ d f a\flat$ as $g^{9>}$ or $e^{IX<}$:

$$g^{9>}\begin{cases} a\flat & 9^> = \text{III} \\ f & 7\ = \text{V} \\ d & 5\ = \text{VII} \\ b & 3\ = \text{IX}^< \end{cases}e^{IX<}$$

i.e., a change of meaning of the 9> to the III, of the 7 to the V, of the 5 to the VII, of the 3 to the IX$^<$ would yield no new nine-three chord, but the same in the minor sense.   On the other hand, every shifting of the numerical indications yields a different chord, *e.g.* :

$$g^{9>}\begin{cases} a\flat & 9^> = \text{V}\ a\flat \\ f & 7\ = \text{VII}\ f \\ d & 5\ = \text{IX}^<\ d \\ b & 3\ \underline{\underline{\frown}}\ \text{III}\ c\flat \end{cases}e\flat^{IX<},\ \text{or also}\begin{cases} a\flat & 9^> = 7\ a\flat \\ f & 7\ = 5\ f \\ d & 5\ = 3\ d \\ b & 3\ \underline{\underline{\frown}}\ 9^>c\flat \end{cases}b\flat^{9>}$$

But since the function of the nine-three chord always remains the same ($D^{9>}$ or $S^{IX<}$ do not actually mean two different things, but are different expressions for the same thing), a modulation by means of enharmonic alteration of one or more of its notes, cannot otherwise be determined with certainty than by indication of the change of meaning of one of these notes.   Taking $b\ d f a\flat = D^{9>}$ and $S^{IX<}$ in C-major (C-minor) as starting-point, we shall find in

$$D^{9>}\underset{\underline{\underline{\frown}}}{\overset{(3}{\underset{9>)}{=}}}D^{9>}\ \text{or}\ S^{IX<}\underset{\underline{\underline{\frown}}}{\overset{(IX<}{\underset{III)}{=}}}S^{IX<}\ \text{or}\ D^{9>}\underset{\underline{\underline{\frown}}}{\overset{(3}{\underset{III)}{=}}}S^{IX<}\ \text{or}\ S^{IX<}\underset{\underline{\underline{\frown}}}{\overset{(IX<}{\underset{9>)}{=}}}D^{9>}$$

that it changes uniformly to $d f a\flat\ c\flat$, the dominant nine-three chord of E♭-major or E♭-minor, etc.   It becomes evident from this trial that there is scarcely any object in writing the formula $D^{9>}$ or $S^{IX<}$ twice or of placing $D^{9>}$ next to $S^{IX<}$ (unless one had in mind a bass-progression which would be bad for $D^{9>}$, but good for $S^{IX<}$, *e.g.*, for $b\ d f a\flat$ the step in the bass from f to c, which could only be approved of for $S^{IX<}$, as f would be fundamental

K

note [V], for $\mathit{D}^{9>}$ on the other hand bad, as f would be seventh [7]); it will therefore be sufficient to indicate the change of meaning over the *one* formula $\mathit{D}^{9>}$ or $\mathit{S}^{IX<}$, but naturally avoiding the change from major into minor numbers, and *vice versâ*. Then the result of changes of meaning of $b\ d\ f\ a\flat$ as $\mathit{D}^{9>}$ or $°\mathit{S}^{IX<}$ in c-major or c-minor, indicated in a form easily surveyed, is:

(1A) $\overset{(3\ \overline{\infty}\ 9>)}{\mathit{D}^{9>}}$ from $(g)\ b\ d\ f\ a\flat$ into $(b\natural)\ d\ f\ a\flat\ \overset{9>}{c\flat}\ (=\mathit{D}^{9>}$ of E$\flat$-major or E$\flat$-minor).

(B) $\overset{(IX<\ \overline{\infty}\ III)}{\mathit{S}^{IX<}}$ from $\overset{IX<}{b}\ d\ f\ a\flat\ (c)$ into $d\ f\ a\flat\ \overset{III}{c\flat}\ (e\flat)\ (=\mathit{S}^{IX<}$ of E$\flat$-major or E$\flat$-minor).

(2A) $\overset{(9>\ \overline{\infty}\ 3)}{\mathit{D}^{9>}}$ from $(g)\ b\ d\ f\ \overset{9}{a\flat}$ into $(e)\ \overset{3}{g\sharp}\ b\ d\ f\ (=\mathit{D}^{9>}$ of A-major or A-minor).

(B) $\overset{(III\ \overline{\infty}\ IX<)}{\mathit{S}^{IX<}}$ from $b\ d\ f\ \overset{III}{a\flat}\ (c)$ into $\overset{IX<}{g\sharp}\ b\ d\ f\ (a)\ (=\mathit{S}^{IX<}$ of A-major or A-minor).

(3A) $\overset{(7\ \overline{\infty}\ 3)}{\mathit{D}^{9>}}$ from $(g)\ b\ d\ \overset{7}{f}\ a\flat$ into $(c\sharp)\ \overset{3}{e\sharp}\ g\sharp\ b\ d\ (=\mathit{D}^{°>}$ of F$\sharp$-major or F$\sharp$-minor).

(or AA) $\overset{(9>\ \overline{\infty}\ 5)}{\mathit{D}^{9>}}$ from $(g)\ b\ d\ f\ \overset{9>}{a\flat}$ into $(c\sharp)\ e\sharp\ \overset{5}{g\sharp}\ b\ d\ (=\mathit{D}^{9>}$ of F$\sharp$-major or F$\sharp$-minor)

(B) $\overset{(V\ \overline{\infty}\ IX<)}{\mathit{S}^{IX<}}$ from $b\ d\ \overset{V}{f}\ a\flat\ (c)$ into $\overset{IX<}{e\sharp}\ g\sharp\ b\ d\ (f\sharp)\ (=\mathit{S}^{IX<}$ of F$\sharp$-major or F$\sharp$-minor).

(or BB) $\overset{(III\ \overline{\infty}\ VII)}{\mathit{S}^{IX<}}$ from $b\ d\ f\ \overset{III}{a\flat}\ (c)$ into $e\sharp\ \overset{VII}{g\sharp}\ b\ d\ (f\sharp)\ (=\mathit{S}^{IX<}$ of F$\sharp$-major or F$\sharp$-minor).

Other changes of meaning would not really lead to other progressions, but only to differently written ones, *e.g.*, $5\ \overline{\infty}\ 3$ to $d\sharp^{9>}$ $(d\ \overline{\infty}\ c^\times)$ and $5\ \overline{\infty}\ 9>$ to $d\flat^{9>}$ $(d\ \overline{\infty}\ e\flat\flat)$, which have already been introduced above in a simpler manner.

A similar enharmonic change of meaning may be effected with chords of seven-three, not, however, resulting in chords of seven-three, but in imperfect chords of nine-three (without fifth, ^{8} or $^\times$); *e.g.*, $b\ d\ f$ may change meaning to $c\flat\ d\ f,\ b\ d\ e\sharp,\ c\flat\ e\flat\flat\ f,\ b\ c^\times\ e\sharp$ by means of the clang signs:

$$\overset{(3\ \overline{\infty}\ 9>)}{\mathit{D}^7=\mathit{D}^{9>}_3},\qquad \overset{(7\ \overline{\infty}\ 3)}{\mathit{D}^7=\mathit{D}^{9>}_3},\qquad \overset{(5\ \overline{\infty}\ °>)}{\mathit{D}^7=\mathit{D}^{9>}_3},\qquad \overset{(5\ \overline{\infty}\ 3>)}{\mathit{D}^7=\mathit{D}^{9>}_3}$$

also in the minor sense:

$$\overset{(VII\ \overline{\infty}\ III)}{\mathit{S}^{VII}=\mathit{S}^{IX<}_?},\qquad \overset{(III\ \overline{\infty}\ IX<)}{\mathit{S}^{VII}=\mathit{S}^{IX<}_?},\qquad \overset{(V\ \overline{\infty}\ III)}{\mathit{S}^{VII}=\mathit{S}^{IX<}_?},\qquad \overset{(V\ \overline{\infty}\ IX<)}{\mathit{S}^{VII}=\mathit{S}^{IX<}_?},$$

For the easier and more convenient management of the clang signs for these complicated formations, it should not be over-looked that the sign ⬯ always requires the enharmonically altered notation of the note, and that this altered notation in changes of meaning to 3, VII and IX< generally introduces notes with ♯ or ×, whereas in changes of meaning to III, 7 and 9> it generally introduces notes with ♮ or ♭♭, and not the reverse.

We most decidedly caution against the misuse of enharmonic changes of meaning ; for, excepting where they enter as passing illusions (with subsequent retracting), they positively mislead the ear, and are devices founded merely on the limited power of logical comprehension. On the other hand by opportunely turning ambiguity to advantage, effects of the most surprising beauty can be attained, like mystical views of remote domains of the tone-world, inaccessible by ordinary paths. It remains to be specially remarked that such ambiguous enharmonic harmonies may at times be figured in a sense different from that determined by the context, *e.g. :*

Here, as it were, the intensity of the feeling of tonality mocks at the most forcible means of modulation.

Chords of seven-three and nine-three, where not proper to the key, resulted in the first instance from chromatic alteration in connection with that of the fifth-change, but involving an even more marked sense of dominant harmony than was the case with the latter. We now again return within the range of tonal har-mony, so as to fathom the degree of modulating power possessed by harmonic successions which can indeed be understood tonally, but need not ; in so doing we shall again follow the order in which the harmony steps occurred during the gradual extension of our range of observation.

§ 16 MODULATIONS BY MEANS OF THE THIRD-CHANGE CLANGS.

The *third-change* may, similarly to the fifth-step and turn of harmony, be made use of for a simple exchange of keys ; first for really passing from the principal key to that of the tonic parallel, if the aid of rhythmical expedients be also accepted. But also any third-change from a dominant, to a certain extent undoubtedly suggests modulation to the key of the tonic parallel * :

* The following short examples are all to be worked out in several keys, or, at least, to be played at the piano.

(A) from T to Tp: $T \; D \mid T \; .. \atop =°Tp$ $\Big| °T \; D \mid °T.$

(B) from D to Dp: $T \mid D \; {Dp \atop =°D} \Big| °T.$

(C) from S to Sp: $T \mid S \; {Sp \atop =°S} \Big| °T.$

(D) from $°T$ to $°Tp$: $°T \; D \mid °T \; . \atop = Tp$ $\Big| T \; D \mid T.$

(E) from $°D$ to $°Dp$: $°T \; °D \; \Big| {°Dp \atop =D} \; T.$

(F) from $°S$ to $°Sp$: $°T \mid °S \; {°Sp \atop = S} \Big| T.$

Naturally if the modulation is to be regarded as definitely made, another close will be needed to establish the new key.

The leading-tone change, minor-third change, whole-tone change, and tritone change, being transitions to principal clangs of the parallel key, and being readily comprehended in the sense of that key, have similar *modulating power*, which one often enough experiences in minor as endangering the retention of the tonality (*e.g.*, in sequences in which we only too readily pass over to the conception in the major sense).

Possible modulations by means of *leading-tone changes* are :

(A) $T \quad ..^{II<} \atop =°D^{2>} \; 1$ $\Big| °S \; D^+ \mid °T.$

(B) $T \mid S \quad ..^{II<} \atop =°T^{2>1}$ $\Big| °S \; D^+ \mid °T.$

(C) $°T \quad \Big| \; ..^{2>} \atop =^+S^{II<} \; 1$ $\; D \mid T.$

(D) $°T \mid \quad °D \quad ..^{2>} \atop =^+T^{II<1}$ $\mid S \; D \mid T.$

The *minor-third change* may effect modulations in the following manner :

(A) $T \atop = Tp$ $\Big| \; {Sp \atop °S} \; D^+ \mid °T.$

(B) $T \; D \atop =°Dp$ $\Big| \; {Tp \atop °T} \; °S \mid °T.$

(C) $°T \quad °Dp \atop = Tp \quad D$ $\Big| T.$

(D) $°T$ $°S$
$\quad =Sp$ | T S | $T.$

The *whole-tone change* similarly :

(A) T | D $\quad$ Sp
$\quad =°Dp$ $°S$ | $°T.$

(B) $°T$ | $°S$ $\quad °Dp$
$\quad =Sp$ $\quad D$ | $T.$

Likewise the *tritone change:*

(A) T | S $\quad Dp$
$\quad =F$ $°D$ | $°T.$

(B) $°T$ | $°D$ $\quad °Sp$
$\quad =F$ S | $T.$

But all these steps may equally well lead into other keys than the parallel key, by either starting from a different point, or changing meaning in another sense :

1. Modulations by means of leading-tone changes :

(A) T | S $\quad$ II<
$\quad =T$ II< | S D | T (*e.g.*, c-major—f-major).

(B) T | D $\quad$ II<
$\quad =T$ II< | S D | T (*e.g.*, c-major—g-major).

(C) T | $°S^{2>}$ $\quad$ I
$\quad =T$ II< | S D | T (*e.g.*, c-major—d♭-major.)

(D) T | $°Sp$ $\quad$ II<
$\quad =T$ II< | S D | T (*e.g.*, c-major—a♭-major).

(E) T | S $\quad$ II<
$\quad =°D^{2>}$ I | $°S$ D | $°T$ (*e.g.*, c-major—d-minor).

(F) T $\quad$ II<
$\quad =°T^{2>}$ I | $°S$ D | $°T$ (*e.g.*, c-major—e-minor).

(G) T | $°S^{2>}$ $\quad$ I
$\quad =°T^{2>}$ I | $°S$ D | $°T$ (*e.g.*, c-major—f-minor).

(H) T | Sp $\quad$ 2>
$\quad =+S^{II<}$ I | T (*e.g.*, c-major—f-major).

(I) T | Dp
$\quad =+S^{II<}$ 1 | T (*e.g.*, c-major—g-major).

(K) $°T$ | $°S$ $\quad$ 2>
$\quad =°T$ 2> | $°S$ D | $°T$ (*e.g.*, a-minor—d minor).

(L) $^{\circ}T \mid {}^{\circ}D \quad \overset{{}_{2>}}{\underset{}{\cdot\cdot}}$

$\qquad = {}^{\circ}T \; \overset{{}_{2>}}{\cdot\cdot} \mid {}^{\circ}S \; D \mid {}^{\circ}T$ (*e.g.*, A-minor—E-minor).

(M) $^{\circ}T \mid {}^{\circ}D \quad \overset{{}_{2>}}{\cdot\cdot}$

$\qquad = {}^{+}S^{\mathrm{II}<} \; {}_{1} \mid D^{+} \mid {}^{+}T$ (*e.g.*, A-minor—G-major).

(N) $^{\circ}T \qquad \overset{{}_{2>}}{\cdot\cdot}$

$\qquad = {}^{+}T^{\mathrm{II}<} \; {}_{1} \mid S \; D \mid T$ (*e.g.*, A-minor—F-major, etc.).

2. Modulations by means of minor-third changes :

(A) $T \mid S \quad \overset{S\!p}{}$

$\qquad = T \; S\!p \; D \mid T$ (*e.g.*, C-major—F-major).

(B) $T \mid D \quad T\!p$

$\qquad = T \; S\!p \; D \mid T$ (*e.g.*, C-major—G-major).

(C) $T \mid D\!p \quad \cancel{D}$

$\qquad = S \; D \mid T$ (*e.g.*, C-major—G-major).

(D) $T \mid \cancel{D} \quad T\!p^{\mathrm{III}<}$

$\qquad = T\!p \; D \mid T$ (*e.g.*, C-major—D-major).

(E) $T \mid D\!p \quad \cancel{D}$

$\qquad = T\!p \; D \mid T$ (*e.g.*, C-major—G-major).

(F) $T \mid \overset{{}_{3>}}{\cdot\cdot} \quad S$

$\qquad = S \; D \mid T$ (*e.g.*, C-major—E♭-major).

(G) $^{\circ}T \mid {}^{\circ}D \quad S^{\mathrm{III}<}$

$\qquad = S \; D \mid T$ (*e.g.*, A-minor—G-major).

(H) $^{\circ}T \mid {}^{\circ}\cancel{D} \quad T^{\mathrm{III}<}$

$\qquad = S \; D \mid T$ (*e.g.*, A-minor—D-major).

(I) $^{\circ}T \mid {}^{\circ}S \quad {}^{\circ}T\!p$

$\qquad = S^{2>} \; D \mid T$ (*e.g.*, A-minor—F-major).

(K) $^{\circ}T \mid S\!p \quad {}^{\circ}S$

$\qquad = {}^{\circ}T\!p \; {}^{\circ}S \mid {}^{\circ}T$ (*e.g.*, A-minor—D-minor).

(L) $^{\circ}T \mid {}^{\circ}D\!p \quad {}^{\circ}T$

$\qquad = {}^{\circ}T\!p \; {}^{\circ}S \mid {}^{\circ}T$ (*e.g.*, A-minor—E-minor).

3. Modulations by means of whole-tone changes :

(A) $T \mid T\!p \quad \cancel{D}$

$\qquad = S\!p \; D \mid T$ (*e.g.*, C-major—G-major).

(B) $T \mid D\!p \quad T\!p^{\mathrm{III}>}$

$\qquad = S\!p \; D \mid T$ (*e.g.*, C-major—D-major).

(C) $T \mid {}^{\circ}S \quad S$

$\qquad = S\!p \; D \mid T$ (*e.g.*, C-major—E♭-major).

(D) T | $\overset{}{\not{D}}$ $\quad$ $D\!p^{\text{III}\prec}$ |
$\qquad =Sp \quad D$ | T (*e.g.*, C-major—A-major).

(E) T | $\overset{}{\not{D}}$ $\qquad D\!p^{\text{III}\prec}$ |
$\qquad =S_{\text{VII}}^{\text{III}\prec} \quad D$ | $°T$ (*e.g.*, C-major—A-minor).

(F) T | $D^{3\succ}$ $\quad T$ |
$\qquad =Sp \quad D$ | T (*e.g.*, C-major—F-major).

(G) $°T$ | $°Tp$ $\qquad °\overset{\circ}{\cancel{S}}$ |
$\qquad =°Dp \quad °S$ | $°T$ (*e.g.*, A-minor—D-minor).

(H) $°T$ | $°Sp$ $\qquad °Tp^{3\succ}$ |
$\qquad =°Dp \quad °S$ | $°T$ (*e.g.*, A-minor—G minor).

(I) $°T$ | D^{+} $\qquad °\overset{\circ}{\cancel{D}}$ |
$\qquad =°Dp \quad °S$ | $°T$ (*e.g.*, A-minor—F♯-minor).

(K) $°T$ | $\cancel{S}$ $\qquad °Sp^{3\succ}$ |
$\qquad =°Dp \quad °S$ | $°T$ (*e.g.*, A-minor—C-minor).

(L) $°T$ | $\cancel{S}$ $\qquad °Sp^{3\succ}$ |
$\qquad =D_{3\succ}^{\prime} \quad °S$ | T (*e.g.*, A-minor—C-major).

(M) $°T$ | $S^{\text{III}\prec}$ $\qquad °T$ |
$\qquad =°Dp \quad °S$ | $°T$ (*e.g.*, A-minor—E-minor).

4. Modulations by means of tritone changes :

(A) T $\qquad \overset{}{\not{D}}$ |
$\qquad =S \quad Dp$ | T (*e.g.*, C-major—G-major).

(B) T $\qquad$ | $\overset{}{\not{D}}$
$\qquad =\cancel{F}$ $\quad$ | $°D \quad °S$ | $°T$ (*e.g.*, C-major—E-minor).

(C) T | Tp $\qquad \cancel{S}$ |
$\qquad =+T^{\prime\succ} \quad S$ | T (*e.g.*, C-major—F-major).

(D) T | $\cancel{S}$ $\qquad °T$ |
$\qquad =S \quad Dp$ | T (*e.g.*, C-major—A♭-major).

(E) $°T$ $\qquad \cancel{S}$ $\quad$ |
$\qquad ==°D \quad °Sp$ $\quad$ | $°T$ (*e.g.*, A-minor—D-minor).

(F) $°T$ $\qquad$ | $\cancel{S}$
$\qquad = \cancel{F}$ | $S \quad D$ | T (*e.g.*, A-minor—F-major).

(G) $°T$ | $°Tp$ $\qquad °\overset{\circ}{\cancel{D}}$ |
$\qquad =\cancel{F} \quad °D$ | $°T$ (*e.g.*, A-minor—E-minor).

(H) $°T$ | $\qquad \overset{}{\not{D}}$ $\quad T^{\text{III}\prec}$ |
$\qquad ==°D \quad °Sp$ | $°T$ (*e.g.*, A-minor—C♯-minor).

§ 17. MODULATIONS BY MEANS OF BOLDER HARMONIC PROGRESSIONS.

Nicety of feeling as regards the nature of modulation will be specially formed by means of such turns as are intelligible within the key and abstain as far as possible from notes foreign to the scale. The harmonic progressions now to be discussed with regard to their modulating power introduce foreign notes more and more, so that the paralysing of their modulating tendency is scarcely possible. In tonal harmony the steps in question result from the connecting of the contra-clang of the tonic with the parallel clangs, *i.e.*, clangs which are all only indirectly intelligible (for even the contra-clang of the tonic is that undeniably in a certain sense : its third has the effect of a chromatic note and may not be doubled).

1. *Modulation by means of leading-tone steps.* Analogous to the tonal form of the step ($^{\circ}Sp—D^{+}$ and $Dp—^{\circ}S$ in major and minor) every leading-tone step as representing both dominants, has the effect of pressing directly towards the tonic skipped, and, therefore, if proceeding from other harmonies, it induces modulation :

(A) $Tp \quad ^{\circ}\overset{\circ}{S}$ |
$\quad =Dp \quad ^{\circ}S$ | T [$^{\circ}T$] (*e.g.*, C-major—F-major or F-minor).

(B) $D \quad T^{3>}$ |
$\quad =Dp \quad ^{\circ}S$ | T (*e.g.*, C-major—G-major).

(C) T | $S \quad Dp^{\text{III}\,\triangleleft}$ |
$\quad =^{\circ}Sp \quad D^{+}$ | $^{\circ}T$ (*e.g.*, C-major—A-minor).

(D) T | $S \quad Tp^{\text{III}\,\triangleleft}$ |
$\quad =^{\circ}Sp \quad D^{+}$ | $^{\circ}T$ (*e.g.*, C-major—D-minor).

(E) T | $S \quad T$ |
$\quad =^{\circ}Sp \quad D$ | T [$^{\circ}T$] (*e.g.*, C-major—F-major or F-minor).

(F) $^{\circ}Tp \quad D$ |
$\quad =^{\circ}Sp \quad D^{+}$ | $^{\circ}T$ [T] (*e.g.*, A-minor—E-minor or E-major).

(G) $S \quad T^{\text{III}\,\triangleleft}$ |
$\quad =^{\circ}Sp \quad D^{+}$ | $^{\circ}T$ (*e.g.*, A-minor—D-minor).

(H) $^{\circ}T$ | $^{\circ}D \quad ^{\circ}Sp^{3>}$ |
$\quad =Dp \quad ^{\circ}S$ | T (*e.g.*, A-minor—C-major).

(I) $^{\circ}T$ | $^{\circ}\overset{\circ}{D} \quad ^{\circ}Tp^{3>}$ |
$\quad =^{+}Dp \quad ^{\circ}S$ | T^{+} (*e.g.*, A-minor—G-major).

(K) $^{\circ}T$ | $D \quad ^{\circ}T$ |
$\quad =Dp \quad ^{\circ}S$ | $^{\circ}T$ (*e.g.*, A-minor—E-minor).

But the *rôle* of the leading-tone steps is not as yet at an end. After the experiences we have had (p. 116) as regards the figuration of harmonies by leading-notes (auxiliary notes), there will be no cause for wonder that finally in place of all three notes of the harmony, their respective upper and under seconds may enter ; by this means so-called *auxiliary harmonies* arise, which in the first place have no modulating power and are understood only as figuration.   As they are feigning consonances, they share with all feigning consonances the peculiarity that they may be treated as real harmonies (with doubling of the feigning fundamental note) ; if one of the leading-notes be a note of the key otherwise capable of being doubled, nothing stands in the way of its being doubled here also.   For C-major and A-minor we obtain the auxiliary harmonies :

with some of which we have already become acquainted under other names [(*a*) as *S*, (*c*) as °*Sp* in major, (*g*) as *D*, (*l*) as +*Dp* (in minor)]. It is more convenient to write the auxiliary harmonies in three parts than in four; in four-part writing it will be preferable to call to aid an auxiliary note in the opposite direction:

But it is remarkable that the contra-leading-tone steps do not so unconditionally tend towards a tonic skipped as other far-reaching steps (pp. 52, 146, etc.), but rather lead us to expect a fifth-step or turn of harmonies in the same direction:

Probably the effect produced is due to a confusion of the leading-tone step with the chromatic-semitone step; assuming the latter [167 (c)—(d)] in place of the former, the progression corresponds entirely to our experiences; the succession c^+—$c\sharp^+$—$f\sharp^+$ may then be expressed as (S) $[S]$ D T, or also S D D, and is intelligible.

2. *Modulation by means of third-steps.* The only third-steps in tonal harmony (not taking intermediate cadences into consideration) are Tp—$°S$ and S—^+S in major, $°Tp$—D^+ and D—$°D$ in minor. But in another sense the third-steps require greater attention. Namely if—considered purely harmonically without having regard to scales—the plain-fifth clang is nothing more than the nearest related partial note of the tonic clang, detached, so to speak, and rendered independent as representative of its own clang, the idea suggests itself of rendering the third-note independent in the same fashion, separating it from the clang of the tonic and confronting it with the latter as the bearer of its own clang; then a kind of dominant significance will attach to the third-clang of the major tonic, similar to that of the plain-fifth clang, and the contra-third clang may also lay claim to a kind of under-dominant significance, while in minor, here as everywhere, the relations will turn out exactly reversed. The under-

dominant effect of $a\flat^+$ in C-major we have hitherto defined as
$^\circ S\!p$, the upper-dominant effect of $^\circ g\sharp$ in A-minor as $^+D\!p$, e^+ in
C-major we first became acquainted with as (D) $T\!p$ and $^\circ c$ in
A-minor as $(^\circ S)$ $^\circ T\!p$. *But there can be no doubt that the third-
clang is capable of closing directly to the tonic,* without any sense of
an elision being felt; e^+—c^+ does not close as if $^\circ e$ had been
skipped, $^\circ c$—$^\circ e$ not as if c^+ had been skipped, nor does $a\flat^+$—c^+
need the mediation of $^\circ c$, or $^\circ g\sharp$—$^\circ e$ that of e^+. The formulas
are :

168.

$(D)[T\!p]$ T $(^\circ S)[^\circ T\!p]$ $^\circ T$ $^\circ S\!p$ T $^+D\!p$ $^\circ T$

(D) $T\!p$ T $(^\circ S)$ $^\circ T\!p$ $^\circ T$ $^\circ S^{\mathrm{VI}}$ ^{VII} T D^6 $^\circ T$

Their cadential effect and direct harmonic intelligibility will
be all the clearer and more certain, the more massive and pon-
derous the tone-complex is by which it is sounded, *i.e.*, the less
the *progression of the several parts* strikes the ear. But herein
also lies the reason why the third-step can never have equal rights
with the fifth-step. Harmony is certainly the fountain-head from
which all music flows, but the diatonic scale is the primeval bed,
the banks of which the stream may at times overflow, but into
which it is always forced again. The scale recognises *chromatic
progression* only as *passing through an intermediate degree,* never
as a cadential member of a melodic formation ; *the chromatically
altered note always appears like an approach from the preceding
note to that next following.* But all third-steps contain a
chromatic step ; if intended as a close, the part which has to
execute the chromatic step seems disagreeably wanting in motive
for its progression. In 168 (a)—(d) the $g\sharp$—g, $a\flat$—a, $e\flat$—e, $c\sharp$—c
as cadential steps are not quite logical. Since the second note
of the step belongs to the clang of the tonic, the first is, properly
speaking, tending away from it, and so our indication of the
third-clangs hitherto as dominants of the third-change clangs or
as third-change clangs of the dominants, is, for melodic reasons,
certainly justified. The $g\sharp$ in 168 (a) should by right proceed to
a before going to *g*, similarly the $a\flat$ in 168 (b) first to *g* and then

to *a*, the *e♭* in 168 (*c*) first to *d* and then to *e*, the *c♯* in 168(*d*) first to *d* and then to *c* [*cf.* 168 (*e*)—(*h*)].

It is possible to obtain real cadential significance for the third-steps, if the possibility of confounding chromatic steps with leading-tone steps be taken into account (which we have already verified in the opposite sense, p. 164), but at the cost of the clang-unity, in place of which the feigningly consonant dissonance enters :

169.

$$Dp^{\overset{4>}{}} \qquad T \qquad °Sp^{2<} \quad °T \qquad S^{VII<} \qquad T \qquad D^{:>} \qquad °T$$

But the feigningly consonant nature of this formation allows of the doubling of the feigning fundamental note, so that in reality the effect of a third-step arises.

Though we can prove the cadential power of third-steps only conditionally, yet, on the other hand, their modulating power is all the more beyond doubt, and it acts in the sense of the intermediate relation disclosed at 168. If now we make third-steps from other clangs of the tonal harmony, we obtain the modulations :

(A) $T \qquad Dp^{III<}$
$=°Tp \quad D \qquad$ | $°T$ (*e.g.*, C-major—A-minor).

(B) $S \qquad Tp^{III<}$
$=°Tp \quad D \qquad$ | $°T$ (*e.g.*, C-major—D-minor).

(C) $S \qquad \overset{-}{S} \quad °Sp \quad °S$ | $+T [°T]$ (*e.g.*, C-major—F-major [F-minor]).
$=T$

(D) $D \qquad (D) [Dp]$
$=°Tp \quad D \qquad$ | $°T$ (*e.g.*, C-major—E-minor).

(E) $D \quad °Tp$
$=T \; °Sp \; °S$ | $°T [T^+]$ (*e.g.*, C-major—G-minor [G-major]

(F) $\overset{-}{S} \qquad S^+$
$=°Tp \quad D \quad$ | $°T$ (*e.g.*, C-major—B♭-minor).

(G) $Dp \qquad T^{3>}$
$=Tp \quad °S \qquad$ | T (*e.g.*, C-major—G-major).

(H) $\overset{-}{D} \qquad D^{3>}$
$=Tp \quad °S \quad$ | $T [°T]$ (*e.g.*, C-major—D-major [D-minor]).

(I) $\overset{\circ}{S}p \quad T$
$\quad=\overset{\circ}{T}p \quad D \;\Big|\; \overset{\circ}{T}$ (*e.g.*, C-major—F-minor).

(K) $\overset{\circ}{T} \quad \overset{\circ}{S}p^{3\!>}$
$\quad=Tp \quad \overset{\circ}{S} \;\Big|\; T$ (*e.g.*, A-minor—C-major).

(L) $\overset{\circ}{D} \quad \overset{\circ}{T}p^{3\!>}$
$\quad=Tp \quad \overset{\circ}{S} \;\Big|\; T$ (*e.g.*, A-minor—G-major).

(M) $\overset{\circ}{D} \quad \mathcal{D}\!\!\cdot$
$\quad=\overset{\circ}{T} \quad Dp \quad D \;\Big|\; T^{+}\,[\overset{\circ}{T}]$ (*e.g.*, A-minor—E-major [E-minor]).

(N) $\overset{\circ}{S} \quad (\overset{\circ}{S}) \quad [\overset{\circ}{S}p]$
$\quad=Tp \quad \overset{\circ}{S} \;\Big|\; T$ (*e.g.*, A-minor—F-major).

(O) $\overset{\circ}{S} \quad {}^{+}Tp$
$\quad=\overset{\circ}{T} \quad Dp \quad D \;\Big|\; {}^{+}T\,[\overset{\circ}{T}]$ *e.g.*, A-minor—D-major [D-minor]).

(P) $\mathcal{D}\!\!\cdot \quad \overset{\circ}{D}$
$\quad={}^{+}Tp \quad \overset{\circ}{S} \;\Big|\; {}^{+}T$ (*e.g.*, A-minor—B-major).

(Q) $\overset{\circ}{S}p \quad T^{\mathrm{III}<}$
$\quad=\overset{\circ}{T}p \quad D^{+} \;\Big|\; \overset{\circ}{T}$ (*e.g.*, A-minor—D-minor).

(R) $\tilde{S} \quad S^{\mathrm{III}<}$
$\quad=\overset{\circ}{T}p \quad D^{+} \;\Big|\; \overset{\circ}{T}$ (*e.g.*, A-minor—G-minor).

(S) ${}^{+}Dp \quad \overset{\circ}{T}$
$\quad={}^{+}Tp \quad \overset{\circ}{S} \;\Big|\; {}^{+}T$ (*e.g.*, A-minor—E-major).

But the third-steps open up to us another quite new path, and the result will entirely satisfy us as to the apparent slighting of the third-clangs compared with the fifth-clangs ; for, in point of fact, the third-clangs could not lay claim to perfectly equal rights, for the simple reason that their relation to the tonic is more distant than that of the fifth-clangs. The third (*cf.* Introduction, p. 3) is the fifth note in the series of naturally related notes (in major and in minor sense) ; the fifth, on the other hand, is the third note of the series. How, then, if we could prove that from the clang of the 5th partial note over that of the 3rd a forcible close to the principal clang would be made, *i.e.*, that the fifth-clang after the third-clang leads back to the principal clang ? If, in the first place, we build up harmonies of the same mode, the following successions result :

170.

Here the chromatic note ($g\sharp$, $a\flat$) no longer causes any disturbance, because, though its diverging tendency is felt, it is cancelled by the forcible logic of the progression.

But not only does the return from the third-clang over the fifth-clang to the principal clang, by means of clangs corresponding in mode to the series in question, appear normal and logical, but we find also a series of clangs of the same mode, whose principal notes present in succession a clang of the opposite mode, likewise forming a return :

171.

though, perhaps, the ear will slightly object to 171 (*b*), in consequence of its not being accustomed to the progression.

But third-clangs are also readily followed by a fifth-step in the same direction, which is, no doubt, explained by the leading-tone step formed as total result ; the latter, which by itself is not easily intelligible, will then rightly be divided into a third-step and a fifth-step.

172.

$$T \quad °S\flat \qquad T \; (D)[T\flat] \qquad °T \; (°S)[°T\flat] \qquad °T \; D\flat$$
$$\quad = D \; T \qquad \quad = S \quad T \qquad \quad = °D \quad °T \qquad = °S \; °T$$

But we must here beware of delusions ; whether the third clang be the expected sequel of the two first, or the second be a natural connecting member between the two others, I should not like to decide ; anyway, the latter conception of the case has long been familiar to us in intermediate cadences.   Certainly it is very instructive and strengthens comprehension to bring a large number of chords under one common point of view ; in this case, therefore, to understand only the third clang as the principal point of the progression, and to attach further conclusions to it : then we should again have reached the leading-tone step with its tendency to another fifth-step forward.   So as not to lose the thread in the labyrinth of possibilities shown here, it will be necessary to remain conscious of the solid foundation, the strictly tonal logic, according to which, in the first place, all lowered notes tend to proceed downwards and all raised ones upwards, a law against which, *e.g.*, examples 172 (*a*)—(*d*) only seemingly offend. *Every leading-tone progression denotes a return, every chromatic progression an onward impulse ;* if these two sentences be applied to the examples, the result will be found entirely satisfactory.

　3. *Modulation by means of minor-third steps.* We may sum up the remaining steps briefly, since the impelling forces of modulation have gradually been disclosed to us, and only a few new applications of the same points of view remain to be considered. The last investigation cleared the way for understanding minor-third steps as possible only in regard to a third, principal clang. The steps c^+—a^+ and c^+—$e2^+$ must be referred to the clangs f^+, $°e$ and $a2^+$, $°g$ respectively, and similarly $°e$—$°c\sharp$ and $°e$—$°g$ to a^+, $°g\sharp$ and c^+, $°b$ respectively, *i.e.*, the following ways of proceeding from minor-third steps appear quite logical:

$$c^+ — a^+ — e^+\,;\quad a^+ — c^+ — f^+\,;$$
$$c^+ — e\flat^+ — a\flat^+\,;\quad e\flat^+ — c^+ — g^+\,;$$
$$°e — °c\sharp — °g\sharp\,;\quad °c\sharp — °e — °a\,;$$
$$°e — °g — °c\,;\quad °g — °e — °b.$$

These progressions occur, to be sure, in tonal harmony:

In C-Major :

$$°c — °a — °e$$
$$°S —^+Sp— Tp$$

In A-Minor :

$$e^+ — g^+ — c^+$$
$$D^+ — °Dp — °Tp$$

but there they have not the sense of real closes (returns) to the last clang, but rather that of *deceptive closes ;* but if their actual cadential power be beyond doubt, we cannot do otherwise than make room for the third-clangs and minor-third clangs within tonality, besides fifth-clangs and their parallel clangs ; but we shall not require new signs for them, particularly as on account of the chromatic steps their direct power of making a cadence to the tonic appeared problematical. We need only recognise the harmonic successions :

In Major :

$$T— \quad °Sp \quad — ^+S—T$$
$$T—(D)[Tp]— \quad D—T$$
$$T— \quad °Tp \quad — \quad D—T$$
$$T—(D)[Sp]— \quad S—T$$

In Minor :

$$°T— \quad ^+Dp \quad —D^+—°T$$
$$°T—(°S)\,[°Tp]— °S —°T$$
$$°T— \quad ^+Tp \quad — °S —°T$$
$$°T—(°S)\,[°Dp] — °D —°T$$

as independent cadences, *i.e.*, not to be compared to intermediate cadences ; they are, however, not bilateral, but *one-sided cadences*, as in their case only one side of the relationship is doubly represented. Under the same category come the leading-tone steps with insertion of an intermediate harmony, both proceeding and returning:

In Major:

(A) T — $°Sp$ — $\overline{S}$ — $+S$ — T

(B) T —$(D)[Tp]$—$(D)[Dp]$— D — T

In Minor:

(C) $°T$— $+Dp$ — $\overline{D}$ — $°D$ —$°T$

(D) $°T$—$°S[°Tp]$ —$°S[°Sp]$ — $°S$ — $°T$

in which the inserted clang is always as closely connected to the next as possible (*cf.* the lower brackets). The simplest forms of one-sided cadences are T—$+S$—$°S$—T, $°T$—$°D$—D^+—$°T$, T—Sp—S—T, T—Tp—S—T, $°T$—$°Sp$—$°S$—$°T$, T—Dp—D—T, $°T$—$°Dp$—$°D$—$°T$, etc., which are logical, because they proceed from tonic to dominant by means of notes in common, or similarly return from dominant to tonic. Anyway, such cadential formations are, so to speak, only half ones, and should not be regarded as principal bases of harmonic motion, but rather as accessory forms.

§ 18. MODULATION BY MEANS OF THE MOST FAR-REACHING HARMONY STEPS.

The *tritone-step* may be found between the chord of the Neapolitan sixth ($\overline{S}$) and the major upper-dominant, as well as between the chord of the Lydian fourth ($\overline{D}$) and the minor under-dominant; it is one of the most interesting substitutions for the whole-tone step, and forcibly circumscribes a tonic (which may be either $+T$ or $°T$). If it proceeds from any other harmony, it produces a change of key:

A. In Major:

(A) $°Sp$ — $\overline{D}$
    $=\overline{S}$ — D | T [$°T$] (*e.g.*, c-major—g-major [g-minor]).

(B) S —
    $=\overline{S}$ — D | T [$°T$] (*e.g.*, c-major—e-major [e-minor]).

(C) T —
    $=\overline{S}$ — D | T [$°T$] (*e.g.*, c-major—b-major [b-minor]).

(D) D —
    $=\overline{S}$ — D | T [$°T$ (*e.g.*, c-major—f♯-major [f♯-minor]).

('E) $D\flat$ — $°\overset{°}{\text{S}}$ |
  $=\cancel{B}$ — $°S$ | $T\ [°T]$ (*e.g.,* c-major—f-major [f-minor]).

(F) $T\flat$ — |
  $=\cancel{B}$ — $°S$ | $T\ [°T]$ (*e.g.,* c-major—b♭-major [b♭-minor]).

B. In Minor :

(G) $+D\flat$ — $°\overset{°}{\text{S}}$ |
  $=\cancel{B}$ — $°S$ | $°T\ [+T]$ (*e.g.,* a-minor—d-minor [d-major]).

(H) $°D$ — |
  $=\cancel{B}$ — $°S$ | $°T\ [+T]$ (*e.g.,* a-minor—f-minor [f-major]).

(I) $°T$ — |
  $=\cancel{B}$ — $°S$ | $°T\ [+T]$ (*e.g.,* a-minor—b♭-minor [b♭-major]).

(K) $°S$ — |
  $=\cancel{B}$ — $°S$ | $°T[+T]$ (*e.g.,* a-minor—e♭-minor [e♭-major]).

(L) $°S\flat$ — $\cancel{D}$ |
  $=\cancel{S}$ — D | $°T[+T]$ (*e.g.,* a-minor—e-minor [e-major]).

(M) $°T\flat$ — |
  $=\cancel{S}$ — D | $°T[+T]$ (*e.g.,* a-minor—b-minor [b-major])

(N) $°D\flat$ — |
  $=\cancel{S}$ — D | $°T[+T]$ (*e.g.,* a-minor—f♯-minor [f♯-major]).

The *contra-whole-tone change* is represented tonally as the transition from the minor under-dominant to the second upper-dominant ($°S$—$\cancel{D}$), and may naturally as such modulate to the key of the dominant :

A. In Major :

(A) $°S$ — $\cancel{D}$ |
  $=°\overset{°}{\text{S}}$ — D | T (*e.g.,* c-major—g-major).

(B) $S\flat$ — |
  $=°\overset{°}{\text{S}}$ — D | $°T\ [+T]$ (*e.g.,* c-major—e-minor [e-major]).

(C) $T\flat$ — |
  $=°\overset{°}{\text{S}}$ — D | $°T\ [+T]$ (*e.g.,* c-major—b-minor [b-major]).

(D) $T^{3>}$ — |
  $=°\overset{°}{\text{S}}$ — D | $+T\ [°T]$ (*e.g.,* c-major—d-major [d-minor]).

(E) $D^{3>}$ — |
  $=°\overset{°}{\text{S}}$ — D | $°T[+T]$ (*e.g.,* c-major—a-minor [a-major]).

L

B. In Minor:

(F) $D+ \quad —\overset{\circ}{\underset{\circ}{S}}$
$=\!\!\not{D} \quad —\!\!°S$ | $°T$ (*e.g.*, A-minor—D-minor).

(G) $°D\!p \quad —$
$=\!\!\not{D} \quad —°S$ | $T [°T]$ (*e.g.*, A-minor—F-major [F-minor]),

(H) $°T\!p \quad —$
$=\!\!\not{D} \quad —°S$ | $T [°T]$ (*e.g.*, A-minor—B♭-major [B♭-minor]).

(I) $T^{\text{III}<} —$
$=\!\!\not{D} \quad — °S$ | $°T [+T]$ (*e.g.*, A-minor—G-minor [G-major]).

(K) $S^{\text{III}<} —$
$=\!\!\not{D} \quad —°S$ | $+T [°T]$ (*e.g.*, A-minor—C-major [C-minor]).

This step is particularly easy to write, if both harmonies are introduced with sevenths, in which case two tied notes and two chromatic steps are possible :

173.

$S^{\text{VII}} \qquad \not{D}^{7} \qquad D^{7} \qquad \mathcal{S}^{\text{VII}}$

The *chromatic-semitone change* will be most easily intelligible as the progression $°S\!p—{}^{+}S\!p$ (in C-major $= a♭^{+}—°a$) or of $^{+}D\!p—$ $°D\!p$ (in A-minor $= g♭^{\textstyle\cdot}_{<}—g^{+}$), or again as the transformation of $°S\!p$ into $\mathcal{S}^{\text{VII}}_{\text{III}<}$ (in A-minor $= f^{+}—°f♯$) or of $D\!p$ into $\not{D}^{7}_{3>}$ (in C-major $= b—b♭^{+}$). Where it proceeds from other harmonies, the progression will correspond :

A. In Major.

(A) T | $\quad S —\not{D}$
$=°S\!p—\mathcal{S}^{\text{VII}}_{\text{III}<} \quad D$ | $°T$ (*e.g.*, C-major—A-minor).

(B) T | $\quad S— D^{3>}$
$=°S\!p \;—\mathcal{S}^{\text{VII}}_{\text{III}<} \quad D$ | $°T$ (*e.g.*, C-major—F-minor).

(C) T | $\quad S — \not{D}$
$=°S\!p— {}^{+}S\!p \quad D$ | $+T$ (*e.g.*, C-major—A-major).

(D) T | $\quad S — D^{3>}$
$=°S\!p—{}^{+}S\!p \quad D$ | $+T$ (*e.g.*, C-major—F-major)

(E) $\quad T$ | $\not{D}^{7<}$
$=°S\!p$ | $\mathcal{S}^{\text{VII}}_{\text{III}<} \quad D$ | $°T$ (*e.g.*, C-major—E-minor).

(F) T | $\mathcal{D}^{7<}$
    $=°Sp$ | ^+Sp D | ^+T (*e.g.*, c-major—e-major).

(G) T | $D—$
    $=°Sp—{}^{\varsigma}{}^{VII}_{III<}$ D | $°T$ (*e.g.*, c-major—b-minor).

B. In Minor :

(A) $°T$ | $°D — S$
    $=^+Dp—°Dp$ $°S$ | $°T$ (*e.g.*, a-minor—c-minor).

(B) $°T$ | $°D — S$
    $= Dp—\mathcal{D}^7_{3>}$ $°S$ | ^+T (*e.g.*, a-minor—c-major).

(C) $°T$ | $D — S^{III<}$
    $=^+Dp—°Dp$ $°S$ | $°T$ (*e.g.*, a-minor—e-minor).

(D) $°T$ | $D — S^{III<}$
    $= Dp—\mathcal{D}^7_{3>}$ $°S$ | ^+T (*e.g.*, a-minor—e-major.

(E) $°T$ | $S^{VII>}$
    $=^+Dp$ | $\mathcal{D}^7_{3>}$ $°S$ | T^+ (*e.g.*, a-minor—f-major).

(F) $°T$ | $S^{VII>}$
    $=^+Dp$ | $°Dp$ $°S$ | $°T$ (*e.g.*, a-minor—f-minor).

(G) $°T$ | $°S —$
    $= Dp—\mathcal{D}^7_{3>}$ $°S$ | ^+T (*e.g.*, a-minor—bb-major).

The student should also work out a number of possible modulating applications of the augmented-second change, double-third change, augmented-sixth change, and augmented-third change, analogous to the models given above ; this will be an excellent practice for his powers of conception, and will cause him to return with pleasure to simpler forms.

§ 19. Independent Creation of Musical Sentences. Period Formation.

The student who has earnestly and assiduously endeavoured to fathom the laws of harmonic logic, will no longer need the prescription of definite harmonic successions in his work. As we have accustomed him from the first to dispense with a given part (which for the *thorough-bass* student is always set), and by means of the continuous indication of the tonal functions made him more and more familiar with the innermost nature of harmony, he will for a long time have felt the strict directions for the connecting of harmonies irksome, and perhaps already have tried on his own account to form intelligible sentences. Every gifted pupil will try to soar beyond his school-work ; and we will now not only give him full freedom to do so, but directly set him the task of showing whether he has learnt to think musically. We shall still need to give him a few explanations as regards the nature of musical rhythm.   If his sentences are to turn out satisfactory, not only harmonically but musically in general, he must first learn how the laws of symmetrical construction, hitherto only scantily suggested, may be specialised, on what foundation they rest, and of what exceptions they admit.

Music is the art of symmetry in succession ; just as in architecture the eye seeks out the parts of a form which are symmetrical with one another, so in music the ear desires to perceive parts symmetrical with one another in succession, and from them with the help of memory to build up and understand the whole work of art.   To comprehend music by listening is, therefore, more difficult than to take in a structure by looking at it ;   the latter remains in its place and leaves the mind time for the gradual penetration into details, after first grasping the principal outlines—in music the opposite way is absolutely prescribed : whoever does not comprehend the smallest symmetries can never penetrate so far as to understand the whole. Besides, the work of art in sounds hurries past so rapidly and irrecoverably that there is but one comfort, viz., listening to it again, so that it may perhaps be understood at a second or third hearing, if this was not possible at the first.

The blocks out of which music is built are the bars, but not in the sense that what is contained between two bar-lines would correspond to the smallest independent ideas (motives) ;   the comparison between music and architecture holds to a greater extent than is at first apparent, for in structural art also, single blocks do not correspond to motives ;   rather—covered with sculptures or in fret-work—only when firmly joined together do they yield motives which are partly worked on one stone and partly on the next.

A bar in the first place consists of two *time-beats*, *i.e.*, divisions of time of medium duration practically corresponding to the speed of the pulse, which for human beings serves as the most natural subdivision of the course of time ;   these time-units are perceived by the ear through change of the tone-substance, or by interruption of the sound (rests).   The two beats of the bar form the first small symmetry ;   the second, so-called *accented*, beat closing the symmetry is, as such, rendered prominent by lingering on it—but as a rule very slightly—(accent), and besides, the connection of the two beats is made clear by the increase from the unaccented beat to the accented—*crescendo*.   The accented beat may be twice as long as the unaccented, and this fact gives rise to *triple measure*.   The accented beat, then, may be followed by a silent one (rest), or the accented note be sustained during an extra beat, or finally, it may be followed by another note. Thus, in the first place, the primitive beginnings of all musical form take root in these subdivisions of time :

In notation the bar-line has, for about three hundred years been placed before the accented beat; it does not, therefore actually divide off bars, but marks their points of stress:

Not the beat before the bar-line (the up-beat), but the beat afte the bar-line is called the first beat (the *point-of-stress note*). Th unaccented beat following the accented one in triple measure is in the first place, to be regarded as a prolongation of it as a sig of its accent, but it may introduce new tone-substance, first, in sense of belonging to the accented beat (thus, *e.g.*, in the synco pation of the third and first crotchets followed on the secon crotchet by the resolution of the dissonance, p. 117). But finall this second beat may even be detached from the first, and b referred to the next accented one:

by which means a much more restless formation, rather foreign t the original form of triple measure (♩|♩), arises (with doubl up-beat).

But now bars combine in symmetries in the same manner a time-beats, *i.e.*, the first (unaccented bar) is answered by a secon (more accented); then, also, these *two-bar groups* are confronte with one another and form *half-periods* of four bars, two of whic (the *fore-section* [protasis] and *after-section* [apodosis]) make u the largest normal form, the *sentence* or *period* of eight bars:

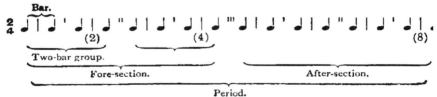

Or :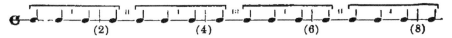

Of the same import as these rhythmical formations we have those in 𝄵 (²/₂), ²/₈, ³/₈, and ³/₂ measure, only differing in the manner of writing (for which, naturally, there are important æsthetic reasons). If every two such bars be contracted into one great bar (⁴/₄, ²/₄, 𝄴𝄵 [⁴/₂], ⁴/₈, ⁶/₈, ⁶/₂), then the bar-line belongs to the point-of-stress note of the more accented of the two bars, *e. g.* :

Unfortunately, composers often do not proceed quite correctly in this matter, and place the bar-lines to the points of stress of the 1st, 3rd, 5th, and 7th bars, so that then all cadential effects are removed to the middle of the bars, and consequently the bar-line does not fulfil its task. Conversely, also, composers often write bars too small, which, according to the tempo, contain only one time-beat. If we look upon the limits of the fluctuation of the rate of the pulse as normal for those of time-beats (between 60 and 120 M.M.), then we must count every two bars as one in notations like the following :

Therefore, particularly in measures of three beats, it is important to see clearly, whether the time-beats given in the notation are really time-beats, or, on the other hand, whether the whole bar-values correspond to beats, or, finally, whether the long and short values have the effect of time-beats of differing length (so, *e.g.*, in ³/₄ ♩ = 150, it is very convenient, and therefore correct, to look upon the values ♩|♩ ♩|♩ continuously as time-beats).

The same principle which is the reason for a slight lingering on the accented beat of the bar, and which gives rise to the bar of three beats (the ancient Greeks even recognised the ratio 2 : 3 for the duration of the two beats), *i.e.*, the principle of clearly distinguishing the single symmetries by marking the accented beats, stipulates the familiar *pauses on the points of stress of the two-bar groups*, or at least on those of the half-periods, which we find so frequently in folk-songs, chorales, etc. :

In more developed art this simple means of subdivision is occasionally replaced by an idealised one, namely, that of the prolongation of the accented beat for the duration of three beats, which gives rise to *three-bar rhythm :*

Here we may remark that the long accented beat does not necessarily entail a complete cessation of all sound-motion ; especially the after-section, which, as answer to the first four bars, has more the character of unity, favours a continuous motion. But altogether three-bar rhythm may abandon its original sense in the same way as triple measure.

This, then, is the normal *eight-bar construction* (we retain this name even for the actual twelve-bar period of continuous three-bar rhythm, still using the numbers 2, 4, and 8 for the principal points of rest—the concluding values of the several symmetries).

As regards the relation of rhythmical form to harmony, a few remarks have already been made (that dissonances on the un-accented beat, entering and proceeding by step of a second [passing-notes], are not striking ; that dissonances falling on the accented beat are best prepared by tying ; that cadential effects [perfect close, half close, deceptive close] are possible only on time-values which conclude greater symmetries ; that harmonies, coming on unaccented beats, between repeated ones coming on the accented beats, have the effect of figuration).   We may now say generally that *accented beats are really the bearers of harmony effects*, and that, *the more accented a beat is, the more decidedly will a harmony effect be expected of it.*   This may be explained thus : *every point of stress of a symmetry represents a unit of higher order ; i.e.,* beyond the motion in plain time-beats, we are conscious of the units of bars, and of bar-groups, and finally of half-periods or even periods :

1. Motion in crotchets :

2. Motion in minims :

3. Motion in semibreves :

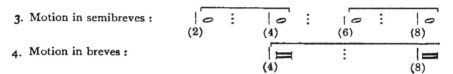

4. Motion in breves :

A glance at a modern orchestral score in many parts, proves the correctness of this explanation (*e.g.*, look at the first movement of Beethoven's c-minor Symphony, with its harmonies for the wind, entering at the 4th and 8th bars, and each time being sustained through four bars ; this same movement also contains sufficient examples of motion in semibreves and minims, besides figurative motion in quavers not hitherto discussed). The above scheme also shows clearly that the first bar is to be understood as a higher kind of up-beat to the second, and similarly the second to the fourth, and the fourth to the eighth.

The simplest deviation from the eight-bar period, set up as norm, is the omission of the unaccented beat, the up-beat to the first bar at the beginning. Then, as it were, motion in minims enters in place of motion in crotchets, and the latter comes in subsequently :

Similarly, also, the unaccented bar may be entirely missing at the beginning, so that the first value represented belongs to motion in semibreves :

etc.

(4)

but, nevertheless, the second bar-motive may be introduced complete (with up-beat) in crotchet motion :

etc.

(2)   (4)

Beginning, thus, *with accented beats* (without up-beat to the first bar, without first bar, without first bar-group—indeed, without foresection [commencing *ex abrupto*]) does not stipulate any sort of irregularities as regards the further course of the work, *i.e.*, all the following periods may be complete. But in conformity to the laws of artistic modelling, the peculiarity of a theme caused by its commencing on an accented beat, will often be retained by it in the course of elaboration, *i.e.*, imitations of it will again be incomplete at the beginning ; but this will by no means stipulate gaps in the following symmetrical construction ; on the contrary, *extensions of the endings* generally arise, *i.e.*, the scheme is filled up by appendages to the cadential values, *e.g.* :

Here the fore-section begins with the accented beat of the second bar, and the after-section with the accented beat of the sixth bar, and the following period enters similarly again ; the eight-bar construction is, however, retained consistently. *Extended endings need by no means consist of sustained notes,* and may even proceed in crotchet motion or even smaller (figurative) species ; but they must be intelligible as *appendages to the close (appended motives).*

But it is also possible to interrupt the strict symmetry by commencing with accented bars, and dropping the missing un-accented bars altogether, *e.g.* :

Here the first and fifth bars are constantly omitted.

Conversely appendages to cadential values are possible at any time, without the new members having to commence incompletely on that account :

Here, at the end of the fore-section and after-section, the last two-bar group is repeated (which is equally possible with the same or similar tone-substance as with different) ; likewise after every second bar the accented bar may be repeated [(2), (2a); (4), (4a); (6), (6a)], or at the end of the whole period the after-section may be repeated. It is also possible at the end of the period first to repeat the whole after-section, then the last two-bar group, and finally only the eighth bar.

Peculiar disturbances of symmetry arise from the contraction of endings with new beginnings, particularly from the coinciding of the cadential bar with the beginning bar of a new period $(8 = 1)$; but contractions of smaller form-members are also possible ($4 = 5$, indeed even $2 = 3$, and $6 = 7$); also in such a manner that repetitions of cadential members overlap (*e.g.*, the repetition of the after-section with $8 = 5$). It will be sufficient for the harmony student to practise the more important forms; first of all, entirely regular constructions, then three-bar formations, then those with elision of the unaccented beginning bars of half-periods, then close-repetitions, and finally formations converting the eighth bar into first or second. It will be wiser for the present merely to study bolder overlappings in the works of the great masters, without as yet attempting to practise them.

EXERCISES 301—305 (free Invention of Harmonic Periods).

(301) Formation of regular eight-bar periods in $\mathbb{C}$, $\mathbb{C}$, $^5/_4$ ($\downarrow | \downarrow$), and $^6/_8$ ($\downarrow . | \downarrow .$) measures, which, in the fore-section, remain in the principal key, and, in the after-section, modulate (for each modulation a new example in a different key is to be written):

A. (Major): (A) to the upper dominant by means of $T^6 = S^6$.
(B) ,, ,, ,, $S^6_{1<} = D^7$.
(C) ,, ,, ,, $T^{3>} = {}^\circ S$.
(D) ,, parallel key by means of $Sp = {}^\circ S$.
(E) ,, ,, ,, $Sp^{III<} = S^{III<}$.
(F) ,, ,, ,, $D = {}^\circ Dp$.
(G) ,, parallel of the dominant by means of $Tp = {}^\circ S$.
(H) ,, ,, ,, ,, $S = \mathcal{S}$.
(I) ,, ,, ,, ,, $Sp^{V<} D = {}^7_{5>}$.
(K) ,, under-dominant by means of $\mathcal{S} = S$.
(L) ,, ,, ,, $D^{3>} = Sp$.
(M) ,, ,, ,, $D^{7}_{{}^5_3>} = S^{VII}$.

B. (Minor): (A) to the parallel key by means of $S^{VI} = S^6$.
(B) ,, ,, ,, $S^{III<} = \mathcal{D}$.
(C) ,, ,, ,, $T^{VII}\natural = \mathcal{D}^\circ\natural$.
(D) ,, minor upper-dominant by means of $T^{VII}\natural$
$[= S^{VII}$.
(E) ,, ,, ,, $S^{VII}_{III<} = D^7$.
(F) ,, ,, ,, $D = D^{6>}_4$.
(G) ,, minor under-dominant by means of ${}^\circ\mathcal{S} = {}^\circ S$.
(H) ,, ,, ,, $S^{VII} = T^{VII}\natural$.
(I) ,, ,, ,, $Tp = {}^\circ Dp$.
(K) ,, parallel of the minor under-dominant by
[means of $\mathcal{S} = S$.
(L) ,, parallel of the minor under-dominant by
[means of ${}^\circ\mathcal{S} = Sp$

(302) Formation of regular eight-bar periods which can be added to those of 301, and which, having emphasised the new key by one or more cadences in the fore-section, modulate back to the original key. The return modulations are to be effected at :

A. (Major) : (A) by means of $T^{7}\natural = D^{7}.$

(B)   ,,   ,, $D^{7}_{3>} = S^{6}.$

(C)   ,,   ,, $Sp = Tp \; °S \; D_{4}.$

(D)   ,,   ,, $S^{VI} = S^{6}.$

(E)   ,,   ,, $T^{VII} = \underset{b}{\not{\!\!4}}{}^{9}\natural.$

(F)   ,,   ,, $S^{I>} = \not{S}^{V\cdot I}.$

(G)   ,,   ,, $T^{I>}_{V<} = (D^{9>}) \; Sp.$

(H)   ,,   ,, $°T \; \not{S} = Dp \; S$

(I)   ,,   ,, $\underset{b}{L}{}^{9>} = S^{6<}_{I<}.$

(K)   ,,   ,, $T^{I<} = \underset{b}{\not{\!\!4}}{}^{7}.$

(L)   ,,   ,, $D^{I<} = (D) \; Sp.$

(M)   ,,   ,, $T^{3>} = °S.$

B. (Minor) : (A)   ,,   ,, $T^{I<} = (D^{7}) \; °S.$

(B)   ,,   ,, $S^{I<}_{6<} = \not{D}^{9>}.$

(C)   ,,   ,, $\not{D}^{9}\natural = T^{VII}\natural.$

(D)   ,,   ,, $T^{III<} = D.$

(E)   ,,   ,, $T^{I>} = \not{S}^{VII} \; (°S).$

(F)   ,,   ,, $D^{7>}_{\underset{3}{5}>} = S^{VII}.$

(G)   ,,   ,, $S^{III<}_{V<} = \not{D}^{7}.$

(H)   ,,   ,, $T^{III<} = S^{III}.$

(I)   ,,   ,, $°Sp = \not{S}.$

(K)   ,,   ,, $S = \not{S}.$

(L)   ,,   ,, $Tp \; ..^{VII} = S^{VII}.$

These exercises may at first be executed in four parts, note against note, but not stiffly written in notes of the same duration, but, on the contrary, in order to incite the imagination, pregnant with rhythmical motives like the following sixteenth model example [cf. 301 (A)—(H) and 302 (A)—(H)] ; the omission of the up-beat or of the first unaccented bar may already be allowed in these exercises (without shortening the form) :

(Sixteenth model example.)

(303) Formation of periods in three-bar rhythm,

    (1) by means of the insertion of an unaccented bar after the 2nd, 4th, 6th, and 8th bars (cf. above, p. 177);

    (2) by means of the elision of the 1st and 5th bars (order of the bars ‖: accented—unaccented—accented :‖) ;

    (3) by means of the insertion of a close-repetition after the 2nd, 4th, 6th, and 8th bars.

Take for the order of modulation of these periods :

A. In Major :

(A) to the second upper-dominant by means of $T^6_{I<} = D^7$.

(B)   ,,   ,,   ,, $D^6 = S^6$.

(C)   ,,   ,,   ,, $D^{3>} = {}^{\circ}S$.

(D)   ,, parallel of the dominant by means of $Tp^{VII}\natural = S^{VII}$.

(E)   ,,   ,,   ,, $S = \bar{S}$.

(F)   ,,   ,,   ,, ${}^{\circ}S \cdot \overset{VII<}{\underset{V}{\cdot\cdot III}}_{<} = D^{9>}$.

(G)   ,,   ,,   ,, $T^{6<} = \not{D}^{9>}_{5>}$.

B. In Minor :

(A) to the second ${}^{\circ}$ upper-dominant (or second ${}^{+}$ upper-dominant)

                                  [by means of ${}^{\circ}Tp = \bar{S}$.

(B)   ,,   ,,   ,, $D^{VII}\natural = S^{VII}$.

(C)   ,,   ,,   ,, $T \cdot \overset{VI}{\underset{V}{III}}_{<} = \bar{S}^{IX<}$.

(D)   ,, dominant of the parallel by means of $T^{\cdot VI} = S^6$.

(E) to the dominant of the parallel by means of $S^{\text{III}<} = D$.

(F)   „   „   „ $D^{\text{VII}>} = S^{7<}$.

(G)   „   „   „ $D^{\text{VII}}_{\text{I}>}\natural = \text{\it/\!\!\!/}^{9>}$.

(304) Formation of four-bar half-periods leading back, so that the periods in 303 may be repeated after them; but the latter are, in this case, to be divested of modulation in their second half, and to close in the principal key (as in the seventeenth model example). These exercises are to be written in three instead of four parts, and in three separate exercises a free figuration is to be carried through, first in the highest, second in the middle, and third in the lowest part; then, two exercises are to be written with distribution of the figuration between the three parts. Special rules for three-part writing are not needed. In addition to the means of figuration made use of hitherto, the occasional introduction of unprepared dissonant notes on accented beats may be employed (accented auxiliary notes, suspensions), as also leaping to foreign notes on the unaccented beat, which proceed by step of a second to chord-notes falling on accented beats ([feigning] passing notes by leap). The seventeenth model example points out these notes by asterisks.

The returns to the principal key in these *intermediate half-periods*, which, as stated, are to consist of four bars, and not three, are to be effected by the following changes of meaning, which may take place at once (as a rule these intermediate half-periods, which may grow into full eight-bar intermediate periods, remain for some time on the dominant of the principal key, causing the re-entrance of the latter to be expected with heightened suspense [Mixolydian]) :

A. (A) by means of $T^{7}\natural = D^{7}$ to the key of the dominant, whose tonic is again turned into dominant by adding $7\natural$.

(B) by means of $D^{3>}$ to the key of the dominant, and then by means of $D^{7}_{3>} = S^{6}$ to the principal key.

(C) by means of $S^{7}_{7}\natural = D^{7}$ directly to the principal key.

(D) by means of $T^{\overset{\text{VI}}{\text{III}}<} = D^{7}$ to the parallel key, and from there by means of $^{\circ}S = Sp$ to the principal key.

(E) by means of $T^{\overset{\text{I}>}{\text{VI}}} = S^{\text{VII}}$ to the parallel of the under-dominant, from there by means of $^{\circ}T = Sp$ to the principal key.

(F) by means of $^{\circ}S = Tp$ directly to the principal key.

(G) by means of $\overline{S} = S$ directly to the principal key.

B. (A) by means of $T^{\text{I}>} = \overline{S}^{\text{VII}}$ (or $T^{5>}_{3>} = \overline{S}^{\text{VII}}$) directly to the principal key.

(B) by means of $D^{5>}_{3>}$ to the $^{\circ}$dominant, from there by means of $T^{\text{III}<} = D$ to the principal key.

(C) by means of $^{\circ}\overline{S} = {}^{\circ}S$ to the $^{\circ}$dominant, and from there again by $^{\circ}\overline{S} - {}^{\circ}S$ to the principal key.

(D) by means of $T^7 \natural = S^{VII}$ directly to the principal key.

(E) by means of $S\!p = {}^{\circ}S$ to the ${}^{\circ}$dominant, from there by means of $D^{5>}_{3>}$ to the principal key.

(F) by means of $T^7 \natural = D^7$ to the parallel key, then by $S\!p = {}^{\circ}S$ to the principal key.

(G) by means of $\overline{S} = S$ to the parallel key, then by means of $S^{7<} = S^{VII>}$ to the principal key.

(*Cf.* 303, 2 B D, with mixed figuration.)

(Seventeenth model example.)

In this example, partly on account of the short kind of bar, the dividing off of the half-periods is rather intrusive; this immediately becomes more tolerable if to the fourth and eighth bars confirmation be appended (to be inserted in 174):

(305) Formation of eight-bar periods with insertion of closer confirmations:

(1) by repeating every accented bar (2nd, 4th, 6th, 8th);

(2) by repeating the accented groups of half-periods (1—4, 3a—4a, 5—8, 7a—8a) ;

(3) by repeating the whole after-section (1—8, 5a—8a).

These periods, extended by insertions, should include modulation and return ; the examples in major should modulate in the fore-section to the dominant, parallel of the dominant, second dominant, or dominant of the parallel, making use at pleasure of the expedients shown, and in the after-section restore the principal key ; the minor examples may make modulations to the parallel key, ° dominant, second ° dominant, or parallel of the ° dominant, and in the after-section return to the principal key. The exercises will gain in interest (because forming small finished compositions), if a second period be appended to the first, either in the form here asked for, or in the three-bar rhythm of Exercise 303, for major in the key of the under-dominant, ° under-dominant, or under-third, for minor, in the ° under-dominant or parallel of the under-dominant ; it should join on without modulation and be repeated ; but the repetition is not to come to an independent close, but to make the return modulation, and, in place of the cadential eighth bar, let the beginning of the repetition of the first period enter (8 = 1), as in the following eighteenth model example. These pieces may also be thought out and written down for piano. Directions as regards figuration, etc., we shall dispense with entirely, and leave free play for invention, also with respect to the number of parts, which may be increased or lessened at pleasure :

(Eighteenth model example.)

To promote skill in the management of parts, and as another preliminary exercise in reading score, a few attemps at *six-part writing* are to follow, for which the exercises in former chapters may be used.   Six-part writing is more unwieldy than four- or five-part ; it necessitates still more doubling than the latter, and cannot entirely avoid crossing of parts.   But the doubling of real thirds by parallel motion is still forbidden, as also the doubling of dissonances (excepting simultaneous passing notes in two parts). Six-part writing is more conveniently read and worked out as 3 + 3 parts, or in case of need 4 (upper) + 2 parts.   These exercises should be worked out on six staves, so as to attain quickness in reading score, and the mezzo-soprano clef and the high bass clef (baritone clef) are to be added to those hitherto practised.   The following nineteenth model example is the working-out in six parts of Exercise 198 :

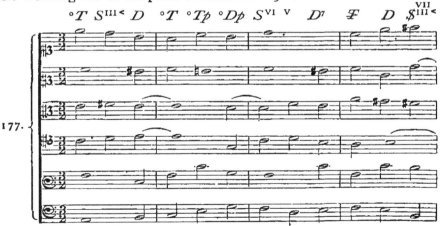

(Nineteenth model example.)

$$D \quad {}^{\circ}T \quad \mathcal{S} \quad D^{6}_{4} \quad \pm \quad ? \quad \mathcal{F} \quad D \quad .. \quad {}^{\circ}T$$

§ 20. PEDAL-POINT AND MODULATING SEQUENCE.

We must still mention two formations, one of which adds to the complication of note combinations to the utmost extent, and the other puts the feeling of tonality to the strongest test by means of modulations heaped on one another. We do not class the two together without reason; for their combination is not only possible, but first shows the full force and real significance of each. Neither of them is entirely strange to us now. Simpler pedal-point formations have occurred repeatedly in our exercises when a harmony was figured with foreign notes (*e.g.*, Exercise 258: $D^{4\ {}^{8\ 7\ 5\ 7\natural}_{6\ 6\flat\ 5\flat}}_{3}$); sequences are familiar to us, at least tonally, from § 11, and intermediate cadences have already introduced us nearly up to the modulating sequence. The whole circuit of harmony is rounded off by the insertion of these key-stones.

The pedal-point has developed historically from the *chord of six-four* by means of increased figuration and gradually more extended ornamentation of the suspended fourth or sixth, or of both, over the sustained dominant fundamental chord at the last close of the period. The primitive forms of pedal-points are therefore $D^{4\ \downarrow}$, $D^{6\ 5}$, $D^{4\ {}^{6\ 5}_{3}}$, $D^{4 \longrightarrow {}^{8\ 7}_{3}}$, $D^{4 \longrightarrow {}^{8\ 7}_{6\ -\ 5}}_{3}$, etc.; also the shake on the third or fifth of the dominant formerly almost indispensable for closes, comes under this category (6—5 or 4—3 in rapid alternations), and if the turn be added at the end or the slide up to it at the beginning, or if both shakes be combined, the relation to the pedal-point becomes all the more striking. The small cadenzas formerly (up to Haydn's time) interpolated as a matter of course at the stereotyped pauses on the chord of six-four at the close of sonata or concerto movements, with their wide scope

M

(*e.g.*, D. G. Türk advised those who did not know how to improvise a proper cadenza to be satisfied with making a shake), illustrate most clearly the history of the origin of the pedal-point.

The extent of a pedal-point varies a great deal according as it just fills out the last bars of a symmetrical construction, or comes to a standstill at the 6th bar (by which it will generally be introduced), stipulating the repetition several times of the group 5—6, or again entirely breaks through the symmetry, and independently forms whole periods, or even series of periods, by itself. But the two bars 6—7 of a regular eight-bar period will be sufficient to prove the value of this peculiar effect, *e.g.* (in five parts) :

The chords indicated with * are among the most complicated that can occur (with from 3 to 4 dissonances of a second) ; our figuring, which allows of separating the sustained bass-note (to which the name pedal-point, in the narrower sense, belongs), and indicating the chords resulting above it in the manner hitherto employed without the pedal-note, lessens the horrors of such formations to such a degree as tallies with the effort required of the ear in comprehending them. The first example did not even need a rounded bracket, but could be indicated throughout in relation to the principal tonic. The following one goes a step further, and inserts a few intermediate dominants :

Both examples close with short pedal-points on the fundamental note of the tonic.

The combination with the modulating sequence increases to

the utmost the call for power of tonal perception, which in the pedal-point finds, as it were, a tangible embodiment. The nature of the modulating sequence differs from that of the tonal sequence, in that not only a melodic formula, but also a *harmonic* one is imitated in it, *i.e.*, that a succession of functions is repeated in other keys; if, in so doing, the mode of the tonics were never altered, and the size of the intervals in progression strictly retained, the sequence would soon reach the end of notation, *i.e.*, the limits of representation, and could only be continued by means of enharmonic alteration:

Progressions of this sort, which are familiar to all singing masters as a form of accompaniment for exercises in *messa di voce* on notes rising or falling by degrees, are naturally of extremely doubtful artistic value. On the other hand, the formations related to them, which only retain the formulas of functions, but vary the size of intervals in progression and the mode of tonics reached with regard to the principal key (*half tonal sequences*), are of far greater importance, *e.g.*:

$$S\ D^7\ T\ (^{\circ}S\ D^7)\ Sp\ (^{\circ}S\ D^7)\ Dp\ (S\ D^7)\ S\ (S\ D^7)\ D$$
etc.

The result is naturally nothing more than a tonal sequence to the several harmonies of which intermediate cadences are made.

There is nothing to hinder such a formation from being supported by a pedal-note; indeed, with a little caution, it is possible to build up a strictly modulating sequence at some length over a pedal-note:

These detailed explanations will suffice to enable the student
to analyse the most elaborate pedal-points, such as the celebrated
one on D in the third movement of Brahms' German Requiem.
To teach him, however, how to *practise* anything so ambitious
does not come within the scope of a book like the present one.

EXPLANATION OF THE TERMINOLOGY AND THE CHORD SIGNS IN ALPHABETICAL ORDER.

(All explanations are also given in the text).

CLANG is the harmonic unit resulting from the combination of a principal tone with its fifth and third on the same side. As the fifth and third may be taken either from the overtone series or the undertone series, we have two clangs, the over-clang (major-chord) and the under-clang (minor-chord), *e.g., c* with its over-fifth, *g,* and over-third, *e,* gives the *c* over-clang or *C* major chord, *c e g ; e* with its under-fifth, *a,* and under-third, *c,* gives the *e* under-clang or *A* minor chord, *a c e.*

CONTRA-, as addition to the indication of an interval, means that it is conceived in a direction opposite to the clang mode, *e.g., a* is the contra-fifth (V) of the *E* major chord.

CONTRA-CLANG (turn of harmony) of any chord is the clang of opposite mode formed from its prime ; *e.g., f a♭ c (= °c)* is the contra-clang of *c e g (= c⁺).*

CROSSING OUT a number means omission of a harmony tone corresponding to the number (which, therefore, can only be 1, 3, or 5, or I, III, or V) ; *e.g., D̶⁶₈* means Dominant with the sixth and without the fifth ; but the omission of the prime is indicated by crossing out the clang sign (*e̶⁷, D̶⁷, S̶ᴵˣ*, etc.). Also in the indication of the leading-tone substitutes (*B̶, S̶,* etc.) the omission of the Prime is understood.

DOMINANT (abbreviated *D*) is the clang lying a fifth higher than the Tonic; *⁺D* = major over-dominant, *i.e.,* Dominant being a major chord (usually simply *D*), *°D* = minor over-dominant, *i.e.,* Dominant being a minor chord.

HARMONY STEPS. The terminology of harmony steps starts from the indication of the interval of the principal tones (primes), which is qualified, according to the clang started from, as either plain or opposite (contra-) ; sequences of clangs of equal mode are called "steps," sequences of clangs of opposite mode, "changes." Suppose, *e.g.,* the interval of the principal tones to be the *fifth c g ;* if we start from *c⁺, g* is the plain fifth (in the major sense) ; if from *°g, c* is the plain fifth (in the minor sense). If we start from *°c, g* is contra-fifth, if from *g⁺, c* is contra-fifth. Therefore *c⁺—g⁺* and *°g—°c* are plain-fifth steps, *⁺g—⁺c* and *°c—°g,* contra-fifth steps ; *c⁺—°g* and *°g—c⁺,* plain-fifth changes, *°c—g⁺* and *g⁺—°c* contra-fifth changes. We call plain, in major, all intervals resulting from ascending fifth- and third-steps; in minor, all intervals resulting from descending fifth- and third-steps. The whole-tone is to be conceived as double fifth-step (*e.g.*, $c\ d =$ *c—g—d*), the leading-tone, as combination of a fifth-step and a third-step in the same direction (*e.g.*, $c\ b\ =\ c$—g—b); the tritone-step, as a combination of two fifth-steps with a third-step (*e.g.*, $c f\sharp\ =\ c$—g—d—$f\sharp$); the minor-third is to be considered as major-sixth, *i.e.*, as connection of the fifth-tone and the third-tone, *e.g.*, $e\ g$ as $[C]$—g—e', or as $[b'']$—e'—g; this interval is to be regarded as plain when it proceeds from the fifth-clang (*e.g.*, for $C\ g\ e'$, from g^+) to the third (in the case mentioned, therefore, in the direction of the ascending harmonic natural scale); a simple and easily surveyed rule is this : *an interval is plain when it ascends from a major chord, towards the side of the ♯ tones, or descends, from a minor chord, towards the side of the ♭ tones.* We call plain, therefore, the third-steps c^+—e^+, and $^{\circ}c$—$^{\circ}a\flat$, the minor-third steps c^+—a^+, and $^{\circ}c$—$^{\circ}e\flat$, the chromatic steps c^+—$c\sharp^+$, and $^{\circ}e$—$^{\circ}e\flat$, the double-third changes c^+—$^{\circ}g\sharp$, and $^{\circ}e$—$^{\circ}a\flat$, etc. All harmony steps can also be understood as being made backwards (retrograde); the retrograde plain steps, then, externally present the same appearance as the advancing contra-steps, and the reverse ; while the plain and contra-changes cannot interchange their rôles (*i.e.*, a retrograde plain-fifth change still appears as a plain-fifth change, not as a contra-fifth change); the contra-changes are always the most complicated of the successions of clangs whose principal tones form the same interval.

INTERVALS (second, third, etc.), and the numbers designating them (2, 3, etc.) are considered only rarely and exceptionally in this book as well as in all other writings of the author, as the simultaneous sounding of two notes. They, rather, serve, as a rule, only to indicate and characterise single *notes* in their position relative to the prime of an over- or under-clang. Therefore, augmented, diminished, and similarly complicated intervals are mentioned only on the occasion of giving instruction as to the management of the single parts (avoiding intervals difficult to sing); generally the expression "third" means the *third-tone* of a clang (therefore, only one, not two notes), "sixth," similarly, the *note* which lies at the distance of a whole-tone from the fifth.

LEADING-TONE SUBSTITUTE is the chord of opposite clang mode arising from replacing the prime of a clang by its minor contra-second (second of the side opposite to the clang principle). We indicate the major chord substituted in this way for minor chords by a ⋗ through the clang sign, thus : $\mathcal{F}$, $\mathcal{B}$, $\mathcal{S}$, the minor chords similarly substituted for major chords by a ⋖ through the clang sign, thus : $\mathcal{F}$, $\mathcal{B}$, $\mathcal{S}$. $\mathcal{F}$, therefore, in *a* minor is $a\ c\ [e]\ f\ (=f^+)$, $\mathcal{B}$, in *c* major, $f\sharp\ [g]\ b\ d\ (=\ ^{\circ}f\sharp)$, etc. Inasmuch as the ⋗ through a clang sign sufficiently indicates the leading-note from *above* to the prime of a *minor* chord—which leading-note, when substituted

for the prime, changes the minor chord into a major chord—the °
can be dispensed with.

LETTERS (SMALL) indicate the primes of clangs ; for instance,
$c^+ = c$ over-clang (c major chord), $°e = e$ under-clang (minor
chord under e, therefore A minor chord) ; where the clang sign
($^+$, °) is wanting, the $^+$ is to be considered as omitted (a major
chord prescribed), unless italic numbers indicate the minor mode
(see NUMBERS).

LETTERS, CAPITAL (T, D, S) indicate the functions of clangs, as
Tonic, Dominant, and Subdominant.

NATURAL are those plain (*q.v.*) intervals which are component
parts of the clang ; therefore the 1 (8), 3, 5 of the over-clang
(major chord) and the I (VIII), III, V of the under-clang
(minor chord) ; also the minor seventh (7, VII), for instance, in
the c major chord, b♮, in the A♭ major chord, g♮2, in $°c$ (= F minor
chord), d, etc. In cases where a natural interval is to be indicated explicitly as such (for instance, where a chromatically
different form of it preceded or was to be expected), a ♮ may be
added to the number, which, however, has no altering significance, but only indicates the same interval that would be prescribed by the number without the addition ; for instance, T^{VII}♮
= minor tonic with *natural* (*i.e.*, minor) under-seventh, in A minor,
f♯ a c e.

NUMBERS (1—9, I—IX) indicate tones according to their distance (interval) from the prime of an over- or under-clang ; all
Arabic numbers indicate intervals counted upwards, all Roman, intervals counted downwards ; they indicate, at the same time, the
clang mode, so that also in minor the ° is omitted whenever numbers are used along with the clang sign. In particular 1, 3, 5 (I, III,
V) indicate the essential parts of the clang (prime, [major] third,
[perfect] fifth) ; 2 (II), the major second ; 4 (IV), the perfect
fourth ; 6 (VI), the major sixth ; 7 (VII), the minor (!) seventh ;
8 (VIII), the perfect octave ; 9 (IX), the major ninth. Alterations of these values, which are the properly normal, are indicated
by ⋖ (= raising a semitone) and ⋗ (= lowering a semitone).
The position of a number *under* the clang sign or the repetition
points (..) replacing it, indicates that the tone prescribed by the
number is to be given to the bass part ($_3^c$, ᵢᵢᵢ, ᵥ̇) ; the position
over the letter or the points ($^c_{\dot{c}}$, $^I_{\dot{c}}$, ^{III}) indicates that it is to be
given to the highest part. Numbers after the letters or points
(c^δ, e^{VII}, ..^{VI}) prescribe only the addition of the indicated tone to
the harmony, without defining its position. It is a proof of the
simplicity of our method of chord signs that tones which would
require double raising (⋚) or double lowering (⋛), never occur,
and cannot even be comprehended.

PARALLEL CLANG (abbreviated p) of a Tonic, Dominant, or Subdominant is that clang which stands to it in the relation of the
Tonic of the parallel key to the Tonic of the principal key. For

instance, c major and A minor, G major and E minor, are parallel keys, therefore g^+ is the parallel clang of $°b$ (E minor), c^+ the parallel clang of $°e$ (A minor), and conversely $°e$ and $°b$ are parallel clangs of c^+ and g^+. The clang mode of the Tonic, Dominant, and Subdominant is indicated also in the compositions Tp, Sp, Dp, in the manner explained above (major by a $^+$ or without any addition, minor always by a $°$), and the mode of the parallel clang is always the opposite. For instance, in Tp the Tonic is a major chord (because there is no $°$ to the T), the parallel clang, therefore, a minor chord, in $°Sp$, the subdominant a minor chord, its parallel clang, therefore, a major chord. Any numbers relating to the management of the parts always follow the mode of the *parallel clang*, for instance Sp, because the third of the parallel clang of the major Subdominant is a minor third (III).

PLAIN is applied to an interval, when it is conceived from the principal tone of a clang in the sense of its mode; therefore, from a major chord the upward intervals are plain, from a minor chord, the downward (from c^+, a is plain sixth = 6, from $°e$, g is plain sixth = VI); intervals conceived in the opposite direction receive the addition of *contra-* to their name; for instance, b is the minor contra-second (II $<$) of the c major chord. Cf. *Harmony steps.*

SECOND UPPER-DOMINANT is the Dominant of the Dominant ($\mathcal{D}$, $°\mathcal{D}$); second under-dominant is the Subdominant of the Subdominant ($\mathcal{S}$, $°\mathcal{S}$).

SIGNS:

$<$ (with a number) means "raised a semitone;" $>$, "lowered a semitone."

$=$ meaning "converted to," always indicates a change of the tonal functions, that is to say, a modulation; for instance, $T^6 = S^6$, means "Tonic with sixth" converted to "Subdominant with sixth."

$\approx$ means "enharmonically changed to;" for instance, $\mathcal{D}^{9>}$ converts, in A minor, $g\sharp\,b\,d\,f$ into $b\,d\,f\,a\flat$ by means of changing the $3\,g\sharp$ into the $9> a\flat$ which is enharmonically identical with it; the chord sign, therefore, indicates a modulation into c major or c minor to whose $L^{9>}$ the chord in its new writing corresponds.

( ), the round brackets, emancipate the indications of tonal functions from the Tonic of the principal key; the Dominants, etc., indicated in such brackets have their meaning by reference to the chord following immediately after the brackets, whether it be a principal clang (D, S, $°S$, D^+) or a feigning consonance (Tp, $°Dp$, $\mathcal{S}$, $\mathcal{B}$, $S^{III<}$, etc.); for instance, (D^7) $°Sp$ = Dominant seventh of the following minor Subdominant parallel (in c major: $e\flat\,g\,b\flat\,d\flat$). There are cases where the chord to be conceived as Tonic of the functions in

( ) does not follow at all; if, in such a case, it precedes, the reference of the bracketed indications to it can be shown by an arrow pointing backward, for instance $\overleftarrow{S}\,(S)$; if it neither precedes, nor follows, it is indicated, after the round brackets, in square brackets [ ] (see the following).

[ ], the square brackets, indicate a harmony as the conceived tonic of functions indicated in round brackets immediately before it. The chord indicated in square brackets, then, is omitted, skipped, in its place another one, that is not expected, follows.

. . means the *repetition of the preceding harmony ;* after brackets ( ) it means repetition of the chord preceding the brackets. After complicated signs with dissonances, it means only the continuation of the principal harmony, not of the dissonances, for instance, in $D_4^6\,\overset{+}{.}$, the continuation of the Dominant harmony, but with the $_4^6$ proceeding to $_3^5$. D_4^6 .., however (without numbers or $^+$ with the), would indicate the continuation of the chord of six-four.

SUBDOMINANT (abbreviated S) is the clang lying a fifth lower than the Tonic ; ^+S = major Subdominant (Subdominant being a major chord), usually simply S; $^\circ S$ = minor Subdominant (Subdominant being a minor chord).

TONIC (abbreviated T) is the clang from which the key is named, therefore, in c major, the c major chord (c^+), in A minor, the A minor chord $(^\circ e)$; the Tonic of the minor key is indicated by $^\circ T$, the major Tonic, in contradistinction (see *Variant*) to it, by T^+, but usually simply by T.

VARIANT is the Tonic of opposite mode, in c major the c minor chord, in A minor the A major chord. It is indicated by $^\circ T$ and T^+ respectively.

ALPHABETICAL INDEX.

(The numbers indicate the pages.)

AUGENER Ltd.
18 GREAT MARLBOROUGH STREET,
63 CONDUIT STREET (Regent Street Corner) & 57 HIGH STREET, MARYLEBONE,
LONDON, W. 1.